THE GREAT FEAR

THE GREAT FEAR

STALIN'S TERROR OF THE 1930s

JAMES HARRIS

OXFORD
UNIVERSITY PRESS

OXFORD
UNIVERSITY PRESS

Great Clarendon Street, Oxford, OX2 6DP,
United Kingdom

Oxford University Press is a department of the University of Oxford. It furthers the University's objective of excellence in research, scholarship, and education by publishing worldwide. Oxford is a registered trade mark of Oxford University Press in the UK and in certain other countries

First Edition published in 2016

Impression: 2

Published in the United States of America by Oxford University Press
198 Madison Avenue, New York, NY 10016, United States of America

British Library Cataloguing in Publication Data
Data available

Library of Congress Control Number: 2015947524

ISBN 978–0–19–969576–8

Printed in Great Britain by
Clays Ltd, St Ives plc

Acknowledgements

In one way or another, I have been working on the terror for at least two decades. Many people, groups, and institutions have contributed to the evolution of this book in that time. My ideas have developed in the process of correspondence, conversations, and arguments with many colleagues. Those who know me best will know that I enjoy the arguments particularly. Nothing refines ideas as well as the heat of argument and the hammer blows of counter-evidence forcefully presented. My fellow postgraduates at Chicago similarly loved a tussle, and they helped set me on a productive track. Sheila Fitzpatrick, my Ph.D. adviser, encouraged me to continue working on the terror after the Ph.D. A review essay she asked me to write in the early 2000s crystallized some of the ideas at the core of this book. Arch Getty has been a fantastic mentor, colleague, and friend. No one knows the sources better than Arch, and no one is more generous of time and effort to help those of us who want to invade his territory. This book would have been immeasurably weaker without his input.

Many colleagues have commented on chapters, or the seminar and conference papers on which they were based. Those who attended my terror conference in 2010 helped me at a critical time in the writing of the book. In particular, I want to thank Bill Chase, Gabor Rittersporn, Anna Geifman, Wendy Goldman, David Brandenberger, Sarah Davies, Arfon Rees, Matt Lenoe, Iain Lauchlan, Melanie Ilic, David Shearer, Paul Hagenloh, Lynne Viola, Ronald Suny, Alistair Kocho-Williams, David Priestland, Jorg Baberowski, Roger Reese, Vladimir Khaustov, Larisa Malashenko, Vladimir Nevezhin, Oleg Khlevniuk, Robert Hornsby, Joe Maiolo, Alex Kilin, and Gennadii Shaposhnikov. I am indebted to the University of Leeds for granting the research leave necessary to complete the writing of this book, and to the Arts and Humanities Research Council for funding half the leave period. Teaching time has been very useful too. For five or six years I have been teaching a module on 'Stalinist Terror' to the excellent MA students at the University of Leeds. I have learned a lot from the discussions I have had with them. One in particular, Peter Whitewood, went on to complete a Ph.D. on the subject, and to shape my view of the terror in the Red Army, and the mass operations. Finally, without the help of the archivists and archives in Russia, this work would have been unthinkable. The staff at RGASPI, RGVA, AVPRF, GARF, RGAE, TsDOO SO, and GAAO SO have been an immense help, and a pleasure to work with.

Contents

Contents

Abbreviations

APRF	Archive of the President of the Russian Federation
ARCOS	All-Russian Cooperative Society
AVP RF	Archive of Foreign Policy of the Russian Federation
Basmachi	Group fighting Soviet power in Central Asia during and after the Revolution
Cheka	All-Russian Extraordinary Commission for Combating Counter-Revolution and Sabotage
Comintern	Communist International
Decembrists	Participants in an unsuccessful 1825 uprising
Donbas	Don Basin
Duma	State parliament formed in 1906 under Nicholas II
dvurushnichestvo	'Double dealing' (praising policy in public and working to undermine it in private)
dvurushnik	'Double dealer'
FSB	Federal Security Service
Gosplan	State Planning Commission
GPU	State Political Administration
Gulag	Main Administration of Camps
INO OGPU	Foreign Department of the OGPU
Izvestiia	national state newspaper
Kadet	member of the Constitutional Democratic Party
kolkhoz	collective farm
Komsomol	All-Union Youth League
krai	Territory
kulak	Wealthy peasant
KVZhD	Chinese Far Eastern Railway
Lubianka	Building containing the offices of the political police in Moscow
Mensheviks	Faction of the Russian Social-Democratic movement
NEP	New Economic Policy
NKVD	People's Commissariat of Internal Affairs
obkom	Regional committee of the Communist Party

oblast′	Region
OGPU	Consolidated State Political Directorate
Oprichnina	Ivan the Terrible's secret police organization
Orgburo	Organizational Bureau of the Central Committee
Osoaviakhim	Union of Societies of Assistance to Defence and Aviation-Chemical Construction in the USSR
People's Will	Revolutionary movement responsible for the assassination of Alexander II
Petliurovite	Supporter of Simon Petliura's movement for Ukrainian independence
Politburo	Political Bureau of the CC
polpred	Equivalent of ambassador
polpredstvo	Soviet equivalent of an embassy in the early years after the Revolution
Pravda	Communist Party's national newspaper
Rabkrin (RKI)	Workers' and Peasants' Inspectorate
RGASPI	Russian State Archive of Social and Political Socio-Political History
RGVA	Russian State Military Archive
RSFSR	Russian Soviet Federative Federated Socialist Republic
ruble	Unit of Russian/Soviet currency
Secretariat	Secretariat of the Central Committee
skloki	'squabbles'; or factional infighting
Sovnarkom	Council of People's Commissars
SR	Member of the Socialist Revolutionary Party
Strel′tsy	Russian guardsmen (sixteenth to eighteenth centuries)
TASS	Telegraph Agency of the Soviet Union
Time of Troubles	A violent interregnum, 1598–1613
USSR	Union of Soviet Socialist Republics
VKP(b)	All-Union Communist Party (Bolshevik)
VSNKh	Supreme Council of the National Economy
White Guard	Associated with the White forces during and after the Civil War

Introduction

Between the winter of 1937 and the autumn of 1938, approximately three-quarters of a million Soviet citizens were subject to summary execution and their bodies dumped in mass graves. More than a million others were sentenced to lengthy terms in the labour camps of the Gulag. Many of those did not survive the ordeal. This was not the only episode of mass repression in the history of the USSR but it was by far the most devastating. It ranks among the horrific episodes of state violence in a century characterized by violent states. Commonly known as 'Stalin's Great Terror', it is also among the most misunderstood moments in the history of the twentieth century.

It is certainly baffling. The terror gutted the ranks of engineers, factory directors, and other economic specialists and managers after three solid years of economic growth in which all major plan targets were met. Indeed, the arrests and execution provoked an economic crisis by depleting managerial talent and instilling a fear of taking even the most elementary decisions. The terror raged through the armed forces on the eve of the Nazi invasion. The deaths of thousands of officers and military specialists of all ranks contributed directly to the disastrous opening campaigns of the war. The wholesale slaughter of party and state officials, up to and including the overwhelming majority of the party Central Committee, was in danger of making the Soviet state ungovernable. The majority of these victims of state repression in this period were accused of participating, or 'potentially' participating, in counter-revolutionary conspiracies. Almost without exception, there was no substance to the claims and no material evidence to support them. In 1937–8, there was no meaningful threat to the Bolshevik revolution, to the regime, or to Stalin personally. By the time the terror was brought to a close, the majority of victims were not high-ranking officials, or for that matter people with any particular connection to powerful people or places. Most of the victims were ordinary Soviet citizens, workers, and peasants, for whom 'counter-revolution' was an unfathomable abstraction. In short, this episode of extraordinary political violence was wholly destructive, not merely in terms of the incalculable human cost, but also in terms of the interests of the Soviet leaders, principally Joseph Stalin, who directed and managed it.

Attempts to make sense of the terror have long been complicated by the paucity of sources. No government is candid and open about the work of its political police, but the Stalin regime was among the most secretive of all time. What we knew about 1937–8 began with what little the regime wanted the domestic and international public to know. Much of what it chose to publicize was the story of the purported counter-revolutionary activity of small groups of former oppositionists surrounding Politburo leaders of the 1920s who had competed with Stalin in the power struggle after Lenin's death. Newspaper articles and trial transcripts explained how Leon Trotsky, Grigorii Zinoviev, Lev Kamenev, Nikolai Bukharin, Alexei Rykov, and others did not accept Stalin's victory in the 1920s, and into the 1930s resorted to ever more desperate measures to unseat him, including conspiring with the main enemies of the revolution: the capitalists and fascists. Again this story had only the most tenuous connection to underlying events, but because there were so few sources, this part of the broader terror phenomenon naturally tended to become the centrepiece for historians. The explanation that still grips the public imagination presents the terror as the culmination of Stalin's struggle for total power. The so-called 'Moscow Trials' are presented as the weapon with which Stalin served the coup de grâce that removed the Leninist old guard and allowed him to promote a new generation of officials who were personally loyal to him.

Robert Conquest popularized this view in his 1968 book *The Great Terror*.[1] It has been in print almost continuously since then, long past

1. Robert Conquest, *The Great Terror* (London, 1968). Almost twenty years earlier, Isaac Deutscher had presented a similar, though much briefer, account in his *Stalin: A Political Biography* (Oxford, 1949). See also contemporary memoirs like Alexander Barmine, *Memoirs of a Soviet Diplomat* (London, 1938); Walter Krivitsky, *I was Stalin's Agent* (New York, 1939); Victor Kravchenko, *I Chose Freedom* (New York, 1946); Alexander Orlov, *The Secret History of Stalin's Crimes* (New York, 1953); Boris Nicolaevsky, *Power and the Soviet Elite* (New York, 1965).

the point at which new evidence established that the central argument was untenable. Popular histories tend to personalize major historical events, and blaming the bloodthirsty tyrant bent on total personal power made a great—and morally comforting—story. In blaming one man for the deaths of millions, Conquest escaped the almost impossible narrative challenge of representing the variety of victims and perpetrators and the complex history of political violence in the USSR, and in the Russian Empire before it. Conquest was not alone in approaching the subject this way. In his 'Secret Speech' to the 20th Party Congress in 1956, Nikita Khrushchev blamed the political violence of the Stalin era on the dictator and his 'Cult of Personality', but in that case Khrushchev was not just trying to package a good story. He was communicating to the thousands of perpetrators, particularly among the party elite, that their participation in the mass repression would not be prosecuted. He made it clear that Stalin alone would take the blame, though he knew, and they knew, that the reality was much messier.

In the 1970s and 1980s, historians and political scientists chipped away at this dominant Stalin-centred 'strong state' view by exploring issues beyond the personality and actions of the leader: the role of Bolshevik ideology; the ways in which the bloody Civil War made the party more centralized and violent, the social preconditions of Stalinism and the importance of conflicts and tensions between central and regional officials, among other things.[2] In 1985, J. Arch Getty delivered a broadside to the very foundations of Conquest's explanation with his book, *Origins of the Great Purges*. Where Conquest saw one man's pursuit of total power, Getty saw a system in disarray, lurching from crisis to crisis, and lashing out at its own 'shadows'.[3] Getty's vision of a 'weak state' was a perfect counterpoint to Conquest's 'strong state'. When the Soviet system collapsed in 1991, and literally millions of archival files

2. See e.g. Robert Tucker (ed.), *Stalinism: Essays in Historical Interpretation* (New York, 1977); Sheila Fitzpatrick, *The Civil War as a Formative Experience* (Washington, DC, 1981); Graeme Gill, *The Origins of the Stalinist Political System* (Cambridge, 1990).

3. J. Arch Getty, *Origins of the Great Purges: The Soviet Communist Party Reconsidered, 1933–1938* (Cambridge, 1985). Getty's more recent work has explored Stalin's role in the Terror in considerable detail, though he has not explicitly addressed the strong state/weak state paradox explicitly in these works. See J. Arch Getty and Oleg V. Naumov (eds), *The Road to Terror: Stalin and the Self-Destruction of the Bolsheviks, 1932–1939* (New Haven, 1999); J. Arch Getty and Oleg V. Naumov, *Yezhov: The Rise of Stalin's Iron Fist* (New Haven, 2008).

were opened to scholars, it was easy enough for both sides to find evidence to support their radically different positions: evidence both of a supremely powerful, hyper-centralized state, and evidence of confusion, insubordination, and fear. There were no easy and quick answers. It took time to digest and make sense of the immense volume of documents. The greatest archival 'revelation', to the extent that there were any, was that the overwhelming majority of victims were ordinary Soviet citizens—workers and peasants—rather than party and state elite, as was commonly assumed. That was surely a serious blow to those who thought the terror was the culmination of Stalin's quest for total power. The workers and peasants were no serious obstacle to that. At roughly the same time, however, with the release of a large part of Stalin's personal papers in 2000, it was becoming clear that in the 1930s the state was hyper-centralized and power concentrated in Stalin's hands. Stalin was, as one historian put it, 'master of the house'.[4] There seemed to be plenty of evidence to support both sides of the argument.

This book presents a general history of the terror that attempts to resolve the weak state/strong state paradox. It took shape in the long ebb and flow of archival releases in the last twenty years.[5] The first wave of releases, after 1991, gave historians an extraordinarily detailed picture of decisions taken by official bodies from the very apex of the system down to the district level. The second wave, almost ten years later, opened the personal papers of senior officials, including Stalin. These papers included a substantial part of the incoming information—foreign and domestic intelligence, opinion summaries, newspaper clippings, and reports of all kinds—on which these leaders based their decisions. When one looked at the decisions in the light of the information received, it was possible to glimpse how Soviet leaders

4. Oleg Khlevniuk, *Master of the House: Stalin and his Inner Circle* (New Haven, 2009).
5. James Harris, 'The Purging of Local Cliques in the Urals Region, 1936–7', in Sheila Fitzpatrick (ed.), *Stalinism: New Directions* (London, 2000), 262–85; James Harris, 'Resisting the Plan in the Urals, 1928–1956: Or Why Regional Officials Needed "Wreckers" and "Saboteurs"', in Lynne Viola (ed.), *Contending with Stalinism: Soviet Power and Popular Resistance in the 1930s* (Ithaca, NY, 2002), 201–27; James Harris, 'Was Stalin a Weak Dictator?', *Journal of Modern History*, 2 (2003), 375–86; James Harris, 'Encircled by Enemies: Stalin's Perceptions of the Capitalist World, 1918–1941', *Journal of Strategic Studies*, 3 (2007), 513–45.

were interpreting that information, and misinterpreting it.[6] The Bolsheviks had come to power in 1917, in the midst of the Great War, German occupation, mass desertion, and general social disorder. Seizing power in Petrograd and Moscow was not easy, but in the effort to take power in the rest of the Russian Empire they faced an array of very powerful enemies: the White armies, the Germans, the foreign armed forces determined to sustain the eastern front, and that substantial part of the domestic population for whom the promised 'dictatorship of the proletariat' was unwelcome. In short, it was entirely clear why the Bolsheviks should have wanted, and have gone to great effort to develop, effective systems for gathering information on the activities and intentions of their enemies.

By the early 1920s, the Bolsheviks had won the Civil War, but they knew that they had a long way to go before they had built the utopia of their dreams, and that there were still many groups, domestically and internationally, that would not want them to succeed. It was only sensible that they should direct the apparatus of intelligence gathering to keep a careful watch. In the years that followed, the Soviet leadership received a steady stream of disturbing reports of international alliances of capitalist powers bent on invading the USSR: 'bourgeois' engineers, other specialists, academics, wealthy peasants, non-Russian ethnic groups and nationalities, army officers, former oppositionists, and many others working to undermine Soviet power from within. The reports in most cases grossly exaggerated, or even invented, the threats they purported to analyse. These 'threats' were not simply invented to serve cynical political ends. They cannot be explained as merely the product of some psychopathology. This book explains how a dysfunctional relationship between information gatherers and Soviet leaders emerged, and how it substantially explains Stalin's terror of the 1930s. The state was supremely powerful, but it perceived that it was weak. In the autumn of 1936, the Stalin regime thought that invasion was imminent. At the same time, it thought it was under siege from multiple, interlocking conspiracies that could, in the event of war, trigger defeat, the end of the revolution, and the restoration of capitalism. Stalin and

6. Together with Sarah Davies, I addressed the themes of information gathering and perception/misperception most recently in *Stalin's World: Dictating the Soviet Order* (New Haven, 2014), part 1. See also James Harris, 'Intelligence and Threat Perception: Defending the Revolution, 1917–1937', in James Harris (ed.), *Anatomy of Terror: Political Violence under Stalin* (Oxford, 2013), 29–43.

his inner circle believed that the potential fifth column had to be eliminated if the regime, and the revolution, were to survive. War did eventually come in 1941, and the regime inevitably faced a measure of collaboration, but it would have been stronger and more united had it not lashed out at largely non-existent conspiracies in the 'Great Fear' of 1937–8.

The story of the 'Great Fear' does not begin in 1917 with the revolution and the Bolshevik seizure of power. We will see that the exaggerated fear of foreign and domestic threats was exacerbated by certain traits of Bolshevism and the early experience of the Bolsheviks, but few threats—real or perceived—troubling the Bolsheviks after 1917 were entirely without precedent. Some dated back to the very origins of the Russian state. A brief sketch of threat perception in Russian history shows that the exaggerated vision of the enemy was not an exclusively 'Bolshevik' phenomenon, let alone the product of the psychological traits of a single leader. On the contrary, most of the fears that underpinned Stalin's recourse to terror in 1936–8 had been experienced by many generations of Russian rulers before. Many of the persistent insecurities of Russia's rulers were directly inherited by the Bolsheviks. In no sense did they make the terror inevitable. They cannot explain the exceptional violence of state repression under Stalin. But the actions of the Bolsheviks after the revolution cannot be fully understood without reference to the insecurities built into the very structure of Russian history.

Power and insecurity in Russia, 980–1917

The Eurasian plain is not an obvious place for the emergence of a great empire. The first records of the existence of the Slavs are found in Byzantium—where they were traded as slaves by the Vikings. It was an exceptional challenge to cultivate the soil given the short farming season but the surpluses they managed to generate allowed them to pay tribute to more powerful groups who could protect them from attack. This basic protection supported the spread of Slav communities, consisting mostly of fifty to sixty people working the land together. The original communities gradually dissolved into larger groups dominated by a single family. At the cusp of the millennium, in the 980s, through a combination of conquest and negotiation, Prince Vladimir of Kiev became the first 'super-prince', the first ruler who could lay a claim to represent *Rus'*, as the sum of the Slav lands and people came to be known. Vladimir's achievement was immense, but the practical realities of their power were rooted in an elaborate court hierarchy in which the ruler had to contend with powerful princes who continued to have considerable power in their own right. By the middle of the twelfth century, the unitary Kievan state was in decline as the princes increasingly asserted their separate power. The final blow was delivered by Chingiz Khan and the Mongol invasion of 1237–41, and for the next 250 years, the Slav princes were forced to collect tribute for the Mongols. Though this was an undisguised humiliation, those princes who won favour with the Mongols extended their power enormously in this period, and none benefited more than the princes of Moscow.

By a combination of luck and design, they avoided the power struggles that had fatally weakened Kiev. From 1389 to 1589 Muscovy had only five rulers, in no small part because they dealt with threats to the unity of the state in a more ruthless manner. Principalities were absorbed into Moscow by conquest and the penalty for challenging the Muscovite 'Grand Prince' was death or exile. Political violence was a typical response to any threat to state power. A new and unprecedented political system emerged in these two centuries. By the mid-sixteenth century, the princes who had been absorbed into the Muscovite state had been transformed into servitors or servants of their sovereign. The Muscovite rulers, who now called themselves 'Tsar' to assert their dominance, did not merely control the land and people. They owned them. The whole of Russia had become their property, or 'patrimony'. This sort of rule, without any limits or conditions, is without parallel in medieval Europe. The total concentration of power and resources allowed the Muscovite state not only to break free of Mongol rule, but to expand relentlessly to the south and east across the Eurasian plain. Yet it would be a mistake to assume that meant that the Russian autocrat felt entirely secure. The power of life and death over the old princes and boyars was not an ironclad guarantee of political stability.

The absence of any independent power and their status as the property of the Tsar did not mean that the elite had no separate aspirations. They did not forget their own princely lineage, and occasionally conspired against the ruler. In turn, their conspiracies provoked countermeasures that heightened political violence. In the 1540s, Prince

Andrei Shuiskii tried to take advantage of the death of Vasilii III when his son and successor Ivan (Ivan IV) was only 3 years old. Ivan was saved through the intervention of other leading families who did not want the Shuiskiis to succeed, but not without a string of murders, executions, and arrests that scarred the future Tsar. Ivan IV—Ivan the Terrible as he is commonly known—was haunted by the spectre of disloyalty among the elite, such that he formed a private court (ruling circle) known as the *oprichnina*. Its members (*oprichniki*) were ordered to seek out and destroy enemies of the Tsar. They orchestrated an orgy of violence, murdering thousands of people of all ranks from princes to peasants, and exiling many others. Mass terror sent out an emphatic signal of Ivan's power and of his attitude to those who would conspire against him.

In 1682, the death of the childless Tsar Fedor III provoked another round of boyar jockeying, this time combined with a revolt of the *strel'tsy* as the palace guards were known. Yet again a future Tsar, this time Peter I, then aged 10, witnessed scenes of exceptional violence in the Kremlin. Peter's response was to form the Preobrazhenskii Prikaz, which became the first proper secret police force in Russia, with the power to detain and question any individual regardless of rank, suspected of treasonous actions—or thoughts. As with the political police forces that followed through to Stalin's day, they acted as judge, jury, and executioner. And yet, the political police could not guarantee an end to political intrigue. Between 1741 and 1801 there were three successful coups leading to the violent death of the reigning monarch. Catherine the Great began her thirty-four year reign in July 1762 by deposing her own husband, Peter III. She maintained a close relationship with the head of the political police, Stepan Sheshkovskii, whom she valued for his ruthlessness and efficiency. She valued him further still after the French Revolution culminated in the execution of the French King and inspired the fear of a 'French infection' in Russia.

In the end, there were no revolutionary events in Russia in Catherine's time, but the notion of a 'French infection' was not misplaced. At the beginning of the eighteenth century Peter the Great had turned Russia to the west against the will of much of the Russian elite. But by Catherine's time, the process of westernization had progressed to the point of being irreversible. Through education and travel, the elite came to feel more at home in the capitals of Europe than on their estates in the Russian heartland. As they witnessed at first hand the emerging political freedoms and economic development of Europe, many longed for Russia to experience the same. It was not long before these feelings turned into political action. By the nineteenth century, the great boyar and princely families no longer entertained serious thoughts of conspiring against the Tsar in the royal court. Indeed since before Peter's time, the power of the court had been shifting to a bureaucracy where position was determined largely by talent rather than rank or status. There continued to be conspiracies against the Tsar, but they no longer originated in court. The Decembrist uprising of 1825 inaugurated a new and even more unsettling age for the autocracy: the age of revolutionaries.

It would be a stretch to call the Decembrists 'revolutionaries', though the Bolsheviks were later inclined to remember them as such. These officers of the Russian Imperial Guard, many of princely pedigree, did not generally want to overthrow the autocracy, but rather to ensure that liberal reforms initiated by Tsar Alexander I were deepened and extended. In a pattern that would become familiar across the nineteenth century, some were disappointed and radicalized when the Tsar retreated from reform at the first sign that change was creating instability. They formed secret societies in which they could share their views freely, and in that context, the more radical among them exerted an exceptional influence. When Alexander I died suddenly on 19 November 1825, they took advantage of a brief interregnum to force events. When negotiations showed no sign of progress, Nicholas ordered his artillery to open fire on demonstrating 'rebels'. Those who were not blown to bits quickly fled the scene. Like so many of his predecessors, Nicholas relied heavily on his political police chief. General Alexander Benckendorf became the second most powerful person in the Russian Empire and a close confidant of the Tsar. He built an impressive network of spies that infiltrated all the groups and institutions that were likely to harbour 'liberals'—the sort of people who might support the sort of constitutional ideas circulating in Europe. Nicholas and his successors were, nevertheless, fighting a losing battle. Their hesitation to introduce meaningful political and economic reforms meant that they fell further and further behind developments in Europe. To many educated Russians, the continued existence of medieval institutions, from the patrimonial autocracy to the institution of serfdom, was intolerable.

Before the analysis turns to the rise of the Bolsheviks and the many other revolutionary groups that contributed to the collapse of the autocracy in 1917, it is necessary to observe other sources of insecurity for Russian rulers. In the middle of the nineteenth century, two other threats, unresolved across the centuries, were deepening the anxieties of the autocrat. The focus on high politics has meant that we have ignored the population at large. Why should they matter when they were, for the most part, nothing more than the property of the landed elites? Indeed, most of the Russian peasantry had absorbed with their mother's milk a myth of a benevolent Tsar surrounded by rather less benevolent advisers. But there was a limit to the protection the myth offered, and in some ways, the myth presented its own dangers. Against a background of long-standing grievances about their status as serfs and their treatment at the hands of their owners, succession crises excited rumours that the rightful and just Tsar was being usurped. In these conditions, someone claiming to be the legitimate heir could raise peasant armies in their tens of thousands and march on the capital. Four times, between 1600 and 1800, the regime was forced to bring in the full force of the imperial army in order to survive a peasant rebellion. By the middle of the nineteenth century, the threat of peasant rebellion was only growing, particularly as the long awaited emancipation settlement—freeing the peasants from their status as serfs—set onerous conditions that only deepened the misery of their conditions.

The fear of popular and elite hostility, of hidden and not so hidden conspiracies against the Tsar's rule, was compounded by a further sense of vulnerability. From the earliest origins of the Slavs to the Russia of today, the threat from enemies at home was magnified by the threat of enemies abroad. The Eurasian plain lacks obvious natural defences, and from the start the Slavs were only one among many groups fighting for land and resources. Early successes at securing the lands around present-day Kiev were followed by crushing defeat in the Mongol invasion and more than 200 years of occupation. By the sixteenth century, the Muscovite state was bumping into major powers in the south and west: the Ottoman Empire, Poland, Lithuania, and Sweden. All of them had their spies (and supporters) in the Russian imperial court, and tried to take advantage of succession crises, peasant rebellions, and other domestic disturbances to seize territory and even power. At the height of the Time of Troubles, there were large numbers of Polish, Lithuanian, and Swedish soldiers on Russian soil and a Polish King in the Kremlin. The new Romanov dynasty ultimately saw off that threat, but not the underlying problem of her international security. In the eighteenth century, arguably the period of her greatest imperial expansion to the east, Russia fought nine major wars in the west and south. Without any resolution of those conflicts, Russia then faced a titanic struggle against the combined forces of the Napoleonic army, then dominating continental Europe. Russia's size and resources combined with her relative weakness and backwardness made her an irresistible target. The ultimate defeat of Napoleon did little to change that. More than a century later, this was exactly what Stalin had in mind when he told a conference of his leading economic officials that 'we are 50–100 years behind the advanced countries. Either we make up that difference in ten years, or they will crush us.'[7]

A fourth source of perceived vulnerability for the Russian empire lay in the very success of the imperial expansion. As the empire grew, it absorbed ever larger numbers of non-Russians, most of whom lived on western and southern borders. The 1897 census revealed that out of a population of over 125 million, less than 56 million were native Russians.[8] Most of the non-Russian peoples had been the objects of military conquest, and many continued to put up a ferocious resistance long after the prospect of independence had faded into the past. While almost 37 million others were fellow Slavs, not all of them were happy with Russian dominance. The 8 million Poles in particular considered the Russians their implacable enemies, and towards the end of the nineteenth century, despite—and probably because of—a programme of Russification, even the 22 million Ukrainians (called 'little Russians') were showing early signs of turning against their 'bigger brothers'.[9]

The expansion of empire had made Russia the largest country in the world, with thousands of miles of borders that were almost impossible to police. Those borders were populated on the one side with ethnic groups many of whom were hostile to the Russians, and on the other side by countries with which Russia was often at war. It was a toxic combination. Those countries with interests along Russia's southern

7. I.V. Stalin, *Sochineniia* (13 vols., Moscow, 1947–51), xiii (Moscow, 1951), 38–9.
8. By native language. The numbers of Russians were probably exaggerated by the census takers. N. A. Troinitskii (ed.), *Pervaia vseobshchaia perepis' naseleniia Rossiiskoi Imperii* (St Petersburg, 1905).
9. Geoffrey Hosking, *Russia and the Russians* (London, 2002), ch. 8.

and western borders were in a position not only to destabilize Russia's periphery, but to use the porous borders and sympathetic non-Russian population as spies and saboteurs. The only way the regime could protect itself against the dangers on the periphery was by maintaining a colossal standing army—which poor and backward Russia could ill afford.

Alexander's Great Reforms laid the foundations of an impressive industrialization drive that promised to build Russia's military and economic might, shore up central power, and restore national security. But in the process, it did the opposite. The reforms badly tore Russia's social fabric. The emancipation settlement left the gentry in terminal decline and the peasantry indebted and dangerously angry. Industrialization was drawing peasants in their millions into urban centres, faster than they could be adequately housed. Low pay, long hours, and poor working and living conditions provoked labour unrest. In the end, the reforms did nothing to assuage the revolutionaries. Rather, they excited them into action. Alexander II, the Liberator, was assassinated on 13 March 1881 when a member of the revolutionary group calling itself 'The People's Will' lobbed a bomb at his carriage. By the early twentieth century political assassination became a sort of national pastime. The enforcers of the regime's reactionary policies were their favourite targets. Minister of the Interior Dmitrii Sipiagin was murdered in 1902 and his successor Viacheslav von Plehve in 1904. The Tsar's uncle, the governor-general of Moscow, was assassinated in the same year. These were the most prominent victims, but thousands of other lesser government officials fell victim to the bullet and bomb in a rising tide of revolutionary violence.

Meanwhile, a series of humiliating defeats in the Russo-Japanese War in the course of 1904 was intensifying popular disillusion with the backwardness and corruption of the autocracy. Appeals for political reform from liberal groups combined with popular demonstrations, mass labour unrest, large-scale peasant uprisings, protests and violence among national minorities on the periphery, terrorist attacks, and multiple military mutinies, to leave the regime teetering on the brink of collapse. Political concessions won in October 1905 were broadly celebrated, though Nicholas II considered them to be a shameful betrayal of the dynasty. Rather than accept the inevitability of political change, he used the relative calm that followed to re-establish central control, and by means so brutal as to immediately betray the spirit of the concessions. Police investigations into subversive activity were radically simplified, and civilian suspects passed to secret military courts without legal representation, where they could face a sentence of death.

They also undertook to infiltrate all the major revolutionary groups, and with extraordinary success. 'Provocateurs' rose through their ranks, allowing the police to track their members, and anticipate their plans. The revolutionaries no longer knew whom they could trust, and who were sending their comrades to the gallows and into exile. By the time they finally seized power in 1917, the Bolsheviks had spent well in excess of a decade in a state of high anxiety, determined to realize their vision of a proletarian revolution, but never entirely sure which of their comrades genuinely shared that vision, and which of them were only acting, taking money from the enemy in order to undermine the movement from within. Distrust became an instinct, necessary for survival. At the same time, the revolutionaries learned painfully, and at first hand, that a repressive police state could make subversive activity very difficult. The almost total suspension of civil liberties, the mass surveillance, and the power to arrest, imprison, exile, and even execute suspected revolutionaries without legal niceties had their effect. The old regime was brought back from the brink, at least until the beginning of the war.

Russia's involvement in the First World War began with the same burst of patriotic sentiment seen elsewhere in Europe, but it dispelled rather more quickly in Russia. Crushing military defeats and the rapid loss of territory to the invading Germans played the largest role, but by no means the only role. State finances were in no condition to support a prolonged conflict. Raising taxes is never popular, but a punishing new burden to pay for military incompetence and the resultant appalling loss of life on the front was doomed to excite protest. In March 1917, a small demonstration in the capital marking International Women's Day set off a chain of events that brought an end to the Romanov dynasty. That same day, the Putilov munitions plant, the city's largest employer, locked out its increasingly militant labour force with which it was in dispute. Thousands of angry workers joined the demonstration, which descended into a bread riot. When soldiers were ordered to shoot on the demonstrators after three days of rioting, they chose instead to join them. The Tsar had lost control of the capital, and was without any available troops to restore order. After a brief and unsuccessful attempt to calm the situation by passing power to his brother Grand Duke Mikhail, the Duma took charge. It was Russia's greatest chance to establish a liberal democratic government, but the circumstances could not have been less conducive to success. While liberal forces held to their principled concerns about legitimacy, Russia was collapsing about their ears. The war effort went from bad to worse. The supply of food to the cities remained unstable. Peasant and nationalist uprisings intensified. The population at large was left to think that if this was what liberal democracy looked like, they didn't want it. Circumstances favoured the Bolsheviks. A disciplined, conspiratorial organization, decisive leadership, and the broad sympathy of urban workers underpinned their successful coup d'état at the beginning of November.

In the months and years that followed, it was inevitable that they would develop the same sense of vulnerability experienced by the old regime. They too faced succession struggles. They too faced hostile foreign powers. They too had to defend thousands upon thousands of miles of porous borders. They too would have to deal with the perennial problem of nationalism on the periphery. None of the fears that drove the Bolshevik apparatus of repression was unprecedented. Indeed, there is an argument to be made that they were built into the structure of Russian history. There were unique circumstances, personalities and conditions that made Bolshevik political violence more extreme than anything witnessed under the Tsars, but it would be too simple to attribute them, as many have done, to one psychopathic dictator or his evil ideology. The analysis that follows explores the many, very real threats faced by the Bolshevik regime after 1917, but also the particular evolution of systems for the collection and interpretation of information on those threats. It will show how, by the middle of the 1930s, the regime had become convinced that it faced multiple, interlocking conspiracies capable of overthrowing it. The information-gathering systems were presenting to Soviet leaders a compelling, detailed, and nuanced picture of threats that, in most important respects, did not exist.

I

Fear and violence

The Bolsheviks seized power in Petrograd in early November 1917 with remarkably little violence. The authority of central government had so badly disintegrated by the autumn that the coup met little or no resistance. Most famously, the Provisional Government, meeting at the Winter Palace, dispersed after they heard the shattering glass from a single blank shell fired by the battleship *Aurora*. The group sent to seize control of the Central Telegraph Office got most of the way there before they realized that they had no armed support. They proceeded nonetheless and found it sufficient merely to declare that they were now in control.[1] The uprising began on 7 November and already the next day power had passed to the Soviets. But this was not fated to be a peaceful transition. It took almost a week of fierce street fighting before the Bolsheviks were able to take control of Moscow, and this was only the beginning. As Leon Trotsky took charge of the task of building a 'Red' army capable of extending control and defending the revolution, anti-Bolshevik forces were gathering on the outskirts of the central provinces, preparing to wipe out the revolutionary menace. It took three years of an exceptionally violent civil war to secure victory. Well in excess of a million soldiers were killed, and civilian casualties were considerably greater—almost ten times as many, and far in excess of the casualties suffered in the course of the First World War. The brutal tactics employed on both sides—bombing, gassing, and executing the military and civilian population alike—defy the contemporary imagination. There can be no doubt that the violence of the Soviet state under Stalin had roots in the violence of the Civil War, but was it the Civil War that made the Bolsheviks violent, or the Bolsheviks

1. Robert V. Daniels, *Red October: The Bolshevik Revolution of 1917* (New York, 1967).

who made the Civil War violent? Did Lenin's terror lead to Stalin's terror of the 1930s? The answers are not obvious, and bear exploration.

The revolutionaries were a generally violent lot, but the Bolsheviks were not leaders in that field. Assassinations and bombings were the specialism of the Socialist Revolutionaries and particularly their terrorist wing which sought to provoke a revolution by decapitating the old regime. By contrast, the Bolsheviks dreamt of a popular revolution in which they would be acclaimed as the natural representatives of Russian working masses. But they knew that workers and peasants needed help to overcome the resistance of the possessing classes. The Bolsheviks were Marxists, and good Marxists are good historians. They were deeply aware of previous revolutionary episodes and why they had failed. They did not want to repeat the mistakes of the French Revolution, the events of 1848, the Paris Commune of 1871, and their own 1905. And though many mistakes were made, the most common theme was the error of underestimating the forces of reaction. History dictated to the Bolsheviks that the possessing classes would do everything in their power to strangle the revolution, and they understood that they had to deal with that threat consistently, ruthlessly, and to the end. It was not just about launching their own terror, but also about encouraging and channelling popular unrest against the 'counter-revolution'. They were not inclined to glorify revolutionary violence, but they would not shrink from it in defence of the revolution, as Trotsky made clear when he famously quipped: 'We shall not enter the kingdom of socialism in white gloves on a polished floor.'[2]

They had a brief period of relative calm before the counter-revolution began in earnest. While the Bolsheviks seized power in Moscow and a raft of other provincial towns and cities, the generals of the imperial army argued with politicians of the Provisional Government about how to respond to the revolution. Fatefully, they never came to a consensus, and never adequately coordinated their action,[3] though in the course of 1918 they had effectively hemmed the Bolsheviks into the central provinces around Moscow by Generals Kaledin, Wrangel, and

2. E. H. Carr, *A History of the Bolshevik Revolution: The Bolshevik Revolution, 1917–1923* (London, 1950), i. 165.

3. The main source of conflict was over the form of government they were fighting for: a restoration of the autocracy, a constitutional monarchy, or a liberal democracy? The disagreements made a unified command unlikely.

Denikin in the south, Iudenich in the north and west, and Admiral Kolchak in the east. The so-called 'White' armies were soon joined by a variety of foreign forces, including the Americans, British, French, Germans, Czechs, and Turks, who were in one sense continuing to fight the First World War on Russian soil, and in another, attempting, as Churchill put it, to help the Whites 'strangle Bolshevism in its cradle'. The decisive battles took place in 1919.

After a promising start to the year, the Red Army could not seem to contain Denikin's counter-offensive from the south and west. By October, the 'Reds' had abandoned Kursk, Voronezh, and Orel. Moscow was under immediate threat. At the same time, Iudenich's armies were advancing on Petrograd. The 'Whites' were on the threshold of victory, but they were not able inflict the coup de grâce. The closer victory appeared, the less willing they were to coordinate their actions, and the more each military leader sought to impose his vision of the Russian future. Effectively, they gave the Bolsheviks the opportunity to slip from the tightening noose and regroup.

The turning tide of the war in late 1919 and into 1920 did not make the struggle any less brutal. Both sides conscripted their armies at gun point and shot deserters. Both sides commonly executed captured soldiers and commanders. Both sides requisitioned grain and property without regard to the populations they left without food and shelter. Both deported entire communities whom they suspected of disloyalty. The Bolsheviks went one step further, proposing in 1919 to exterminate the entire Cossack elite of the Don region in reply to their cooperation with Denikin.[4] The exceptional violence can be explained only in part in terms of the exigencies of war. The Reds and Whites were fighting for control of a country in near total collapse. They were barely able to provide food and shelter for their fighting forces. The civilian population was bound to suffer and prisoners of war even more so. In any civil war, loyalties are bound to be divided, ambiguous, wavering. Most participants want nothing more than to survive, and change sides as the momentum of war serves that goal. But such mass defections were intolerable in a finely balanced conflict. Commanders threatened death for disloyalty, a move that was as logical as it was inhumane. The readiness with which murderous commands were both issued and carried

4. Peter Holquist, '"Conduct Merciless Mass Terror": Decossackization on the Don, 1919', *Cahiers du Monde Russe*, 1–2 (1997), 127–62.

out owes equally as much to the dehumanising effect of war itself. The Civil War followed on the heels of four years of brutal warfare against the Germans. Commanders and conscripts alike had become inured to the sight, the smell, and the meaning of death.[5]

There was a further dimension to the Bolshevik practice of violence: ideology. The seizure of power in 1917 had presented them the opportunity to realize in practice their dreams of an ideal society free of exploitation and inequality. For them, this was no utopia, it was the inevitable trajectory of history and they had the chance to be the midwives of the glorious future of all mankind. They passionately believed that theirs was a perfect and unique vision, and that resistance to it, any alternative vision, was inevitably blinkered by ignorance and self-interest. Resistance had to be overcome because this glorious end justified the most hideous of means. Trotsky was exploring this logic when he wrote: 'If human life in general is sacred, we must deny ourselves, not only the use of terror, not only war, but also the revolution itself... [and yet] to make the individual sacred we must destroy the social order which crucifies him.' Red Terror was superior to White Terror in the view of Bolshevik leaders because it was used to support the goal of the liberation of all mankind. White Terror was aimed at defending an old regime that served the venal interests of a narrow elite. The use of state violence was not a matter of principle, but a matter of expediency.[6] They conceived a sort of sacred obligation to destroy any individuals, groups, or institutions that stood between them and their vision. The implications of such an approach extended far beyond the field of battle. Resistance, or what at least appeared to be resistance, was both inevitable and pervasive.

The Bolsheviks were not in a position to dispense wholesale with the old order and build a new state from scratch. The movement had around 20,000 members at the time of the February Revolution and perhaps five times as many by the time of the seizure of power, but they were revolutionaries, and not experienced in public administration. It only made sense to absorb and adapt existing state institutions. They had been able to march into the Central Telegraph office in Petrograd on 7 November 1917 and declare that they were in control,

5. See e.g. Peter Holquist, *Making War, Forging Revolution: Russia's Continuum of Crisis, 1914–1921* (Cambridge, Mass., 2002).

6. Leon Trotsky, 'Terrorizm i kommunizm', quoted from Baruch Knei-Paz, *The Social and Political Thought of Leon Trotsky* (Oxford, 1978), 248–9.

but it was another thing altogether to keep this and other state institutions running smoothly and fully subordinated to their revolutionary cause. By their education and status, the directors of state institutions and private enterprises were among the least likely to support a 'dictatorship of the proletariat'. The broader ranks of the civil service and enterprise administration were little different. Bolshevik rule promised to rob them of all they had and held dear. It should come as no surprise that many of them sought to frustrate the Bolsheviks as best they could. A matter of days after the seizure of power, the Bolsheviks faced a strike movement intended to paralyse the state and economy. By January 1918, almost 50,000 civil servants and other administrators were refusing to work, including 10,000 bank workers, and 10,000 employees of the post and telegraph agencies. The Bolsheviks were convinced that the strike movement was being organized and funded by Russia's richest capitalists, among them P. P. Riabushinskii, A. I. Putilov, and A. I. Vishnegradskii, but they understood that it would not be enough to deal with them alone. Rather, they collected the names of striking employees and sacked 12,000 of them, with the loss of pension rights. Many were then assigned to forced labour in factories or shovelling snow on the streets.[7]

The strike fizzled out shortly afterwards, but the hostility of officialdom remained. The Bolsheviks needed to ensure that resistance did not continue covertly. On 20 December 1917, Lenin pushed the revolution's governing body—the Council of People's Commissars—to establish a group that would deal with the strike and the broader problem of resistance. The All-Russian Extraordinary Commission for the Struggle against Counter-Revolution and Sabotage (Cheka) was formed later that same day. It seemed a rather rushed beginning, but Lenin had sown the seed of what would become an immense and fearsome institution, a political police that would take the lives of millions of Soviet citizens in the coming two decades. It was not a casual decision on Lenin's part, nor for that matter a sign of some hesitation to neutralize threats to the regime. This is clear enough from his decision to put in charge of the Cheka one of his most capable and trusted comrades: Felix Dzerzhinskii. Though the Cheka started its work with 1,000 rubles and a staff of twenty-three, it only took a few months for

7. *Velikaia Oktiabr'skaia Sotsialisticheskaia Revoliutsiia: Entsiklopediia* (Moscow, 1987), 450; K. V. Skorkin, *NKVD RSFSR, 1917–1923* (Moscow, 2008), 65.

Dzerzhinskii to take on a further 600 staff and open branches across the territory controlled by the Bolsheviks.

It was common practice for new institutions to expand on the hoof, but the speed of expansion and the vigour with which it pursued its targets owes much to the rapid deterioration of the situation in early 1918. The Bolsheviks had attempted to end Russia's participation in the First World War with the declaration of a unilateral ceasefire. As much as the Germans were pleased to have the opportunity to shift troops to the western front, they were determined to impose a punishing peace settlement on the Bolsheviks, and their response to Bolshevik posturing was to renew the offensive in the east. The immediate and rapid advance of German troops most worryingly towards the capital presented an immediate threat to the survival of the revolution. The concern of the Bolshevik leadership was not merely the challenge of marshalling a military force capable of countering the German advance, but that opposition to the new regime on the home front would use the opportunity to undermine it from within. While Trotsky threw himself into the task of creating a capable 'Red' Army, Dzerzhinskii stepped up his work to secure the home front. On the same day that the party newspaper *Pravda* warned its readership that 'The Socialist Fatherland is in Danger', the Cheka instructed local administrations (Soviets) to 'seek out, arrest and shoot immediately' those whom they deemed to present a threat to the regime. There were no specific instructions on investigations, or standards of evidence, and there was no basis for appeal. For the first time in what was to become a long history of such episodes, Cheka 'justice' was to be applied without restraint or explicit limits. Where the survival of the revolution was at stake, the end justified the means.

The Cheka did not, as a matter of course, have set procedures for proving guilt or innocence. Matters of legal process were conspicuously ill-defined, and individual judgements played the largest role in determining whether someone held by the Cheka was shot, imprisoned, fined, or released. Out of habit, the families of those arrested were inclined to hire the best lawyer they could afford. The Cheka was quick to issue a statement to the effect that 'lawyer-petitioners confer no advantages, and on the contrary will only make matters worse'.[8] In

8. A. A. Plekhanov and A. M. Plekhanov, *F. E. Dzerzhinskii: Predsedatel' VChK-OGPU, 1917–1926. Dokumenty* (Moscow, 2007), 36.

part, counter-revolutionary crimes were loosely defined because the regime did not have time to investigate and sort through legal niceties. Complaints about the contemporary situation could be classified as counter-revolutionary agitation, but the larger group to lose their lives were deemed guilty by association with class enemies of the regime. As Marxist revolutionaries, Bolsheviks tended to assume not merely that the bourgeoisie and old elites were hostile to them, but that many were actively conspiring against them. For the Cheka—the agency instructed to protect the revolution by uncovering such conspiracies—these assumptions held the power of conviction as a matter of professional duty. Where the fate of the revolution was at stake, their duty was to act decisively and ruthlessly.

As it happened, the danger presented by the German advance was addressed in early March and the recourse to terror proved unnecessary for the time being. The seat of government was moved from the vulnerable Petrograd to the high walls of the Moscow Kremlin. To put an end to the German advance, the Bolsheviks met German demands in the Treaty of Brest-Litovsk. They surrendered the western borderlands of the Empire, including Ukraine, Poland, Finland, and the Baltic region. In so doing, they gave up 26 per cent of the population of the Russian Empire, 28 per cent of its industrial infrastructure, three-quarters of its coal and iron deposits, and rich agricultural land on which over a third of the country's grain was harvested.[9] It was not a popular decision, but it settled the immediate threat to the regime. Unfortunately for the Bolsheviks, the treaty did not offer much respite, because the threat from the Germans was soon replaced by advancing White armies and various foreign forces attempting to unseat the Bolsheviks in order to bring Russia back into the war.

Trotsky's efforts to build the Red Army continued apace, but they were not up to the initial onslaught. In the spring of 1918, the Reds suffered defeats to General Krasnov, north of Petrograd, to Kaledin and the Cossacks on the Don, and to General Kornilov in Ukraine. As the 'loyal' core of the Imperial Army, the Whites had an obvious advantage in terms of military training and experience. The Reds, on the other hand, tried to make the most of their revolutionary credentials. The promise of a workers' state was attractive, but it was every bit as much the threat of a return to the old order that brought soldiers, exhausted

9. Richard Pipes, *A Concise History of the Russian Revolution* (New York, 1996), 175.

from three years of fighting the Germans, back into military service. But it did not bring enough of them to build a volunteer army. As the Whites advanced, the Bolsheviks announced a general mobilization of workers and miners, and two months later, a general conscription of all men between the ages 18 and 40. Conscription was not ideal, but it would have to do.

The conscripted army also needed officers to lead it and that proved to be an even graver challenge for the Bolsheviks. The rank and file soldiers were almost exclusively made up of workers and peasants who were relatively open to Bolshevik propaganda, though class background itself did not guarantee commitment. Imperial officers were another matter. Their education and upbringing meant that they were likely to be hostile to the revolution. Few experienced commanders joined the Reds voluntarily, and because the conscription of military leaders was problematic at best, under Trotsky's supervision, the Red Army came to be led largely by middle-ranking Tsarist officers (called *voenspetsy*), all under the watchful eye of 'political commissars' from the party. It was not a promising basis for an army. Many *voenspetsy* were poorly motivated and not least because they were treated with such suspicion. They often found their instructions countermanded by party officials. Joseph Stalin and Kliment Voroshilov did just that on the southern front in the autumn of 1918, thus provoking a fierce dispute with Trotsky. Stalin believed that the imperial officers were 'psychologically unfit to wage a decisive war on counter-revolution'. Indeed, it was well known that many *voenspetsy*, including unnamed members of the Red General Staff, were White spies. Trotsky narrowly won this particular conflict with Stalin and confirmed that party officials had to submit to the instructions of the *voenspetsy*, but the simmering suspicion and hostility in Red Army command structures was not conducive to a disciplined and coherent fighting force.[10] Through the summer and autumn of 1918, the balance of military engagements was not in the Bolsheviks' favour. Both Moscow and Petrograd looked increasingly vulnerable to White forces. By late autumn, the end of the war in Europe promised to bring tens of thousands more foreign troops against the Red forces.

10. Roger R. Reese, *Red Commanders: A Social History of the Soviet Army Officer Corps, 1918–1991* (Lawrence, Kan., 2005), 32–5.

The dangerous military situation was made that much more dangerous by the threat of subversion. Civil wars are in their nature messy affairs, dividing populations against themselves. The choice for the citizens of the former Russian Empire was relatively clear, either to support revolutionary change or to oppose it, but it was not a question that the majority of the population had posed for themselves. The frequency of peasant unrest, strikes, and mutinies spoke to an anger at being drawn into a conflict few wanted. It was not difficult to find those who were passionately committed to one side or the other, but the majority did not want a new war, and least of all one fought on their doorstep. For most people, the primary commitment was to survival, and whatever contributed to survival constituted a sensible strategy. The consequent weakness of commitment to one side or the other complicated the military campaigns of both Red and White leaders. On balance, the Whites were more concerned about the loyalties of soldiers, and the Reds were more worried about their officer corps, and the course of the fighting had a big impact on loyalties. The side that appeared to be winning tended to gather support more readily, and the losing side could easily find its forces disintegrating. When the tide of battle turned against the Bolsheviks on the eastern front in the late spring of 1918, three Red commanders abandoned their posts, and within a month, a further fifty Red officers joined the Whites. Then discipline among the soldiers almost completely broke down. Large-scale and decisive defections could be a terrible blow, but the more numerous and less conspicuous betrayals were an equally grave danger. Weak commitment and divided loyalties created opportunities for both sides to exploit. It proved to be relatively easy for each side to infiltrate the camp of the other and gather information on troop locations and battle plans, as well as to commit acts of sabotage.[11] The enemy was not just on the other side of the front. The enemy was everywhere. Just about anyone could be quietly helping the other side. For the Bolsheviks on the front the situation echoed the experience of the revolutionary underground that had been thoroughly infiltrated by *Okhrana* provocateurs. No one could be trusted.

The military situation was difficult and dangerous, but the situation on the home front provided little comfort either. The working masses

11. N. S. Kirmel', *Belogvardeiskie spetssluzhby v Grazhdanskoi voine, 1918–1922 gg.* (Moscow, 2008), 60.

were meant to be the foundation of support for the revolution. The Bolsheviks' commitment to end the exploitation by the possessing classes had some appeal both to the workers and peasants, and they made great use of it in their propaganda. In the end it played a major role in the Bolshevik victory, because the Whites only ever looked as if they would return Russia to the past. But communism as an ideal, and Marxism as a philosophy, meant nothing to the largely illiterate population of the new Soviet state. They judged the new Soviet state according to their experience of it. There was some sympathy that the Bolsheviks would have trouble realizing their stated aims in the context of civil war. But that sympathy had very real limits. So, for example, the peasant response to grain seizures by the Red Army was muted by the fact that the Whites' actions were much the same. And yet conflict was inevitable. Bolsheviks failed in their attempts to build a toehold of support in the countryside and break resistance to seizures by encouraging the poorest peasants to share seized grain. Peasant society was more cohesive than they anticipated, and the peasantry wanted nothing more than to be left alone on the land that the Bolsheviks had promised them. Lenin recognized this as early as May 1918, declaring that 'owners of grain who possess a surplus' and do not hand it over, regardless of social status 'will be declared enemies of the people'.[12] The act confirmed the beginning of a long history of conflict between the Bolsheviks and what remained the majority of the population.

The urban working class had generally embraced Bolshevism in 1917 and abandoned more moderate parties in response to the promise of a proletarian state. But the promise of an end to exploitation and 'worker control' in the factories was not compatible with the necessities imposed by the Civil War. The time was not right to hand power to the workers. The management of factories became even more steeply hierarchical, and indeed militarized. Lenin's famous slogan 'He who does not work does not eat' sounded exceptionally mild in the context of an emerging order of 'conscripted' factory labour in which, as in the countryside, those who abandoned their posts were branded 'enemies of the people'. More worrying still for the workers was the gradual return of the old factory bosses and other 'bourgeois specialists'. As with the Red Army and imperial officers, the Bolsheviks could

12. Lynne Viola, *Peasant Rebels under Stalin: Collectivization and the Culture of Peasant Resistance* (Oxford, 1996), 16.

not do without the expertise they alone possessed. Workers could be forgiven for beginning to wonder if they had done the right thing in supporting them. On the surface of it, the new regime was worse than the one it replaced. It did not help that wages shrank and the supply of food in the cities was irregular at the very best. Malnourished and overworked, thousands were dying of typhus, cholera, and influenza every month. To be sure, there remained a solid core of support for the Bolsheviks, especially among working class youth, and a lingering sympathy that the aims of the revolution could not be achieved in the context of civil war, but by their tens of thousands workers simply abandoned urban areas for the countryside. The working class, in whose name the Bolsheviks had seized power, seemed to be heading for extinction. Many who stayed behind retained their enthusiasm for proletarian revolution, but they were far from sure that they wanted the Bolsheviks to lead it.

It was pretty much downhill from there. If the working classes had deeply ambiguous feelings for the new regime, much of the rest of the population was actively conspiring against it. The other revolutionary parties did not disappear after the revolution and the Bolsheviks were open to working with them, but not on any terms. The (Left) Socialist Revolutionaries (SRs), for example, remained in the Soviet government but conflicts over policy came to a head with their opposition to the Treaty of Brest-Litovsk when most resigned their posts. Unable to work towards their own revolutionary aims within the existing revolutionary order, they continued to pursue them outside it and in opposition to the Bolsheviks. They expressed their anger at what they perceived to be the disastrous terms of the peace with Germany by assassinating the German ambassador, Count Wilhelm Mirbach, in an attempt to restart the war. Another SR, Fanny Kaplan, attempted to assassinate Lenin on 30 August 1918. She nearly succeeded. Lenin survived the two gunshot wounds he received that day, but his health never quite recovered. On the same day, another SR fatally wounded S. Uritskii, head of the Petrograd Cheka. They did not limit themselves to these sorts of terrorist acts, for which they had been so well known before the revolution. They were also trying to organize insurrections among workers and peasants, occasionally cooperating with the Whites.

The Mensheviks had no such clear break with the Bolsheviks. They continued to hold posts in government—city and provincial soviets, factory committees, and trades unions—but their 'cooperation' posed a problem for the Bolsheviks insofar as the Mensheviks appeared to be gaining in popularity as disillusion with them was settling in. Rather than let them continue to gain worker support at their expense, they squeezed Mensheviks out of their various positions on one pretext or another. Meanwhile the Anarchists were another matter. There was no pretext of cooperation in this case. Fortunately for the Bolsheviks, they got wind that Anarchists were stockpiling weapons at various strategic locations in central Moscow. After an almighty gun battle, they were disarmed. The Petrograd Anarchists surrendered without a fight two weeks later, but they continued to take part in armed uprisings organized by others long after that.[13]

Members of the more liberal political parties, together with journalists, academics, doctors, teachers, and much of the rest of the cultural intelligentsia, had profound doubts about the Bolsheviks, though there were those who were enthusiastic about the potential of revolutionary change. Many initially refused to cooperate with the new regime, such as teachers, who were intermittently on strike between December 1917 and March 1918. The Bolsheviks were aware that a hard line might permanently alienate these groups, whose cooperation was so desperately needed, but they were aware of the danger of an anti-Soviet fifth column, particularly as White forces were advancing on Moscow and Petrograd. They accepted a measure of autonomy for those groups willing to work with them, but the political police widely used informants among their sympathizers to root out those who secretly, and not so secretly, continued to struggle against Soviet power. Well into 1918, journalists and political commentators had been able to publish opinion critical of the new regime, but by April and May of 1918 the regime was intensely aware of the danger that a free press presented to their ability to rally the uncertain support of the population under their control and closed many journals and newspapers.[14] Of course this did not stop those with strong anti-Bolshevik views from expressing themselves and taking action. The Cheka arrested individual journalists, academics, lawyers, and others whom informers accused of 'counter-revolutionary activity'. Some were genuinely working in underground groups trying to unseat the Bolsheviks, but

13. Plekhanov and Plekhanov, *Dzerzhinskii*, 37–9.

14. Having closed one publication after another in the spring, the Council of People's Commissars passed a directive on 4 Aug. 1918 closing all 'bourgeois' newspapers. See Plekhanov and Plekhanov, *Dzerzhinskii*, 47–51.

others had good reason to be taken aback by the late-night knock on the door from agents of the political police. The Cheka had neither the time nor the resources to conduct thorough investigations, and given the general pall of suspicion that lay over the intelligentsia, they tended to arrest first and ask questions later. But even in the summer of 1918, they generally did ask questions later, and released those who could reasonably establish their innocence.

'Capitalists', from the owners of large plants to the petty traders, were another group that worried the Bolsheviks terribly. It was easy enough to bring enterprises under state control through nationalization, but another thing altogether to sustain industrial production and the flow of food and other basic consumer goods. Most industrialists and owners of major commercial interests had left at the time of the revolution, but many of their senior administrators, engineers, foremen, and others remained. Yet again, the Bolsheviks were desperately in need of the expertise of a group they understood to be fundamentally hostile to them. Yet again, they felt the need to retain what expertise they could while using informants to identify those who tried to undermine the new regime from within. The danger of false denunciations here was particularly acute, given the history of hostility between workers and management which the Bolsheviks had themselves done so much to encourage. It is very difficult to know what was actually happening at the factories, but the Cheka was left with the impression that the sabotage of industrial infrastructure was widespread, and that 'speculation', rather than being a small-scale activity of petty traders profiting by selling dearly commodities in short supply, was a 'counter-revolutionary' strategy of major commercial and banking interests trying to turn the working classes against the Bolsheviks by intensifying shortages.[15]

While such accusations may have been far-fetched, it does appear as though many of the Bolsheviks' extraordinary fears were not far off the mark. Their gravest concern was that anti-Bolshevik forces would combine to weaken the home front while the White armies were advancing on Moscow and Petrograd. Indeed the archives of the White forces make it clear that considerable efforts were being made to organize a fifth column and orchestrate uprisings to smooth the advance of White forces. Secret organizations like 'The Union for the

15. K.V. Skorkin, *NKVD Rossii*, 31.

Defence of the Fatherland and Freedom' and the 'Union for the Rebirth of Russia' consisted at the core of officers of the imperial army. Behind some kind of legal front, they made contact with anti-Bolshevik groups and individuals in an effort to coordinate action. They were deeply aware that small uprisings here and there presented little challenge to the Bolsheviks, but, to quote the memoirs of one organizer, there was a much greater potential in 'a coordinated, broad-based single uprising in several major centres at the moment when more or less serious [White and foreign] armed forces were approaching'.[16] This was the plan through the spring and summer of 1918, and they were not without some success. With funding from the French diplomatic mission, other foreign governments, and old banking and commercial interests, they established armed 'centres' not only in Moscow, but in Yaroslavl', Kostroma, and Rybinsk, among other towns. They gathered right-wing politicians, academics, doctors, and others hostile to the Bolsheviks, even disaffected workers. In Yaroslavl' alone they had over 1,000 sympathizers ready to act. And they did. As White troops approached Moscow, the Yaroslavl' uprising in July 1918 was meant to trigger uprisings in the other centres. Yaroslavl' held out for nearly three weeks, but the chain reaction was not set off. These individuals and groups shared little but a determination to unseat the Bolsheviks, and at the critical moment, coordinated action proved impossible.

The centres lingered, but not for long. After Fanny Kaplan's attempted assassination of Lenin, the Bolshevik approach to the danger of 'counter-revolution' changed sharply. The survival of the revolution appeared to be on a knife's edge. The Red Army were unable to halt the relentless march of the White forces on the capital, while their grip on the home front appeared increasingly tenuous. Their response was to launch a campaign of terror. Lenin perceived that the Bolsheviks had no other choice. His logic was cold and brutal: 'What's better? To capture and imprison, and even to execute hundreds of turncoats from the Constitutional Democrats, ... Mensheviks, SRs (rising up against us) either in arms or in a conspiracy or by encouraging others against Soviet power ... (Either we do that) or we let things

16. V. Zh. Tsvetkov, 'Osobennosti antisovetskoi razvedyvatel'noi raboty podpol'nykh voenno-politicheskikh struktur belogo dvizheniia 1917–1918gg.', in A. A. Zdanovich, G. E. Kuchkov, N.V. Petrov, and V. N. Khaustov (eds), *Istoricheskie chtenie na Lubianke: 1997–2008* (Moscow, 2008), 45, quoting V. Gurko, 'Iz Petrograda cherez Moskvu, Parizh i London v Odessu', *Arkhiv russkoi revoliutsii* (Berlin, 1924), xv. 66–7.

reach the point where Kolchak and Denikin can beat, shoot and crush to death tens of thousands of workers and peasants? The choice isn't difficult...'[17] From that point, the Cheka and other forces defending the revolution no longer asked questions, no longer paid attention to evidence of guilt or innocence. Anyone even suspected of an association with the Whites or other groups hostile to the revolution was whisked off to a concentration camp or shot on the spot. Mass searches and arrests replaced the more targeted tactics of the summer. The regime gave up on their attempts to win over those who wavered in their support for the revolution and relied instead on fear. Indeed, some questioned whether the bourgeoisie could be useful to the regime. As Martyn Latsis, a Cheka leader, put it in November 1918: 'We are not waging war on individual persons. We are exterminating the bourgeoisie as a class. During the investigation, we do not look for evidence that the accused acted in deed or word against Soviet power. The first questions you ought to put are: to what class does he belong? What are his origins? What is his education or profession? And it is these questions that ought to determine the fate of the accused.'[18] On such logic, many thousands of the Russian middle class were murdered in the following year, and they were by no means the only victims. The Red Army fell into the habit of executing captured White soldiers rather than removing them to camps. Villages perceived to have supported the enemy were razed to the ground. Peasants who resisted the seizure of grain were shot on the spot. In the case of the Cossacks, the Bolsheviks set out, in 1919, to exterminate an entire group perceived to be irretrievably hostile to Soviet power. Hundreds of thousands were killed or deported. The Whites also resorted to terror on much the same scale and with similar virulence. The bloodbath continued to the end of the war in 1921, claiming millions of lives.

Fatefully, the opening of the campaign of terror had coincided with a turn in the tide of the Civil War. To be sure there were many more moments of danger, more defeats, and periods of retreat, but the politics of class hatred and summary justice appeared to instil a discipline and steely determination in Bolshevik forces. As Leon Trotsky subsequently observed: 'In the autumn [of 1918] the great revolution really

17. V. I. Lenin, 'Vse na bor'bu s Denikinym', *Izbrannye sochineniia* (Moscow, 1987), ix. 37–8.
18. Quoted from Robert Gellately, *Lenin, Stalin and Hitler: The Age of Social Catastrophe* (London, 2007), 72–3.

occurred. Of the pallid weakness that the spring months had shown there was no longer a trace.'[19] The extreme acts of brutality against the 'forces of counter-revolution' subtly shifted in the minds of Bolsheviks from an unfortunate necessity to a positive expression of the capacity of Soviet power to overcome all obstacles to the realization of its revolutionary aims. There remained many Bolsheviks who were deeply aware that a powerful and unrestrained apparatus of political violence sat uncomfortably with their ideal of human liberation. Even at the height of the Civil War there were those who sought to restrain the Cheka and temper the violence. From time to time, Dzerzhinskii was compelled to defend his organization from those who would reduce its powers and budget. He never gave ground. He glorified the ruthless defence of the revolution. He warned of the dangers ahead. And he generally won the support of his fellow Bolsheviks. Their first three years in power were spent in a life and death struggle in which their sense of ally and enemy, friend and foe, us and them, had been radically simplified. There was no space for ambiguous feelings and doubts, no time to win over the waverers. The mindset was that you were either with us, or you were against us, and if you were against us, you would be destroyed. That pattern of thought survived long after the Civil War had been won.

The exceptional violence of the Civil War had many different sources. There was a long history of political turmoil in Russia, a history of assassinations, coups, uprisings, and civil wars in which power was won and held with bloody force. The Reds and Whites were conscious of it, and had personal experience of it in the years before 1917, when the tactics of both the revolutionaries and the autocratic establishment had hardened sharply. As the revolutionaries resorted to terrorism, the old regime suspended legal norms and exiled, imprisoned, or executed thousands in reply. The decade of reactionary politics that followed the revolution of 1905 was a stark reminder to the Bolsheviks of what would happen if they lost the Civil War and an object lesson that, when in power, ruthless violence can keep you there. The Bolshevik recourse to violence was informed not only by the Russian precedents, but by the history of revolutionary movements in eighteenth- and nineteenth-century Europe which had shown, in their view, not only that revolutionaries had consistently underestimated

19. W. Bruce Lincoln, *Red Victory: A History of the Russian Civil War* (London, 1991), 161.

the forces of reaction, but that violence was synonymous with revolution. The end of the Jacobin phase in France had marked the beginning of the counter-revolution.

The violence of the Russian Civil War was a matter both of theory and of practice. The Bolsheviks were not predestined by their ideological orientation and study of history to rule by violent means, but they were determined not to shy away from violence when, in their view, necessity dictated it. That time arrived decisively when their various enemies exposed their vulnerability on the home front just as the Whites were closing in on Moscow and Petrograd. From there the use of terror broadened and deepened not only because the Bolshevik leadership was convinced of the necessity, but because the party rank and file and the mass of soldiery had been hardened in battle since the beginning of the First World War. The marked improvement in Bolshevik fortunes in the autumn of 1918 seemed to justify terror. Terror gradually came to occupy a place of glory in the history of the revolution. The Cheka won a reputation as the 'sword and shield of the revolution' and the Chekists as 'the best Bolsheviks'.

The question remains how the experience of the Civil War contributed to the political violence of the mid-1930s. Is there a direct line between Lenin's terror and Stalin's terror? There are no easy answers. Certainly the conduct of terror in the 1930s followed familiar patterns. As in the Civil War, the political police was given extraordinary powers, not only to conduct mass searches and mass arrests, but also to act as judge, jury, and executioner. As in the Civil War, hundreds of thousands of Soviet citizens were arrested and, often without any material evidence of a crime, imprisoned, exiled, or shot. Exile to the Gulag was not Stalin's invention. Nor indeed was it Lenin's. Its roots can be traced to Ivan the Terrible in the sixteenth century. So, for that matter, can the roots of political policing and arbitrary arrest and execution: to Ivan's *Oprichnina*. The history of political violence in Russia contributed to the violence both of the Civil War and of the Stalin era, but it cannot explain the events of the 1930s. The historical pattern of violence did not make Stalin's terror inevitable. Nor for that matter did Bolshevik ideology. Stalin was very much Lenin's disciple in the way he understood the history of revolutionary movements and the threat of counter-revolution. Not least because Lenin successfully brought the Bolsheviks through the Civil War, Stalin shared the leader's ideas on strategy and tactics broadly, and specifically as they concerned the application of terror in defence of the revolution. And yet, this kind of explanation of political violence under Stalin as 'Leninism Triumphant' is deeply problematic too, not only because it brushes aside the anti-authoritarian strands of Bolshevism and exaggerates the naked impulse to dictatorship, but also because *objectively*, there was no clear threat to Soviet power, or for that matter to Stalin's power, in the mid-1930s, when terror again reared its ugly head. There was no civil war in the mid-1930s. No alliances of foreign states bent on restoring capitalism. There were no armed uprisings. There was no sabotage or subversion or conspiracies drawing together enemies of the Soviet state.

Or were there?

On the surface of it, the question seems absurd. It is a relatively straightforward task to establish that Stalin's regime faced no substantial or immediate threat in the mid-1930s, or at least nothing that could compare to the threat that provoked the onset of the Red Terror in 1918. And yet the key lies in *perception*, because by the mid-1930s, Stalin, the broader Soviet elite, and much of the Soviet population too, *perceived* that a new Civil War was imminent; that White forces—still at arms on the Soviet borderlands—were preparing to join a coalition of capitalist powers in an anti-communist crusade; that disaffected Soviet citizens were being recruited by foreign agents and domestic enemies of the regime in advance of the attack, and that the regime could not rely on the unambiguous support of the peasantry, the workers, or indeed its own party and state apparatus. The origin and evolution of this misperception is the story of *The Great Fear*. It is not a story of paranoia, at least not in the sense of a clinical condition. Stalin and the many others who shared this fear were coldly rational in the way they processed the information provided to them. Rather, this is a story of the profound flaws in the Soviet systems of information collection and processing. It is a story that has its roots in the Civil War. The flaws in the systems of information collection and the misperception of threat have their roots here. In understanding Stalin's terror, this was the critical legacy of the Civil War: the long Russian tradition of political violence, and the Bolsheviks' determination ruthlessly to combat threats to the revolution were necessary, but not sufficient conditions for the extraordinary violence of the Stalin era. The perception of threat was the trigger.

The experience of Civil War generated a heightened sensitivity to threat. When they seized power in 1917, the Bolsheviks had hoped carry the support of the working masses, but they had few illusions about the challenge of taking and sustaining control over the entirety of the former Russian Empire. Knowledge of the enemy was going to play a critical role, but it was not clear to them from the start that an intelligence service was necessary. The study of Marx and of the history of revolutionary movements convinced them that they understood the ways of counter-revolutionaries. All things being equal, they did not want to reproduce the Tsarist systems of intelligence collection. The earnest beginning of the Civil War, and of the counter-revolution, gave notice that they had no choice. But they had no experience of it, and in contrast to the army or industry, they could not rely on Tsarist 'specialists'. As such the Bolshevik intelligence collection system was staffed by amateurs, and amateurs of a particular intellectual habit. They developed the basic skills of intelligence collection on the job, and not without success. But because of chronic staff shortages and underfunding, the system relied heavily on the interrogation of suspects, and those caught in 'counter-revolutionary acts'. Particularly in the context of a brutal civil war, the methods of interrogation tended not to elicit subtle or nuanced responses from suspects, though they were broadly effective. It is possible now to compare the archives of the White armies with those of the Bolsheviks, and measure roughly how well Soviet intelligence systems worked. There is, as yet, no detailed academic study of the issue, and a detailed analysis is not possible in the confines of this book, but it is clear enough that intelligence gatherers grasped the broad dimensions of the threat to the regime. Bolshevik leaders did not need much more than that because the Red Terror was itself a crude instrument.

To be sure, the Cheka periodically took stock of the intelligence, especially when it had failed to anticipate major White advances or uprisings, but the more detailed, summary analysis of the counter-revolutionary threat was released after the war had been brought successfully to a close. And it is there, in volumes such as the famous *Red Book of the Cheka* (1922),[20] that we can see certain fundamental trends in misperception. Most significantly, the Cheka attributed to their enemies a greater coherence than they possessed. Certainly there were scores of 'conspiracies' organized by White officers, Kadets, SRs, Mensheviks, and foreign adventurers. They tried to gather support from anti-Bolshevik

20. M. I. Latsis, *Krasnaia Kniga VChK*, 2 vols. Reprint ed. A. S. Belidov (Moscow, 1990).

groups and individuals. The documents they left behind expressed their hopes for a united front that could unseat the Bolsheviks. They outlined their efforts to find political programmes around which the diversity of views could rally. Almost without exception they failed, but the Cheka did not grasp the depth of the divisions that inhibited united action. The summary analysis consistently concludes that anti-Bolshevism was a sufficient rallying point: 'in the struggle with the common enemy, all agreed to mutual concessions and compromise: the monarchists agreed to a national council, and the socialists agreed to recognize a military dictatorship and the private ownership of land. These and others all anticipated the arrival in Moscow of the dictatorship of the (White) generals and the destruction of the Bolshevik (government) they so hated.'[21] This was, after all, the lesson of the great revolutionary failures of the previous century: the threat posed by uprisings of the working people united the forces of reaction. In the words of the *Red Book*, they were carrying out the political duty of their class.[22] But it did not apply here. Many opponents of the Bolsheviks wanted to find a common ground, but they could not. The Cheka analysis made it look as if the aristocracy was in league with commercial and industrial interests, and with right-wing and liberal parties who took instructions from the Whites who were cooperating with non-Bolshevik revolutionaries. And all were being financed and advised by foreign capitalist governments. The analysis suggested there were contacts among all these groups. There were passing alliances and efforts at cooperation. But there was too much mutual suspicion and too many stark incompatibilities in their plans for Russia's future for any meaningful concerted action. The analysis was misguided.

The Cheka developed a taste for uncovering grand conspiracies: 'The Council of Public Activists', 'The Union of Land Owners', 'The Commercial-Industrial Committee', 'The Right Centre', 'The Union of Regeneration', and so on. Arrests and interrogations brought new arrests and new 'revelations' of links among these groups. Trials, exile, and execution of 'counter-revolutionaries' coincided with the successful advance of the Red Army. The Cheka was determined to take credit for victory not only because they sincerely believed in the substance of their contribution to victory, but because they knew that there

21. Ibid. 22.
22. Ibid. 16.

remained a core of opinion in the party hostile to the existence of a powerful Bolshevik political police. Documents like the *Red Book* were part of a conscious and focused effort by the Cheka to justify its existence. Fortunately for them, a majority of Bolshevik leaders shared the view that counter-revolutionary conspiracies had been, and would remain, a profound threat to Soviet power.

2

Peace and insecurity

By the beginning of 1920, the outcome of the Civil War was no longer in much doubt. It would take several more years before fighting ceased, but the military threat to the survival of the Soviet state had passed. The White armies were in retreat on all fronts and foreign forces had begun to withdraw. The Bolshevik leadership could now shift their attention to rebuilding a country devastated by five and a half years of total war. The economy lay in ruins and the population on the verge of famine, but the steady advance of the Red Army filled the leadership with confidence that similar victories could be obtained on the 'economic front'. They tried, for a time, to build communism by brute force and at speed, nationalizing all industry, banning private production and trade, enforcing military discipline in the factory, conjuring up super-ambitious multi-year plans, breaking all resistance with teams of leather-jacketed commissars.

This policy of 'war communism' did not work. The economy continued to shrink through 1920 primarily because the continuing seizures of agricultural goods left the peasants with little incentive to increase production. The absence of food stifled industrial production and gave impetus to a black market that made a mockery of the ban on private trade. By the beginning of 1921, peasant riots were threatening to explode into full-scale rebellion. The depletion of food stocks provoked a descent into famine. Criminal gangs roamed the towns and countryside. In late February, the soldiers of the Kronstadt garrison, a group that had played a substantial role in the Bolshevik seizure of power in 1917, rose up against the new regime and its disastrous policies. Lenin and others in the leadership had begun to doubt the efficacy of war communism, but the Kronstadt rising served notice that a sharp turn in policy was needed to prevent a descent into chaos. That turn began with the end of grain seizures (*prodrazverstka*) and their replacement with a tax-in-kind (*prodnalog*). It encouraged peasants to maximize spring sowing on the grounds that they would be allowed to keep a fixed proportion of their harvest. The threat of rebellion was averted, but the measures were too late to forestall a famine. Millions died in the course of the following two years despite the acceptance of food aid from abroad.

The famine strengthened the regime's commitment to the tax-in-kind as an incentive to agricultural production, and that commitment in turn imposed a new logic on economic policy. The regime needed agricultural surpluses to reach urban areas and peasants could not deliver it effectively on their own. Though there was some resistance to the idea, the ban on private trade was lifted. And if peasants were to part with their grain, they would need something to buy. In order to encourage the production of appropriate goods, the regime then lifted the ban on private production. Thousands of small enterprises that had been nationalized were leased to entrepreneurs who were empowered to sell their production at a profit. In essence, the Bolshevik leadership was presiding over a partial restoration of capitalism. Lenin held firm to the logic of the change though it escaped many of his contemporaries. The fastest possible reconstruction of the economy was necessary not merely to ensure the survival of Soviet power, but to create the foundations for the construction of a socialist society in the future. Lenin reasoned that, on the promise of a profit, capitalists could be encouraged to produce the rope with which the Soviet state would later hang them. Even the large-scale enterprise that remained in the hands of the state was subject to the logic of the market. Mines and factories alike were obliged to work at a profit, and were given the right to sell their output to whatever private or state enterprise paid the highest price. The regime even invited foreign capitalists to Soviet Russia to invest in the reconstruction and earn a profit on the same basis.

This 'New Economic Policy' (NEP) did work, though not without crises and controversy. As early as 1923, the harvest was already at 75 per cent of its pre-war level. Food got to the cities and industry began to recover at a furious pace. By 1926, factory production exceeded the level in 1913.[1] The success of this quasi-market economy

1. Measured in 1926–7 rubles. Alec Nove, *An Economic History of the USSR* (London, 1969), 94.

both pleased and troubled Bolshevik leaders. Their first strategy for the construction of communism had failed miserably. Now, a series of ad hoc measures, accommodating the elements of capitalism, was a roaring success. Could NEP lead to socialism? Or would it inevitably lead to the restoration of capitalism? There was plenty of reason to fear the latter. The success of NEP relied on peasants to produce surpluses, but the majority of them remained subsistence farmers. The few who did produce surpluses were the most successful capitalists. 'Kulak' was the regime's term of abuse for this group on which they so heavily depended. Twice in the course of the 1920s, surplus-producing peasants across the country had refused to bring grain to market in protest at the high prices charged for industrial production. The 'kulak' appeared to be in a position to hold the Soviet government to ransom.

Capitalists in the towns were a worry too. Petty traders and other entrepreneurs flourished, while the workers struggled with rising prices. No wonder workers asked themselves what had happened to the dictatorship of the proletariat they had been promised. Were not they supposed to be the ruling class? Opinion in the party was equally divided. It seemed reckless on the one hand to risk the extraordinary benefits NEP had brought, but on the other hand they had to be vigilant to the dangers that NEP presented to their revolutionary ambitions. The universally acknowledged leader of the Bolsheviks, Vladimir Lenin, had died in January 1924 without making adequate provisions for a smooth succession. As a result, the resolution of the policy dilemmas NEP imposed and the debates that ensued became a battleground of the Bolshevik titans struggling to succeed Lenin. Trotsky, Zinoviev, Stalin, Bukharin, and others put forward their competing views through the mid to late 1920s, both in the conviction that they best understood the way forward, and in the determination to seize Lenin's mantle.

On the surface of things, this was a great advance from the dark days of the Civil War when the Bolsheviks clung to power by the narrowest of margins. The strikes and protests of the 1920s bore little resemblance to the riots and rebellion of the Civil War. There was no mass hunger and the factories and plants were buzzing with activity. Bolshevik leaders were locked in struggle, but their differences only concerned how to build on the successes of NEP and realize their common vision of a communist society. Most importantly, they were no longer at war. The Whites had been defeated and driven beyond the borders of the Soviet Union, and the armies of the capitalist countries had withdrawn.

There was no shortage of anti-communist sentiment in the wider world, deepened by the Bolsheviks' efforts to export revolution through the Communist International, but after the years of the Great War—the First World War—public sentiment was powerfully opposed to any return to war. The Bolshevik leaders had every reason to believe that they could debate the future of the revolution confident that Soviet power was secure, both domestically and internationally. And yet historians have largely failed to see that the Bolsheviks substantially misperceived the situation they faced, and that serious anxieties about security lingered in ways that shaped the policy debate and the future of the Soviet Union.

There were several reasons why the Bolsheviks could not shake off their insecurity. Part of the explanation lies in Bolshevik ideology. Following Lenin's theory of imperialism,[2] Bolsheviks were inclined to think that the development of capitalism and of competition for markets inevitably led to war, and that because the success of Soviet socialism constituted an immediate threat to the capitalist order, a showdown between a coalition of capitalist powers and the Soviet Union would come sooner or later. But this is only part of the explanation. The Soviet Union had faced an invading coalition of capitalist powers in the Civil War and it was nothing but prudent to employ Soviet intelligence services to watch lest such a coalition might re-emerge. And yet, by establishing the identification of threats against the regime as the first priority of the intelligence services, a bias was built into the information collected. Deepening this bias was the predisposition of Soviet leaders to disregard, or at least to discount, counter-evidence. At the same time, there was no shortage of evidence of anti-communism in the capitalist world, anti-communist activity, and genuinely hostile intent towards the USSR.[3] The Bolsheviks understood this anti-communism and anti-Bolshevism in class terms: the success of the revolution presented a concrete threat to the dominance of the bourgeoisie in the capitalist states. While the Soviet Union existed, thrived, and rallied communist

2. The manuscript of 'Imperialism, The Highest Stage of Capitalism: A Popular Outline' was completed in 1916. It remains Lenin's best-selling work.
3. Michael Jabara Carley has written extensively on anti-communist sentiment in the inter-war period. See his articles, 'Episodes from the Early Cold War: Franco-Soviet Relations, 1917–1927', *Europe-Asia Studies*, 7 (2000), 1275–1305; 'Down a Blind Alley: Anglo-French Soviet Relations: 1920–1939', *Canadian Journal of History*, 2 (1994), 147–72; 'Behind Stalin's Moustache: Pragmatism in Early Soviet Foreign Policy, 1917–41', *Diplomacy and Statecraft*, 3 (2001), 159–74.

movements abroad, the likelihood of a successful revolution in Europe was substantially greater. Soviet leaders were sure that 'bourgeois' governments would not tolerate the threat to their existence. But the Bolsheviks consistently overestimated both their fear of revolution and their determination to destroy the Soviet government.

The Cheka had reason to want them to. As the Civil War came to a close, pressure rose to restrain the powers of the political police.[4] The Ninth Congress of Soviets in December 1921 decided on a fundamental reorganization of the structure and function of the organization. Stalin co-chaired (with L. B. Kamenev) the commission which oversaw the process.[5] Obscurely renamed the State Political Administration or GPU, the new structure had much more carefully circumscribed rights to investigate and try political cases on its own, and the Commissariat of Justice was granted its demand to review GPU verdicts. Furthermore, in the subsequent three years, the staff of the new organization was allowed to decline by 50 per cent. Feliks Dzerzhinskii, candidate member of the Politburo and the head of the GPU (and Cheka before it), was by no means indifferent to the weakening of his organization. He tried to resist and limit the supervision by the legal organs of their activities.[6] He pushed several times, unsuccessfully, to focus all intelligence-gathering activity in the hands of the GPU.[7] He fought to ensure that the GPU could continue to conduct major operations and that it did not shrink further because of an inability to provide a decent standard of living for its workers. Among party leaders, Trotsky and Kamenev were proponents of further cuts to the GPU budget, whereas Stalin was inclined to defend the organization before the Politburo.[8] Stalin did so perhaps because he understood the role

4. For Lenin's opinion of the need for the Cheka to change its tactics, see V. I. Lenin, *Polnoe Sobranie Sochinenii (PSS)* (Moscow, 1959–1969), xl. 115.
5. V. N. Khaustov, V. P. Naumov, and N. S. Plotnikova (eds), *Lubianka: Stalin i VChK-GPU-OGPU-NKVD, ianvar' 1922-dekabr' 1936*, hereafter *Lubianka: Stalin, 1922–1936* (Moscow, 2003), 11–15.
6. e.g. in Sept. 1922, the GPU pressed for the right to execute without the approval of the Commissariat of Justice 'in exceptional circumstances, and for the right to investigate all crimes and not just cases of counter-revolutionary activity.' Ibid. 64–6.
7. Ibid. 77–8, 103.
8. The Politburo resolved in May 1922 that there should be no shortfall in the provision of wages and supplies to GPU workers, but the GPU like other Party and Soviet institutions faced regular budget cuts through the first half of the 1920s despite Stalin's advocacy. Ibid. 27–9, 37–9, 95–6, 791–2. On Kamenev and the GPU budget, see Donald Rayfield, *Stalin and his Hangmen* (London, 2005), 96.

that the political police could play in the struggle for power after Lenin's death, but he also appears to have been sympathetic to Dzerzhinskii's claims that the work of the GPU was critically important to the security of the Soviet state. Dzerzhinskii repeatedly complained to him that that security would be compromised both by budget cuts and by the limits imposed on it by the Commissariat of Justice.[9]

The best case he could make for strengthening the GPU was rooted in the results of its investigations. If his fellow Politburo members shared his sense of the grave threats that the Soviet Union faced, they would be more inclined to accept his case for more powers, staff, and financing. The Politburo membership was kept well informed of ongoing GPU operations and investigations. In the first half of the 1920s, there were operations against 'banditism' and currency counterfeiting, against 'anti-Soviet elements' in the Russian Orthodox Church, and among intellectuals. But none of these operations of itself would have commanded the attention of the Politburo as critically important to national security. There had to be an existential threat to the Soviet state. For Dzerzhinskii, the breakthrough came with 'Trest' and 'Sindikat-2', and other similar operations in which GPU agents posed as representatives of anti-Soviet organizations in search of material and financial assistance abroad. The agents contacted and ultimately infiltrated various White Russian organizations and obtained information about their plans for anti-Soviet activity, their hopes to organize and unite opposition to the Soviet Union from within, and about the support that they had, supposedly, been promised by the French, British, Polish, Romanian, and other 'bourgeois' governments. Dzerzhinskii now had 'evidence' of the plans and combined efforts of foreign governments and anti-Soviet groups to undermine the Soviet state.[10] At the same time, the intelligence agencies and party officials along Soviet southern borders warned Moscow that the British were trying to destabilize the regime by supporting opposition groups such as the Basmachi, and were supporting and arming anti-Soviet forces in Turkey,

9. Rossiiskii Gosudarstvennyi Arkhiv Sotsial'no-Politicheskoi Istorii (RGASPI) 76/3/362; A. V. Kvashonkin (ed.), *Bolshevistskoe rukovodstvo: Perepiska, 1928–1941* (Moscow, 1999), 277.

10. Richard B. Spence, 'Russia's *Operatsiia Trest*: A Reappraisal', *Global Intelligence Monthly*, 1 (1999), 19–24.

Persia, Afghanistan, and China.[11] The British were indeed very active in these states south of Soviet borders, not so much for the purpose of destabilizing Soviet borderlands, but rather to take advantage of Soviet instability to reinforce their position in those states.

Soviet leaders were also convinced that Britain and France stood financially and militarily behind the Polish forces that attacked Bolshevik Russia in the spring of 1920.[12] When the campaign suddenly went badly wrong for the Poles, and Soviet forces were on the outskirts of Warsaw, a contingent of French military advisers under General Maxime Weygand helped chase the Red Army out of Poland. After a peace was negotiated, the Bolsheviks watched carefully as the French continued to contribute money and arms to the Polish and Romanian armies.[13] For France, close ties with strong and stable regimes in eastern and southern Europe was a critical part of her strategy to contain Germany. Soviet leaders continued nevertheless to see the diplomatic and military ties among Britain, France, the Balkan states, Romania, Poland, the Baltic states, and Finland as evidence of a longer term plan to prepare a new assault on them. This sort of caution was sensible, given that these countries had given refuge to the bulk of the White armies as they had retreated from Russia. Soviet intelligence agencies warned that these states kept hundreds of thousands of White soldiers in arms and ready for war.[14]

The difficulty for Soviet leaders of distinguishing between policy towards them and towards Germany was deepened by the Treaty of Rapallo (April 1922) which set the basis for close Soviet–German relations until the early 1930s. Following Rapallo, any French action against Germany was seen by Soviet leaders as a precursor of action against the Soviet Union. The occupation of the Ruhr in early 1923 was one

11. See e.g. RGASPI 558/11/29/116–116ob for a coded telegram from the Central Asian bureau to Stalin on British support for the Basmachi. Rossiiskii Gosudarstvennyi Voennyi Arkhiv (RGVA) 25895/846/2 has intelligence from the Central Asian Military District on British support for the Emir of Bukhara.

12. RGASPI 558/11/1180/53 from an unpublished collection of Stalin's writings on military issues. See also *Pravda*, 25, 26 May 1920.

13. See e.g. Stalin's commentary in *Pravda* (18 Dec. 1921). This was reprinted in I.V. Stalin, *Sochineniia*, v. 118–20.

14. This was a common theme of communications from the political police and military intelligence in this period, but even the normally sceptical Foreign Ministry was warning of the imminence of war with Poland and Romania in the early part of 1922. See Maxim Litvinov's correspondence with members of the Politburo. RGASPI 359/1/3.

such example. While Soviet leaders were using the crisis to foment a revolution in Germany, they were convinced that neither France nor Poland[15] would tolerate a communist revolution in Germany. They believed that the military force used to crush a revolution in Germany would subsequently be turned on Soviet Russia. Soviet military intelligence suggested that the invasion of Russia was already being prepared. In February 1923, S. S. Kamenev, the commander-in-chief of the Red Army, wrote to P. P. Lebedev, the commander of the Western Army group, that the White Army was being reorganized by the Entente and was supported by a substantial (largely British) fleet that could make an independent landing on the Black Sea coast or be transported to the Soviet western frontiers. Kamenev further warned that, in the event of an invasion, all or any of the states along the Soviet western border, from Finland to Turkey, might enter a state of war with Soviet Russia.[16] Soviet military intelligence was quite wrong here, but subsequent events in Britain and elsewhere reinforced the impression that something was afoot. In May, Lord Curzon, the British Foreign Minister, demanded that the Soviet government withdraw its 'agents' operating against British interests in Asia or face the rupture of diplomatic relations. The action corresponded with reports of a sharp increase in anti-Soviet terrorist activities along Soviet borders.[17] The United States and France firmly supported Britain in what seemed to Soviet leaders to be an attempt to justify an invasion to a European and American public still thoroughly sick of war.

Soviet hopes for the German revolution were, of course, never realized, and as the political situation in Germany stabilized, the fear of invasion calmed. The calm was reinforced as the conservative and anti-Soviet governments of Stanley Baldwin in Britain and Raymond Poincaré in France fell and were replaced by (short-lived) governments on the Left interested in improving relations with Bolshevik Russia. Stalin was quick to point out that this evidence of growing 'respect' for Soviet Russia did not mean that the danger of war had passed. Stalin's many public statements on the continued danger of war strictly adhered

15. The existing cooperation between Germany and Soviet Russia made the Poles very nervous, given that neither state had an interest in Poland's continued independence. A revolution would leave Poland surrounded and doomed to a communist takeover.
16. G. M. Adibekov, Zh. G. Adibekova, L. A. Rogovaia, and K. K. Shirinia (eds), *Politbiuro TsK RKP(b)-VKP(b) i Komintern, 1919–1943: Dokumenty* (Moscow, 2004), 185–202.
17. See Lenin, *PSS*, xliii. 4.

to the logic of Lenin's writings on imperialism, but they were underpinned by concrete detail provided by the Soviet intelligence agencies. It was no secret that the British were actively investing in the east European economies, and providing substantial loans,[18] but the OGPU Foreign Department was inclined to link this financial interest to a military one. They observed frequent meetings of senior British military officers with their east European counterparts. Military intelligence told Stalin that the British were building a disturbing 'military-political and military-economic' influence in the countries along the Soviet western border, especially Poland, Romania, and the Baltic states.[19] They were convinced that the British continued to support counter-revolutionary terrorist groups planning assassinations and destabilizing national minority regions. Soviet leaders were already convinced that the Poles were hard at work trying to destabilize Belorussia and Ukraine, and so they worried about the possibility of an anti-Soviet bloc with Britain and Poland at its core. Of course, no such bloc existed, and the British were determined to avoid entanglements in Europe, but the conviction that it was an ever present possibility deepened when the Soviet leadership witnessed the negotiation of the Treaty of Locarno in the autumn of 1925. The treaty was meant to address unresolved issues in European security, most importantly by ending the isolation of Germany since the First World War. To the Soviets, Locarno was all about drawing Germany away from the USSR and eliminating the remaining obstacles to the emergence of an effective anti-Soviet bloc. Soviet leaders sensibly assumed that Poland, Romania, and the Baltic states were much less likely to wage war on the Soviet Union if there remained a threat to their security from Germany. They concluded that the treaty increased the danger of war against the USSR to the extent that it drew Germany towards the enemies of the Soviet state.

In November 1925, Dzerzhinskii passed to Stalin reports to the effect that Britain was trying to broker a deal that would end the trade war between Poland and Germany and resolve tensions over disputed

18. Zara Steiner, *The Lights that Failed: European International History, 1919–1933* (Oxford, 2005), 283–5.
19. N. S. Simonov, 'The "War Scare" of 1927 and the Birth of the Defense Industry Complex', in John Barber and Mark Harrison (eds), *The Soviet Defense Industry Complex from Stalin to Khrushchev* (Basingstoke, 2000), 35.

borders.[20] A few months later, he reported that the British were canvassing Whites in Prague, Paris, and Constantinople on the possibility of cooperation in an invasion of the USSR. Shortly thereafter, Stalin was told that the Japanese might join the coalition, supported by Zhang Zuolin in China.[21] The 'coalition' was apparently already increasing subversion and espionage in Soviet borderlands in anticipation of military action.[22]

While no such coalition existed, the steady drip of intelligence painted an ever more compelling and detailed picture of one. In May 1926, the democratic government of Poland was overthrown by Josef Pilsudski in a military coup d'état. Dzerzhinskii wrote to Stalin that he thought England was behind the coup and that they promoted Pilsudski in the interests of accelerating plans for an attack on the Soviet Union.[23] The Commissar of Foreign Affairs Georgii Chicherin, who was no alarmist, agreed with the assessment of the threat.[24] France was now also understood to be a major player in the purported bloc. At the time, the French were beginning to realize an ambition to build political and economic influence in east Europe, not least in order to contain Germany and Soviet Russia. French investment, French arms sales and other military assistance to the Poles and the Romanians, and French diplomacy including the Little Entente and alliances with Poland and Czechoslovakia gave Soviet leaders the impression of the strengthening of bonds to aggressive anti-Soviet ends. They failed to see that British and French aims in east Europe were fundamentally in conflict; that neither harboured aggressive intentions, and that neither had nearly as much influence in east Europe as they would have liked. Instead, Stalin was consistently warned that the British and French were gathering forces in Eastern Europe to orchestrate an attack on the USSR that would be spearheaded by Poland. Dzerzhinskii told him that the frequent visits of French military attachés to Poland and

20. RGASPI 76/3/364/23–31.
21. RGASPI 76/3/362/3.
22. On 14 Apr. 1926, Iagoda wrote to Stalin about 'materials in our possession which confirm beyond doubt that on the instructions of the English, the Polish and other general staffs of countries on our western borders have begun broad subversive work against the USSR and have increased their espionage network on our territory... Measures are being taken...' *Lubianka: Stalin, 1922–1936*, 117.
23. RGASPI 76/3/364/57. He had been warning about the anti-Soviet links between England and Poland since the spring of 1925.
24. Ibid., l. 70.

Romania were responsible for the signing of a military convention that was one further step in the organization of a concerted attack on the USSR. In early July 1926, he wrote to Stalin asserting that 'there is an accumulation of evidence which indicates with doubtless (for me) clarity that Poland is preparing a military assault on us with the goal of seizing Belorussia and Ukraine'.[25]

The situation appeared to be fraught, but the Soviet leadership calculated that an attack was not yet imminent. Military intelligence consistently exaggerated the size and might of the Polish armed forces and their potential to join forces with the Romanians, the Whites, and others, but they remained reasonably confident that Pilsudski, and the imagined coalition behind him, was still hesitating to act for fear of the domestic political consequences. If they could rally public opinion, they would invade. For the Soviet leadership, this was the essential background to the ARCOS raid and the rupture of relations with Britain that is commonly understood as the basis for the war scare of 1927. When the British government orchestrated the raid on the London offices of the All Russian Cooperative Society (ARCOS) in May 1927, and claimed to have uncovered documents proving that the Soviet government was engaged in subversive activity, the Soviet leadership saw the action in terms of a new, bolder, and more aggressive effort of the British bourgeoisie to convince the working class not only in England, but on the continent, to support military action against the USSR. In the first week of June, while Stalin was digesting a report on the capture of a purported British spy ring in Leningrad, he was informed that Petr Voikov, the Soviet ambassador to Poland, had been assassinated. He sent a telegram to Molotov: 'I feel the hand of England. They want to provoke (us into) a conflict with Poland. They want to repeat Sarajevo.'[26]

In fact, Britain had nothing to do with the assassination, and no plans to encourage Poland to war. Baldwin was an anti-communist, but the public manifestations of that anti-communism were as much about principle as they were about his efforts and those of his fellow conservatives to convince the British electorate that the Labour Party's

25. Ibid., l. 58.
26. The Leningrad OGPU claimed to have uncovered a British–White Russian network trying organize anti-Soviet activity in Ukraine in advance of an invasion. See A. M. Plekhanov, *VChK-OGPU, 1921–1928gg.* (Moscow, 2003), 285, citing materials from the FSB archive. Stalin's quote is from *Lubianka: Stalin, 1922–1936*, 133–5, 795.

sympathy for the Russian Revolution made it a dangerous force in British politics. In other words, the vociferous anti-communism of the Tories and the British establishment generally was largely directed at a domestic audience, and was not about to underpin an aggressive foreign policy. But that was not the way the Soviet government saw it. They thought they had overwhelming evidence to the effect that war was imminent. That 'evidence' in turn affected the way they looked at the domestic situation. Because war seemed imminent, the wavering loyalty of large segments of the population was much more worrying than it need have been.

Throughout the 1920s, the intelligence services had warned that foreign governments were building networks of agents within the USSR whose task was to undermine Soviet power from within by means of the sabotage of factories and infrastructure, the assassination of officials, and the organization of a fifth column in the event of war.[27] On the surface of it, this made considerable sense. The Soviet government had inherited many of the perennial concerns of the Tsarist regime, including the problem of thousands of miles of poorly protected borders. It presented little challenge for foreign enemies of the Soviet Union to conduct such operations, and GPU infiltration of White organizations abroad uncovered some plots and plans for more. On several occasions in the early 1920s the GPU successfully appealed against budget cuts in order to extend their agent network abroad.[28] Meanwhile, on 10 March 1922, regional GPU organs were instructed to focus their attention on 'transport and enterprises especially important to the economy and strengthen operations to uncover and prevent sabotage by SRs, Kadets and Monarchists; Secure these enterprises from the bombs and arson of counter-revolutionary elements;... [and] take further measures to uncover the espionage activities of foreigners and those with links to foreign diplomatic institutions and counter-revolutionary organizations'.[29] The instruction made sense, in so far as the regional organs were best placed to secure local enterprises facing this supposed threat.

27. Like Boris Savinkov and the 'People's Union for the Defence of the Motherland and Freedom' (Narodnyi soiuz zashchity rodiny i svobody). O. B. Mozokhin, 'Iz istorii bor'by organov VChK-OGPU s terrorizmom', *Voenno-istoricheskii zhurnal*, 5 (2002), 5; V. Chebrikov (ed.), *Istoriia Sovetskikh organov gosudarstvennoi bezopasnosti* (Moscow, 1977), 159–60.

28. On several occasions. *Istoriia sovetskikh organov*, 151; RGASPI 17/162/2/157, 160, and *Lubianka: Stalin, 1922–1936*, 108.

29. *Istoriia sovetskikh organov*, 129–30.

And yet, the local GPU organs did not have the staff, expertise, or funding to undertake successful operations to infiltrate anti-Soviet organizations as their counterparts in the Foreign Department (INO OGPU) did. At best, they maintained a crude surveillance of known SRs, Kadets, Monarchists, 'class aliens', and other individuals and groups suspected of being hostile to the regime and arrested suspects on the basis of 'revolutionary instinct' rather than any material evidence of a crime against the state. That suited central party and GPU organs in so far as they tended to demand that investigations of sabotage result in the prosecution of those responsible. But the situation also presented opportunities for ambitious regional GPU officials. *Preventing* sabotage by 'uncovering' anti-Soviet organizations often won high praise and promotion even if the evidence supporting arrests and prosecutions was largely circumstantial. Consequently, through the 1920s, the GPU, and in turn the party leadership, received a steady stream of reports from the regions detailing successful operations against saboteurs with links to foreign governments.[30]

By the mid-1920s, the growing and increasingly confident Foreign Department of the GPU was passing to the party leadership reports indicating the heightened domestic threat linked to the rising threat of foreign invasion. White Russian military forces and the Polish and Romanian governments backed by the British and French were meant to be increasing espionage and sabotage in anticipation of war.[31] In July 1925, the OGPU was given almost 4 million rubles to improve the guarding of borders.[32] Three months later, Dzerzhinskii insisted on a tightening of security in the Kremlin in response to reports of assassination plots. At the same time he was pushing the Politburo hard to free the OGPU from further oversight of the Commissariat of Justice: 'Now is not the time, politically, to take from us the right to deal with cases involving terrorists, monarchists, Whiteguard groups, and otherwise

30. Politburo resolutions on these reports can be found in RGASPI 17/162. The materials of the Politburo commission that discussed sentences for the accused (Komissiia po politdelam) remain in the Presidential Archive. Some reports were deemed suitable for publication in the national press. See e.g. the case of Kinderman, Volscht, and Ditmarin, *Pravda*, 23 June 1925, and *Lubianka: Stalin, 1922–1936*, 105–6.

31. Some of the reports that Dzerzhinskii received and passed on to Stalin between late 1924 and the first half of 1926 can be found in RGASPI 76/3/331/1–3; 76/3/364/4–8, 12–13, 21–5, 58.

32. This paid for, among other things 2,600 new border guards, 925 horses, 25,000 rifles, thirty 1.5 ton lorries, and 102 motorcycles with sidecars.

restrict our ability to fight counter-revolution.'[33] Through 1926 and into 1927, reports of fires and explosions on the transport system and at major enterprises rose sharply.[34] In the autumn of 1926, VSNKh and OGPU were working out measures to fight sabotage.[35] On 13 January 1927, Stalin ordered the OGPU to report to the Politburo on the measures it had come up with 'to combat fires and explosions and other deliberate attacks on enterprises'.[36] Menzhinskii pleaded that they did not have the resources adequately to defend enterprises from the current threats and subsequently got more money, more troops, a new department to deal specifically with the threat of sabotage, and so-called 'Committees for Cooperation with the OGPU' (*komitety sodeistviia*) in every enterprise under their surveillance.[37] In the summer of 1927, OGPU lecturers toured regional, city, and district party organizations as well as factory committees and general factory meetings in order to draw attention to the new security risks posed by the hidden agents of hostile powers.[38] Significantly, the OGPU was also given the right to try cases of sabotage without having to consult the Commissariat of Justice or the Politburo Commission on Political Affairs.[39] With the perceived increasing danger of war, this right was 'temporarily' extended in June to include cases involving White Russians, spies, and bandits.[40]

By the time Dzerzhinskii died in July 1926, the OGPU was well on its way to recovering from the cutbacks it had faced at the end of the Civil War and the limits placed on it by the Commissariat of Justice. It is likely that concrete acts of sabotage and espionage uncovered by the

33. RGASPI 76/3/362/11. At that stage the OGPU was freed from the oversight of the Commissariat of Justice on appeal to the Politburo. See e.g. RGASPI 17/162/3/56 (Apr. 1926).
34. *Istoriia sovetskikh organov*, 189.
35. Ibid. 191.
36. On the same day, he ordered Voroshilov to report on the danger of war and defence plans drawn up by the Commissariat of Defence. RGASPI 17/162/4/3–4.
37. These committees extended the existing system created in 1922 to prevent the infiltration of party committees by SRs, Mensheviks, and other 'anti-Soviet elements'. 'V. I. Lenin: "Khoroshii kommunist v to zhe vremia est" i khoroshii chekist', *Istochnik*, 1 (1996), 115–19.
38. *Istoriia sovetskikh organov*, 214.
39. Ibid. 191. RGASPI 17/162/4/70, 89, 94–6. Some of these documents are also published in *Lubianka: Stalin, 1922–1936*, 125–8.
40. *Istoriia sovetskikh organov*, 194. It was not long before the Commissariat of Justice was trying to claw these new rights back. See Krylenko's note to the Politburo, 1 July 1927. *Lubianka: Stalin, 1922–1936*, 137–8.

organization, as well as the worsening international situation, put it in a better position to plead its case before the Politburo. When asked about the extraordinary powers of the OGPU by foreign delegations on the tenth anniversary of the revolution, Stalin publicly declared they would be suspended and the OGPU disbanded 'when the capitalists of all countries stopped organizing and financing counter-revolutionary groups, conspirators, terrorists, and saboteurs'.[41] But as the OGPU received more resources, broadened its investigations and intelligence collection, as it eased its way out of the control of the Commissariat of Justice and the publicity given to the danger presented by foreign agents increased, ever more threats to the regime were found. Dzerzhinskii and his successor Viacheslav Mezhinskii passionately believed that they were protecting the regime from very real dangers, but the general lack of rigorous scepticism of the evidence of that threat contributed significantly to the belief. When the Commissariat of Justice accused them of 'excesses', of prosecuting cases on the basis of flimsy evidence, they reacted with scorn, insisting, as Dzerzhinskii did in 1925, that such complaints only helped the regime's enemies.[42]

The domestic threat extended beyond those who had entered the USSR from abroad illegally. Soviet leaders were also worried that substantial parts of the domestic population might be inclined to assist their enemies. The workers were perhaps the least of their concerns, though even in relation to their strongest natural allies, they showed a capacity to frighten themselves. The political police had compiled reports on popular opinion since 1919, but from the early 1920s, the top party leaders were receiving monthly summaries of opinion reports compiled by local organizations. In much the same way as the foreign intelligence tended to inflate any threat, the summaries of popular opinion tended to highlight hostile views and focus on regions where worker unrest was likely to flare up. Reports on the peasantry tended to reflect the regime's predisposition to see the private farmer as naturally hostile to Soviet power. The reports detailed cases of violence against Soviet officialdom in the countryside, but perhaps more worrying to the leadership was the ability and willingness of peasants

41. *Lubianka: Stalin, 1922–1936*, 144. He made a similar statement to Henri Barbusse in Sept. 1927. '"U nas malo rasstrelivaiut": Beseda I.V. Stalina s A. Barbiusom', *Istochnik*, 1 (1999), 101–5.
42. RGASPI 76/3/362/10–11.

to withhold their surpluses and hijack Soviet industrialization plans at the very time the rapid growth of industrial production was necessary to support the readiness to fight a war. As the war scare deepened in 1927, Politburo member Viacheslav Molotov directed the OGPU to compile a special report on the likely response of the population in the event of armed conflict.[43]

The leadership was even more concerned about the real and potential disloyalty of the so-called bourgeois specialists. Despite substantial investment in the training of engineers and other specialists needed for the rapidly growing economy, those with pre-revolutionary training and experience continued to hold key posts not only in major enterprises, but in the state apparatus and the army. The presence of so many 'class aliens'—members of the Tsarist middle class or lower nobility—in such positions of power and authority was a source of grave concern especially in the context of the war scare. The discovery of a 'conspiracy of specialists' was made almost inevitable by the combination of worker hostility towards bosses generally and 'bourgeois' bosses in particular, conflict between 'Red' and 'bourgeois' specialists, OGPU prejudices bred by long-standing operations against intellectuals and those with connections abroad, and a common, genuine hostility among the specialists towards the Soviet regime.

Local OGPU organizations had rich material for their regular reports to the centre on the progress of fulfilling the 13 January 1927 directive, but it was in the coal industry of the North Caucasus region that one OGPU plenipotentiary E. G. Evdokimov, with the Economic Department of the OGPU, began to build a case suggesting a broader conspiracy against the regime. It was, as ever, based on circumstantial evidence. The accused Shakhty specialists did not always work well with party authorities or enterprise directors. They were resented and distrusted by the workers since Civil War days.[44] They were treated with hostility by Soviet-trained specialists. They were critical of the plan and of enterprise directors. They had plenty of contacts abroad in Poland, Britain, and other countries thought to be preparing an invasion of the Soviet Union. But the material evidence of sabotage that

43. Marrku Kivinen, 'Obzory OGPU i sovetskie istoriki', in G. N. Sevast'ianov et al. (eds), *'Sovershenno Sekretno': Lubianka-Stalinu o polozhenii v Strane (1922–1934)* (Moscow, 2001), i/1. 25.

44. Hiroaki Kuromiya, 'The Shakhty Affair', *South East European Monitor*, 2, (1997), 41–64.

appeared to justify the hostility of those they worked with, that made the contacts with foreigners seem sinister, and that spurred on the investigation, came from the assessments of decisions the specialists had made: the flooding of certain mines, the purchase of certain equipment, the use of certain construction methods. K. I. Zonov of the OGPU Economic Department, whose personal file lists his educational level as 'lower', concluded that these decisions were so counter-productive for the efficient functioning of the enterprises for which they worked, that they could only be characterized as deliberate sabotage.[45]

Armed with Zonov's conclusions, Evdokimov took the materials of the investigation to Menzhinskii, who told him to stop the investigation. Menzhinskii's decision may have been a rare assertion of scepticism, particularly in the light of Zonov's qualifications, but it is more likely to have been rooted in his assessment of the importance of the 'bourgeois' specialists to the success of the Soviet economy in general and the Donbas in particular. Evdokimov was not put off though, and he took the risky step of going over his boss's head directly to Stalin. Like Menzhinkii, Stalin saw the dangers in such a move, but he gave Evdokimov his approval to continue the investigation. Scores of specialists were arrested, subjected to lengthy interrogations, and pressured to confess to their crimes.[46] The Politburo first discussed the Shakhty sabotage at the end of February 1928. In a week, a Politburo Commission had been established to review the OGPU materials, and a few days later news of the 'plot' was splashed across the national press.[47] Some Politburo members, notably Aleksei Rykov, argued that the accusations against the specialists were blown out of proportion. Others, like Valerian Kuibyshev, simply shared Menzhinskii's assessment that it was not the right time to attack specialists. But the

45. V. A. Kovalev, the Russian Minister of Justice from 1995, presents a fascinating assessment of the evidence and the conduct of the trial in *Dva Stalinskikh Narkoma* (Moscow, 1995), 48–59.

46. It is not clear what methods the GPU employed for obtaining confessions, but one accused at the Promparty trial testified that he had been interrogated for 18 straight hours, by which time he was ready to sign whatever his interrogators showed him. Ibid. 90.

47. The GPU report on the affair, as edited by Stalin, can be found in RGASPI 558/11/132/1–20. Stalin did not alter the substance of this report, which was widely distributed among party members, enterprise directors, trade unions, and GPU officials in mid-March.

correspondence of most other Politburo members, including moderates Nikolai Bukharin and Mikhail Tomsky, suggests that they genuinely believed that economic sabotage had become a key weapon of hostile capitalist powers in their struggle against the Soviet Union and that that sabotage extended well beyond Shakhty and the Donets Basin.[48] Even Trotsky supported the trial.[49]

And what about Nikolai Krylenko? He had consistently criticized the OGPU for conducting arrests on the basis of flimsy evidence, and here the case almost entirely lacked material proof of guilt. It rested on the technical assessments of someone who was manifestly unqualified and on confessions that had been obtained under duress. Still Krylenko acted as chief prosecutor, defending the use of confessions in evidence and soldiering on when some of the defendants began to retract their confessions.[50] Perhaps Krylenko had no choice but to act as he did in his role as chief prosecutor, but he and the others appear to have acquiesced to Stalin's promotion of the Shakhty trial not so much because they were convinced of the legal case against the accused, but because they accepted the political case for a show trial, convinced that wrecking was going on, that 'bourgeois' specialists in general were hostile to Soviet power, that they were inclined to resist the plan, that they had suspicious contacts with western powers, that a public trial portraying the dangers posed by the specialists was necessary. Of course, rather than reducing the incidence of wrecking, the calls for vigilance generated by the trial resulted in an increase in denunciations and reports of wrecking. In the weeks and months that followed, the Politburo discussed further OGPU investigations of the sabotage committed by specialists in the defence industry, transport, and metallurgy.[51] Each appeared to be part of a growing conspiracy to destabilize the economy in advance of a new foreign intervention.

The fear of a new foreign invasion combined with 'evidence' of serious domestic vulnerabilities necessarily influenced the debates about economic policy, and the struggle to succeed Lenin. The fears gradually turned party opinion away from the New Economic Policy and its quasi-market economy. The logic was clear enough. Surely the

48. *Lubianka: Stalin, 1922–1936*, 155–63; A.V. Kvashonkin et al. (eds), *Sovetskoe rukovodstvo*, 28, 91–4.
49. Hiroaki Kuromiya, *Stalin: Profiles in Power* (London, 2005).
50. Kovalev, *Dva stalinskikh narkoma*, 58.
51. RGASPI 17/162/8/1, 3, 5, 13, 136, 138, 157.

Soviet Union needed to accelerate the tempo of industrialization in order to be better prepared for the inevitable invasion of capitalist powers. Surely the further development of the industrial economy should no longer be dependent on the willingness of the petty capitalist kulak to market his grain. Surely the Soviet Union could no longer afford to permit a strengthening of capitalist and 'class alien' elements, but rather needed to return to the 'communist' methods characteristic of War Communism. Surely now that the economy had recovered, the regime could commit to the sort of fully planned system that had only failed in the context of war and ruin. Indeed, the war scare of 1927 contributed to a sharp turn against NEP and the beginning of what came to be known as the 'Great Break'. It also marked the beginning of the final phase of the struggle to succeed Lenin and the emergence of Stalin's dictatorship. Stalin used the deepening sense of insecurity to his political advantage in the late 1920s, but it is necessary to look more closely at the struggle for power in order to understand how the 'Great Break' and Stalin's increasingly dictatorial power only deepened the propensity of the regime to misperceive and exaggerate the threats to Soviet power at home and abroad.

3

The uncertain dictatorship

The story of Stalin's rise to power has been told many times in scores of biographies and studies of Soviet history, such that there has been an accumulation of received wisdom that demands critical scrutiny. An examination of the archival sources on Stalin's rise to power reveals a great deal not only about the origins of Stalin's dictatorship, but also about how strong and stable his power was both in reality and in perception. The existing literature attributes his rise to a variety of factors, from the use of terror and propaganda to the appeal of his policies, but almost without exception they mention Stalin's position as General Secretary. The common story suggests that, as General Secretary, Stalin used his control over appointments to build a personal following in the party apparatus.[1] The mechanics of this process are sometimes referred to as 'a circular flow of power'.[2] Stalin appointed individual party secretaries and, in return, they voted for him at Party Congresses. It is generally taken as given that Stalin used the power this afforded him to remove his political rivals in the course of his rise to power, and in later years, to remove those officials who had reservations about his policies. In short, the received wisdom is that, by the end of the 1920s, Stalin had a near-total, personal control

1. See e.g. Deutscher, *Stalin*; Adam B. Ulam, *Stalin: The Man and his Era* (New York, 1973); Robert C. Tucker, *Stalin as Revolutionary, 1879–1929* (London, 1974).
2. R. V. Daniels raised the idea in 'The Secretariat and the Local Organisations in the Russian Communist Party, 1921–1923', *American Slavic and East European Review*, 1 (1957), 32–49. But he coined the phrase 'circular flow' in 'Stalin's Rise to Dictatorship', in Alexander Dallin and Alan Westin (eds), *Politics in the Soviet Union* (New York, 1966). See also his *Conscience of the Revolution: Communist Opposition in Soviet Russia* (Cambridge, Mass., 1960) and T. H. Rigby, 'Early Provincial Cliques and the Rise of Stalin', *Soviet Studies*, 1 (1981), 3–28.

over the entirety of the apparatus of state; that his dictatorship was solid and secure.

In the late 1970s and the 1980s, some 'revisionist' scholars began to cast doubt on the idea that Stalin could be sure of the personal loyalty of party officials and that they would unquestioningly execute his will.[3] Since the opening of the archives new evidence has reinforced their views. New studies have clearly shown that party officials pursued agendas defined by their institutional interests and not solely by the will of Stalin or the directives of the central leadership.[4] Recent document collections portray Stalin as nagged by doubts that central directives were being fulfilled.[5] In this, his immediate subordinates were not the problem, but the greater mass of the party and state bureaucracy, pursuing institutional interests and responding to impossible demands from the centre with foot-dragging and deception. Rather than being confident of his control of party officials, Stalin appears to have been obsessed with the spectre of the *dvurushnik* (one who is two-faced, or a 'double-dealer') publicly professing his loyalty to the party line while privately working to subvert it. The new evidence thus seems to contradict the way we have understood the emergence of Stalin's personal dictatorship and to present a more fluid and unstable picture of Soviet power in the 1920s and 1930s.

An analysis of the archives of the Central Committee, and those of Stalin's Secretariat in particular, indicate that while the Secretariat played a crucial role in Stalin's rise to power, it never became a source of personalistic control of the party apparatus as is commonly assumed.

3. Their work has focused mostly on the 1930s and 1940s. W. O. McCagg, *Stalin Embattled, 1943–1948* (Detroit, 1978), parts 2–3; Lynne Viola, 'The Campaign to Eliminate the Kulak as a Class, Winter 1929–1930: A Reevaluation of the Legislation', *Slavic Review*, 3 (1986), 503–24; Getty, *Origins of the Great Purges*; Gill, *Origins of the Stalinist Political System*; Catherine Merridale, *Moscow Politics and the Rise of Stalin: The Communist Party in the Capital, 1925–1932* (Basingstoke, 1990); Gabor Rittersporn, *Stalinist Simplifications and Soviet Complications: Social Tensions and Political Conflicts in the USSR, 1933–1953* (Chur, Switzerland, 1991).

4. See e.g. R. W. Davies, *Crisis and Progress in the Soviet Economy, 1931–1933* (Basingstoke, 1996); E. A. Rees, *Decision-Making in the Stalinist Command Economy* (Basingstoke, 1997); James R. Harris, *The Great Urals: Regionalism and the Evolution of the Soviet System* (Ithaca, NY, 1999).

5. A.V. Kvashonkin et al. (eds), *Stalinskoe politbiuro v 30-e gody. Sbornik dokumentov* (Moscow, 1995); Lars T. Lih et al. (eds), *Stalin's Letters to Molotov, 1925–1936* (New Haven, 1995), published in Russian as L. Kosheleva et al. (eds), *Pis'ma I. V. Stalina V. M. Molotovu, 1925–1936gg.* (Moscow, 1995); A.V. Kvashonkin et al. (eds), *Sovetskoe rukovodstvo: Perepiska, 1928–1941* (Moscow, 1999); Getty and Naumov, *The Road to Terror*.

Stalin could not simply remove his opponents and appoint his allies. From the start, the Secretariat was not able to cope with its task of assigning cadres to party organizations. It assigned them in large numbers in an almost entirely impersonal process. Meanwhile, the party organizations' receiving cadres were profoundly involved in the appointments process. They could, and did, refuse candidates proposed by the centre. The fact of appointment was not sufficient to generate personal loyalty to the General Secretary. Stalin did, however, provide security of tenure to many party secretaries. The gravest threat to their power in the first decade of Soviet power came from political infighting (*sklochnichestvo*) in local organizations. Stalin won the support of secretaries by attacking intra-party democracy and reinforcing their power within their organizations. The political battles over the Lenin succession were exacerbating political infighting locally, and the secretaries were happy to see Stalin stop them. But only in this limited sense was there a 'circular flow of power'. Many party secretaries voted for Stalin at Party Congresses. They helped him defeat his rivals in the Politburo because they had a common interest in it, not because they felt personally beholden to Stalin. In the early 1930s, their interests began to diverge with the crisis of the first Five-Year Plan, punishing grain collections, famine, and the emergence of the 'command-administrative system'. The secretaries had helped Stalin to power, but they may have begun to worry if they had made the right choice. There was nothing they could do about it though. In attacking intra-party democracy, they contributed to a situation in which it was impossible to question the 'Central Committee line'. Where discussion and criticism of central policy was impossible, the foot-dragging and subversion we now see in the new sources was a logical response.

In order to understand how this apparently tense relationship between Stalin and party officialdom emerged in the early 1930s, we must return to the very origins of the Central Committee Secretariat, in the October seizure of power. Following the October coup in Petrograd, the Bolsheviks faced the colossal task of taking control of, and governing, the vast territories of the Russian Empire. They had to shut down, or take over, existing bureaucratic structures from the central ministries down to the local land councils. They had to do battle with other groups competing for power, including Mensheviks, Socialist Revolutionaries, and national minorities seeking to create independent states. By the spring of 1918, they also had to mobilize for civil war. They had long understood that they were undermanned. On the eve of the February Revolution, there were approximately 24,000 members of the Bolshevik underground. By the end of the Civil War, over 700,000 new members had joined the now ruling party.[6]

Registering, assigning, and directing the inflow of new recruits were colossal tasks in themselves. Iakov Sverdlov, a close associate of Lenin, was the first 'secretary' of the Central Committee in charge of personnel questions. With a staff of only six, Sverdlov could only monitor the spontaneous growth of party membership and issue general directives assigning cadres en masse. Though Lenin prized Sverdlov for his organizational skills, it would appear that his Secretariat kept few written records of its activities. Pressures to improve record keeping came from state and party organizations in the centre and regions that were frustrated by the inability of the Secretariat to meet their specific cadre needs.[7] After Sverdlov's death in March 1919, the responsibility for party appointments was formally invested in the Secretariat and Sverdlov's successors[8] undertook to expand the staff in order to meet the ever-growing need for cadres throughout the Soviet Union. By 1921, the Secretariat employed over 600 officials, but it still could not meet the needs of organizations.

Of course, the Civil War had placed considerable extra burdens on the personnel apparatus. The Secretariat worked closely with the Political Administration of the Red Army leadership (*Politicheskoe upravlenie Revvoensoveta*) to mobilize party members to various fronts. While the Soviet state was under threat, the needs of civilian government had not been a top priority, but when victory seemed assured the Secretariat could demobilize and assign tens of thousands of party cadres. Again, any more than the most rudimentary record keeping was impossible. Organizations from the top to the bottom of the new bureaucratic apparatus registered their demands for personnel with specific skills, for work in specific organizations: factory administrations, banks, agricultural co-operatives, and so on.[9] With rare exceptions, all

6. T. H. Rigby, *Communist Party Membership in the U.S.S.R., 1917–1967* (Princeton, 1968), 7–8, 52.
7. Robert Service, *The Bolshevik Party in Revolution: A Study in Organisational Change, 1917–1923* (New York, 1979), 277–95.
8. N. N. Krestinskii, L. P. Serebriakov, Y. A. Preobrazhenskii, and V. M. Molotov.
9. RGASPI 17/34/7.

the Secretariat could do was collect and collate these demands and attempt to meet them in purely quantitative terms.[10]

The low level of any accounting for personal qualities and administrative skills exacerbated existing weaknesses of party and state structures in two fundamental ways. First, the general quality of officialdom was extremely low in terms of basic literacy, administrative skills, and even loyalty to the party. In the process of the exponential growth of the party, the standards for membership had fallen correspondingly. Particularly in the immediate aftermath of the October seizure of power, many had joined the Bolshevik Party in order to take advantage of the privileged access to food, housing, and jobs accorded to members.[11] At the very height of the Civil War, the party leadership had felt compelled to initiate a purge of corrupt and 'morally dissolute' members.[12] The long struggle against the White Armies, combined with political training in the army, did reinforce loyalty to the party, and literacy campaigns raised educational levels, but corruption and incompetence remained serious problems in administration.

Though competent and principled party members were in short supply, that did not mean that there was any shortage of ambitious ones, and the conflict of ambitions presented another, and perhaps more troubling, problem for the Bolsheviks. Not everyone could be a provincial party committee secretary, a department head in a commissariat, even a district party committee secretary or village soviet chairman. Throughout the growing party and state bureaucracy, officials wanted to give orders, not to take them. As the bureaucracy absorbed new cadres, struggles for power erupted at all levels in the drive to capture the 'responsible positions' within and among organizations. Local officials were locked in struggle with cadres sent in from Moscow. New recruits to the party refused to accept the seniority of members with underground experience. Soviet executive committee chairmen refused to follow the directives of the party committee secretaries, local economic councils (*sovnarkhozy*) fought with local trade unions.[13] No senior official could be sure that one of his colleagues was not

10. See RGASPI 17/34/20–6 for statistical tables matching the supply and demand for cadres in 1921 and 1922.
11. See e.g. Rigby, 'Early Provincial Cliques', p. 8.
12. This first party purge was referred to as a reregistration of members. See T. H. Rigby, *Communist Party Membership*, ch. 1.
13. On the variety of conflicts in party organizations, see RGASPI 17/34/110/7–35.

conspiring to take his place. The struggles (*skloki*) pervaded the apparatus, paralysing entire organizations throughout the country.

The task of dealing with these problems fell primarily to the Secretariat. In the fall of 1920, several new departments were created to deal with them. The establishment of the 'Record-Assignment' department was intended to make possible a shift from mass assignments to planned assignments on the basis of the specific needs of organizations. The 'Agitation-Propaganda' department was supposed to raise their ideological awareness. The 'Organization-Instruction' department was directed to bring a measure of consistency to the structure of the apparatus and, by means of a staff of travelling (*vyezdnye*) instructors, to fight corruption and raise the efficiency of administration. It was given an 'Information' sub-department to process the great mass of information received from local organizations, and particularly to summarize their monthly reports on their activities, and a 'Conflicts' sub-department to bring an end to power struggles that pervaded the apparatus.[14]

None of these departments was able to cope with its new responsibilities. Even after demobilization, mass assignments continued to be the order of the day, making any sort of accounting of cadres impossible. In the process of demobilization, the Record-Assignment department was assigning 5,000 cadres a month,[15] but even after that process had been largely completed the numbers remained high. In 1923, the department assigned 14,000 cadres, including 4,000 leading workers.[16] Despite the sheer numbers of those assigned, organizations continued to complain about shortages of skilled officials.[17] Meanwhile, the Organization-Instruction department could not possibly meet its responsibility of instructing weak organizations. Rather, its network of instructors contributed to the work of the sub-departments, investigating and reporting on general trends in the activities of organizations, particularly on the ongoing power struggles.[18] They worked with the Conflict department and the organizations themselves to resolve the worst of the struggles, but they had little success. In 1921, the

14. 'Konstruktsiia rabochego apparata TsK RKP(b)', *Izvestiia TsK* (23 Sept. 1920), 1–5.
15. 'Otchet uchetno-raspredelitel'nogo otdela', *Izvestiia TsK* (28 Mar. 1921), 11.
16. *Trinadtsatyi s"ezd RKP(b), mai 1924 goda. Stenograficheskii otchet* (Moscow, 1963), 120.
17. RGASPI 17/34/15/12–74.
18. See RGASPI 17/67. For a general discussion of the work of the instructor apparatus in the early 1920s, see RGASPI 17/68/17/112–33.

department was receiving over 150 reports of conflicts a month, many from the party officials involved. Hundreds of files were left for months without any response and the backlog was increasing.[19]

The work of the Secretariat was regularly criticized at Central Committee plena and Party Congresses and Conferences. The creation of new departments and the expansion of its staff had done little to improve matters and something had to be done. In his speech on 'intra-party matters' to the Eleventh Party Congress in April 1922, Grigorii Zinoviev emphasized the 'paralysis' of party work caused by the power struggles. He claimed that they had 'become the scourge and calamity (*bich i bedstvie*) of the whole party'.[20] Immediately after the Congress had concluded its work, the Central Committee approved Lenin's draft resolution that assigned Stalin to head the Secretariat and created the position of 'General Secretary'. In assigning a Politburo member to the post, Lenin hoped to lend the Secretariat new authority, though he knew that was not enough. His resolution warned Stalin and the department heads not to get lost in the vastness of the Secretariat's responsibilities, but to stick to questions of a 'genuinely principal importance'.[21] Was this a fateful decision, one that fundamentally changed the course of Soviet history, as so many scholars have contended? Was Stalin able to use his position as General Secretary to build a personal following in the apparatus, to stifle party democracy and defeat his political rivals? Did the members of the Politburo unwittingly place a powerful weapon in Stalin's hands with this decision, or were they burdening him with a bureaucratic millstone?

When Stalin took over the Secretariat in 1922, he introduced several changes to improve its efficiency. The changes he introduced were in keeping with Lenin's instructions not to get lost in the details. One of his first moves was to reduce the responsibilities of the Secretariat in the assignment of cadres. His predecessors had taken responsibility for assignments from the top to the bottom of the apparatus. Stalin encouraged party and state organizations to promote their own cadres, and mapped a limited hierarchy of positions to be staffed under the direction of the Central Committee. The resulting list, known as 'Nomenklatura number 1', included 4,000 senior positions from the

19. 'Otchet org-instruktorskogo otdela TsK za period vremeni s maia 1920 goda po 15 fevralia 1921 goda', *Izvestiia TsK* (5 Mar. 1921), 7–9.
20. *Pravda* (2 Apr. 1922).
21. RGASPI 17/2/78/2.

Presidiums of the People's Commissariats down to the department and section heads, and from the 'bureaus' of regional party committees down to the secretaries of okrug Party organizations.[22] The total number of cadres assigned from Moscow was reduced from approximately 22,500 in the period between the tenth and the eleventh Party Congresses to barely over 6,000 between the twelfth and the thirteenth.[23]

In theory, this allowed the Record-Assignment department to keep more detailed personnel records and to improve its ability to match cadres' skills to the needs of organizations. In practice, the department continued to be swamped with demands for new officials and had little knowledge of the cadres it was passing to the Secretariat for approval. At a meeting of the leading officials of the Organization-Assignment department[24] in early 1927, the poor state of party records was a central topic of discussion. Department officials admitted that in the vast majority of cases, they were assigning party members blindly (*sovershenno sluchaino*).[25] The consensus of the meeting was that the Organization-Assignment departments of party and state bodies had to be strengthened and accounting improved. As it was, unemployed party members tended to head to Moscow to get 'party' jobs and the department was being turned into an employment agency.[26]

One might assume that these concerns related largely to the great mass of lesser posts, but even in the case of appointments to the key positions in the party and state bureaucracies similar issues arose. By 1926, the number of *nomenklatura* posts had expanded again by 50 per cent. As that number expanded and the burdens of the assignments process increased, the consideration given to each appointment decreased. The Organization-Assignment department took no part in appointments at or below the *guberniia* level. It only kept records of decisions that were taken by the local organizations.[27] In the case of

22. RGASPI 17/69/259/101; an example of the list can be found in 17/69/141.
23. RGASPI 17/68/429/24.
24. The sub-departments of the Secretariat were reorganized in 1924. The Record-Assignment department was renamed the Organization-Assignment department. The responsibility for appointments remained unchanged.
25. RGASPI 17/69/140/30.
26. ('Po sie vremia mnogie kommunisty smotriat na Orgraspred kak na birzhu truda...') RGASPI 17/69/140/30, l. 85.
27. See D. I. Kurskii's report of the Central Revision Commission to the 13th Party Congress. *Trinadtsatyi s″ezd*, 132.

more senior positions, the organizations that were to receive the appointees were aggressively drawn in to the appointments process.[28] Seven standing commissions, specialized according to branches of the state and party apparatus, were created within the Organization-Assignment department in order to parcel responsibilities for the appointments.[29] When these commissions discussed specific appointments, they consulted members of the organization to which the appointee would be assigned.[30] In this way, it was ensured that those assigned to key posts were not unknown quantities.

The Organization-Assignment department was concerned that appointees had the appropriate training, experience, and skills necessary to perform effectively. Appointees who were incompetent could be, and were, rejected and sent back to the Organization-Assignment department. Almost a third of appointees were fired within a year.[31] The high rate of turnover was a consequence not only of the low skill levels of appointees. The experience of the group struggles in the early 1920s had shown leading officials the importance of surrounding themselves with people whom they could trust. New appointees who 'did not fit in' (*ne srabotali*) to an organization were also rejected. In order to ensure such a 'fit', some organizations preferred to assign officials on the *nomenklatura* lists without the 'interference' of the centre.[32] The practice did not last long. On the request of the Organization-Assignment department, the Orgburo clarified and reissued the directives on the procedure for appointments.[33] The Organization-Assignment department objected to being totally bypassed, though it did strongly encourage the leaders of state and party organizations to promote candidates from below for its approval. The rapid expansion of the bureaucracy in the 1920s had created terrible shortages of cadres with appropriate administrative skills, such that when faced with a position

28. RGASPI 17/68/60/44.
29. These included the Industry Commission, the Trade Commission, the Soviet Commission, the Cooperative Commission, and the Party Commission; RGASPI 17/69/259/96.
30. RGASPI 17/69/259/96, 17/69/136/131. See also Kurskii's speech to the 15th Congress. *Piatnadtsatyi s″ezd Vsesoiuznoi kommunisticheskoi partii (b): Stenograficheskii otchet* (Moscow, 1928), 164.
31. RGASPI 17/69/136/10–11, 30–1, 136.
32. This was particularly true of the People's Commissars and other central state institutions. RGASPI 17/68/149/141–54. For a description of the unilateral actions of the Commissar of Agriculture Smirnov, see RGASPI 17/69/136/131.
33. RGASPI 17/69/136/167–8.

to fill, the department often had no one to recommend. A leading Organization-Assignment department official observed in early 1927 that 'the system (*khoziaistvo nashe*) is growing, and we don't have new people [to staff it]'.[34] Promotion from within (*vydvyzhenie*) was the preferred method for staffing leading positions, and in encouraging it, the department further strengthened the influence of party and state organizations over the appointments process. If appointees had personal loyalties, they were more likely to be to the organization to which he or she was assigned, rather than to Stalin.

This sense of local loyalties was further reinforced as the Secretariat dealt with the local power struggles. Rather than continue to investigate each case and risk letting the backlog of unresolved struggles increase as his predecessors had done, Stalin encouraged the resolution of conflicts locally. The simplest way to do so was to strengthen the hierarchy of existing party and state organizations, and reinforce the powers of the current 'bosses', most notably, the network of local party secretaries. Following Stalin's speech on organizational matters, the resolutions of the Twelfth Party Congress (April 1923) strengthened the role of party secretaries in selecting 'responsible workers of the soviet, economic, co-operative and professional organizations' in their regions.[35] In effect, the Party secretaries became the main arbiters of the struggles, with the power to remove officials who refused to submit to their decisions.[36]

Not all struggles could be resolved so easily though. Many organizations were unable to settle conflicts on their own, and they continued to appeal to the Secretariat for intervention.[37] In such cases, the Secretariat despatched one of its instructors, who would call an extraordinary conference of the local party committee and attempt to win the censure or expulsion of the weaker of the groups.[38] In cases of truly intractable conflicts, the Secretariat reassigned all parties to the

34. RGASPI 17/69/140/30.
35. *Kommunisticheskaia Partiia Sovetskogo Soiuza v rezoliutsiiakh i resheniiakh s"ezdov, konferentsii i plenumov Tsk* (hereafter *KPSS v rezoliutsiiakh*) (Moscow, 1972–84), iii. 74, 99.
36. The research of the Information department suggests that the regional secretaries were not shy about asserting those powers. RGASPI 81/3/69/189–91. Kaganovich was the chairman of the Organization-Assignment department at the time.
37. See e.g. RGASPI 17/34/112/79, 176; 17/34/114/12, 121. Many more such requests can be found in 17/67 and 17/112, 113.
38. Anastas Mikoian describes his participation in such a case in his memoir *V nachale dvatsatykh* (Moscow, 1975), ch. 2.

conflict and replaced them. For most leading officials unable to work in the face of constant challenges to their leadership, the risk was worth taking. Generally, the worst outcome they could expect was to be assigned to a different institution or region. Most of them accepted the decisions of the Secretariat, though there were exceptions. On several occasions, those who were reassigned complained bitterly and took their cases on appeal to the Central Control Commission, the Politburo, or to Lenin himself. The best known case is the so-called 'Georgian Affair'.[39] Stalin had sent Sergo Ordzhonikidze (then an instructor of the Secretariat) to remove two members of the Georgian Party organization accused of 'local nationalism' in the hotly contested issue of Georgia's participation in the recently established Transcaucasus federation. They were removed in the autumn of 1922 by a decision of the Georgian Party, but not without controversy. Stalin's tactics and Ordzhonikidze's actions—including a physical assault on one of the participants—provoked a great deal of animosity in the process of settling the larger conflict.[40] The case is often cited not because it was typical, but because it incensed Lenin. Less than a year after he had recommended him to the post, Lenin expressed profound reservations about Stalin's 'hastiness and bureaucratic impulsiveness'. Privately, he considered recommending that he be replaced by someone 'more patient, more loyal, more polite and more attentive to comrades'.[41]

'Bureaucratic impulsiveness' was not the only charge levelled against Stalin in his role as General Secretary. Some party leaders were also concerned that the Secretariat was stifling 'intra-party democracy'.[42] Intra-party democracy, meaning not only the election of officials, but also the open discussion of policy issues, had been a subject of considerable debate and controversy since the Civil War had come to a close. Lenin had promoted the ban on factionalism specifically to deal with

39. For more on this, see Jeremy Smith, 'Stalin as Commissar of Nationalities, 1918–1922', in Sarah Davies and James Harris (eds), *Stalin: A New History* (Cambridge, 2005), 45–62.

40. In this case, Stalin was using his position in the Secretariat to pursue a vendetta from his work in the Commissariat of Nationalities. Tucker, *Stalin as Revolutionary*, 224–38; Moshe Lewin, *Lenin's Last Struggle* (London, 1969), ch. 4.

41. Lenin made these comments in his so-called political 'testament', the contents of which were not revealed until after his death.

42. See particularly the comments of Kosior, Rakovsky, and Krasin to the 12th Party Congress. *Dvenadtsatyi s"ezd Rossiiskoi kommunisticheskoi partii (bol'shevikov), 17–25 aprelia 1923 g. Stenograficheskii otchet* (Moscow, 1923).

groups such as the 'Democratic Centralists' and the 'Workers' Opposition' which demanded a more participatory political system. Those 'factions' were crushed, but as the immediate threats to the survival of the Soviet state receded, the question of intra-party democracy returned to the political agenda.

At the time Stalin was named General Secretary, the main subject of correspondence between the Secretariat and party organizations was the struggles for power (*skloki*), rather than conflicts over political principles or policy platforms. Letter after letter referred to the conflicts among individuals and institutions as rooted in 'personal antagonisms', and 'lacking any ideological content'.[43] While there is no evidence to suggest that the Secretariat was enforcing conformity to any set of policies or 'political line', the decision to reinforce the power of party secretaries was hardly conducive to political diversity or open discussion. Party secretaries were always on the lookout for conspiracies against their leadership, and there was no more dangerous time for them than the regular local party conferences, at which key posts were filled by election. It was at these meetings that such 'oppositions' often came out into the open and challenged the authority of existing leaders. For example, a Secretariat instructor's report on the Bashkir Oblast' Party Conference in September 1922 observed that 'the group struggle began only with the discussion of the new composition of the Obkom... All other issues were met with unanimity.'[44] Most often, local party secretaries dealt with the threat by presenting pre-prepared slates of candidates to subordinate party organizations in the run-up to the party conferences. Then, at the party conference itself, the slates were voted on as a whole, and without a discussion.[45] Those officials who challenged the slates were often accused of 'undermining the authority of the Party Committee' or some similar charge and harassed, or expelled from the organization. Supplementing and reinforcing this tactic was the application of the secretary's own powers of appointment. Elected officials or others who were suspected of contemplating a challenge to the party committee leadership could be replaced with someone more 'reliable'.[46] The outlines of what Kamenev and Zinoviev referred to as the 'secretarial regime' were emerging in

43. See e.g. RGASPI 17/67/6/16; 17/67/109/168–9; 17/67/249/68.
44. RGASPI 17/34/112/15, 29–31; 17/34/114/12, 70.
45. RGASPI 17/69/269/54–5.
46. RGASPI 17/68/105, l. 7.

the first years of Stalin's tenure as General Secretary. The reference was not to any dictatorial powers accumulating in the Secretariat. Rather, they referred to the mass of party secretaries who were stifling policy discussions on their own initiative.

In the early 1920s, the situation in the Politburo was similar to that of party committees in the provinces. The Lenin succession was yet another power struggle among ambitious party leaders. Before his death, Lenin had identified the two top pretenders—Stalin and Trotsky—and worried about the consequences of the inevitable conflict between the two. Trotsky's arrogant certainty that he was uniquely suited to lead the revolution after Lenin was well known, as was Stalin's ambition. Stalin would not be restrained by concerns of political principle from using the Secretariat in any way that would further those ambitions. He would squeeze every political advantage he could from it. In his first year as General Secretary, it only seemed to be getting him into trouble. In the face of a direct attack at the Twelfth Congress on the question of intra-party democracy, Stalin was on the defensive. While he argued that the goal of party secretaries to 'build a unified and disciplined leadership group was healthy and necessary', he agreed that 'the means they have employed have frequently not been appropriate'. He also directly denied that the Secretariat was using the Record-Assignment department to exclude the members of political factions: the department was assigning honest and talented comrades, and that was all it did ('Dal'she etogo Uchraspred, poprostu govoria, ne soval nosa').[47]

Lenin's criticisms of Stalin and the Secretariat only a few months before left him politically vulnerable, but Stalin quietly held to his position, understanding its popularity among party secretaries. Through the summer and autumn of 1923, while Lenin's health was declining, divisions in the party leadership were increasingly obvious. Trotsky and other prominent members of the party attacked Stalin and the 'secretarial regime',[48] but only after it was clear that Lenin's condition was hopeless did Stalin drop his defensive tone in public. At the Thirteenth Party Conference in January, only days before Lenin's death, Trotsky's

47. *Dvenadtsatyi s″ezd*, 62, 66.

48. The events of this period are best described in Isaac Deutscher, *The Prophet Unarmed, Trotsky: 1921–1929* (London, 1970), 88–118.

political ally Evgenii Preobrazhenskii railed at the dictatorial methods of party secretaries:

> We must (encourage) a broad discussion of all crucial questions of intra-party life...such that issues of concern to party members can be posed not only by party committees, but also on the initiative of party cells and even individual comrades.

He recommended, among other things, that the 'elective principle be restored to executive party organs (party committee bureaus)'.[49] To any party secretary, the implications of such a policy were immediately clear. They would be open to attack from any disgruntled party member, to say nothing of groups of 'comrades' who might want to topple them from their leadership posts. With Lenin out of the way, unable to apply his overwhelming authority in the party, Stalin could be sure of the support of the delegates. They were, after all, overwhelmingly made up of party secretaries. Stalin told them what they wanted to hear:

> Democracy is not something appropriate to all times and places... Democracy demands a certain minimum of culture (*kultur'nost'*) from the members of (party) cells and organisations as a whole... Of course we need to retreat from it...

Such a statement would have been unthinkable only a year before, but here, it was only the preface to a direct attack on Trotsky. He insisted that what Trotsky was promoting was not democracy, but a 'freedom of group struggle' (*svoboda gruppirovok*) that would be fatal in the 'current conditions' of the New Economic Policy:

> It is not the (Secretarial) regime that is to blame (for the necessity of the retreat), but rather the conditions in which we live, the conditions of the country... If we were to permit the existence of group struggle, we would destroy the party, turn it from a monolithic, united organization into an alliance of groups and factions. It would not be a party, but rather the destruction of the party... Not for one minute did Bolsheviks ever imagine the party as anything but a monolithic organization, cut from one piece, of one will... In the current conditions of capitalist encirclement, we need not only a united party, but a party of steel, capable of withstanding the onslaught of the enemies of the proletariat, capable of leading the workers into a decisive struggle.[50]

49. *Trinadtsataia Konferentsiia Rossiiskoi Kommunisticheskoi Partii (Bolshevikov)* (Moscow, 1924), 106–7.
50. Ibid. 93, 100–1.

The 'retreat' from party democracy proved to be very durable. Secretaries were pleased to repeat Stalin's phrases about the importance of party unity and use them to legitimize the repression of any challenge to their power.

Despite their expanded powers, challenges to the authority of local secretaries remained a fact of political life. In the early 1920s, the general confusion over administrative responsibilities had created a fertile soil for power struggles. Though the administrative hierarchy was gradually set and clarified, political ambitions could not be so easily satisfied and power struggles continued. In part, they were fuelled by policy differences among Politburo leaders. Certainly, some local officials were drawn by conviction to the ideas of the 'opposition', but probably fewer than the reports of the local secretaries would indicate. They often used the label of 'oppositionist' in order to create the impression that cases of local insubordination constituted opposition to the policies of the Central Committee, and not merely the local leadership. At times the labelling was transparent. In their reports to the Secretariat, some secretaries observed that the 'dissatisfied elements' and the 'persistent intriguers' (*neispravimye sklochniki*) in their organizations rallied behind the ideas of the so-called Left Opposition in Moscow.[51]

As a strategy for furthering one's career ambitions, joining an opposition was highly counter-productive. Groups that collectively objected to the so-called 'political line of the Central Committee', or that were labelled as 'oppositionist', were easy to identify and eliminate. Secretaries kept careful records of voting patterns at party meetings and verified them for evidence of support for opposition groups. Suspected members were trailed by the local OGPU, and when evidence was found, their cases were presented to the local Control Commission for expulsion from the party. The Secretariat was kept informed of the names and activities of oppositionists and of the actions taken against them by local authorities.[52] It quickly became apparent to party members in the regions that to join an opposition was political suicide, and, as such, its leaders in Moscow had great difficulty generating support within local organizations.[53] Instead, they

51. See e.g. RGASPI 17/67/249/68; 17/67/285/102; 17/67/378/192; 17/67/193/98.

52. These reports can be found in RGASPI 17/67.

53. A report of the Information department from Dec. 1926 indicated that the overwhelming majority of oppositionist actions (*vystupleniia*) in that year took place in

sent their members out from Moscow to organize demonstrations, speak at party meetings, and distribute 'oppositionist literature'. These 'touring' oppositionists (*gastrolery*) could not be stifled so easily because they had no local status. When they appeared in a given region, the local party committee would gather a team of leading officials to arrange a counter-demonstration.[54] The 'gastrolery' never seem to have presented a threat to the local secretaries, but they were a constant source of irritation.

All this is not to say that the situation of the oppositions was hopeless from the start. Though Stalin sustained and deepened his relationship with party secretaries in the course of the 1920s, the strength of that relationship alone was not sufficient to decide the succession struggle. Policy ideas and political platforms mattered more than machine politics. New archival sources only serve to reinforce our sense of the succession struggle as a see-saw battle of thesis and counter-thesis, of alternative visions of the future of the revolution, presented to the party elite and the broader membership. In his letters to Molotov, for example, Stalin insisted on responding publicly to every speech and article of his rivals. In the summer of 1926, Stalin told Molotov to make sure that Bukharin responded to Zinoviev's criticisms of the foreign policy of the Politburo majority. Zinoviev's views, he wrote, 'are in the air and find support among those in the Comintern with Rightist tendencies'.[55]

For the United Opposition to seek the support of leading party officials generally, and Central Committee members in particular, was a logical strategy. Central Committee members tended to have been in the party longest. They had a higher level of education and stature in the party.[56] They were likely to have been the most independent-thinking of party members, the least beholden to Stalin, the most likely to have been open to the views of the Left. Furthermore, as members of the Central Committee, party statutes assigned them the right to elect

Moscow (222). Leningrad and Odessa were also important centres of oppositionist activity (169 and 139 incidents respectively), but for the rest of the country the numbers were insignificant (most under 10). RGASPI 17/68/105/137.

54. For a particularly vivid and detailed description of the response of a regional committee to the touring oppositionists, see RGASPI 17/67/378, ll. 192–5.

55. Lih et al. (eds), *Stalin's Letters*, 111.

56. Evan Mawdsley and Stephen White, *The Soviet Elite from Lenin to Gorbachev: The Central Committee and its Members, 1917–1991* (Oxford, 2000), ch. 2.

the Politburo. They could, thus, have had a decisive influence in the struggle. And yet neither Trotsky nor any of Stalin's other rivals was able to obtain a majority.

The traditional argument was that Stalin tipped the weight of the Central Committee in his favour by excluding his opponents from it and appointing his supporters, but there is little archival evidence to suggest that Stalin could control the slates of Central Committee members up for election at the Party Congresses in the 1920s, or overtly manipulate its expansion in his favour. Rather, it appears as though Stalin largely carried the Central Committee on the basis of his policies and, in time, on the concrete results they brought. Others have argued that Stalin's position was inconsistent and unprincipled, and there does appear to be evidence to support the view. Alongside Nikolai Bukharin, Stalin had defended NEP from the attacks of the 'Left' (the so-called United Opposition under Trotsky, Zinoviev, and Kamenev), but within months of their defeat and expulsion from the party in late 1927, he had begun to adapt their critique of NEP to orchestrate a break with the 'Right' and with Bukharin. And yet a closer examination of the evidence shows that such a view exaggerates the differences between the Left and the Right. Both groups were careful to portray themselves as proponents of industrialization. The Left called the Right 'kulak sympathizers' who were betraying the revolution, for their determined reliance on trade between town and countryside and protection of the kulak and NEP-men. But the members of the Right faction were not without ammunition. They called the Left's proposed super-tax on the peasants dangerous and unsocialist. They portrayed the Left as 'pessimists' and 'capitulationists' for their constant criticism of central economic policy, which in the mid-1920s was producing unexpectedly impressive results. When the leaders of the Left did propose specific targets for investment, they tended not to be significantly greater than those of the Right. The regional leaders and senior central state and party officials who constituted the bulk of the Central Committee—the group empowered by party statutes to elect the Politburo—had reason to wonder why they should risk supporting the Left.

As Trotsky developed his 'super-industrialist' position, Stalin countered with the concept of 'socialism in one country'. Stalin tried to make a virtue out of the dependence of industry on the development of agriculture. In addition to observing the danger that Trotsky's proposals would lead the peasants to refuse yet again to market their grain, Stalin tried to paint Trotsky's super-industrialism as essentially pessimistic. Trotsky, he claimed, lacked faith in the potential of internal economic forces.[57] Trotsky had argued that the funds generated through the taxation of the peasantry should be spent on importing industrial equipment from abroad. According to Stalin, importing equipment would reinforce Russia's status as an agrarian country, and create a dangerous dependence on the hostile, capitalist world. It was in these terms that Stalin sought to portray himself as the prime advocate of the interests of industry:

> There are two general lines. One proceeds from the assumption that our country should for a very long time remain an agrarian country, should export agricultural commodities and import capital, that we must rely on such a policy and develop this way into the future. This way, in point of fact, demands the curtailment of our industry... This line will lead to a situation in which our country will never, or almost never be able truly to industrialize... This line signifies the retreat from the tasks of construction. It is not our line. There is another line... This line demands the maximal expansion of industry.

He followed with the statement that this expansion would proceed 'in measure and correspondence with those resources which we have'.[58] Stalin's ideas were less impressive for their clarity than for their use of cynical political calculation. His simultaneous support for balanced trade between town and countryside and high tempos of industrial construction was a form of 'centrism'. He dissociated himself not only from Trotsky, but also from the Politburo 'Right', in the person of Bukharin, who most clearly and unequivocally insisted that the growth of industry should proceed from the wealth and success of the agricultural sector.

In the autumn of 1925, Stalin endured the single greatest challenge to his right to speak in the name of the Central Committee. At this time, Politburo members Kamenev and Zinoviev began to criticize 'socialism in one country' and Stalin's cynical centrism. The conflict heated up in the autumn, in the period leading up to the Fourteenth

57. The claim was reinforced by the memory of Trotsky's 'theory of permanent revolution'. Trotsky had suggested that socialism might not be achieved in Russia without the success of socialist revolutions in Europe.
58. *Chetyrnadtsatyi s″ezd Vsesoiuznoi Kommunisticheskoi Partii (Bol'shevikov), 18–31 dekabria 1925 g. Stenograficheskii otchet* (Moscow, 1926), 27.

Party Congress. On the eve of the Congress, these two former allies of Stalin openly attacked the Politburo majority:

> They bandy about loud phrases on international revolution; but they portray Lenin as the inspirer of a nationally limited socialist revolution. They fight against the kulak; but they offer the slogan 'Enrich yourselves'! They shout about socialism; but they proclaim the Russia of NEP as a socialist country. They 'believe' in the working class; but they call on the wealthy farmer to come to their aid.[59]

As Zinoviev and Kamenev had moved away from Stalin's 'centrism' towards Trotsky and the Left, Stalin was compelled to reinforce his association with the leaders on the Right—Bukharin, Rykov, and Tomsky—in order to be sure to retain the majority in the Politburo. However, in the second half of 1925, his association with the Right was becoming a political liability. Bukharin's 'enrich yourselves' comment had given the strong impression that the leadership gave priority to agriculture over industry. The impression was further strengthened when the leadership was forced to reduce its projections for industrial growth in the 1925/26 economic year after the poor harvest of 1925.[60]

Stalin and the Right won a narrow victory at the Fourteenth Party Congress, and the Left continued to try to steal their support, but they failed, largely because they never elaborated a detailed alternative economic programme. Even in early 1927, Bukharin was able to claim that Trotsky's promise of a billion rubles of investment in 1926/27 differed little from the Central Committee's commitment to a minimum of 947 million rubles.[61] They had wasted opportunities, but this was not the worst of their tactical errors. In their impatience with the course of the battle with Stalin and company in Moscow, they had begun actively to organize support in the regions. By the autumn, there were opposition groups in Moscow, Leningrad, Tula, Kharkov, Nikolaev, Tbilisi, Sverdlovsk, and other regional centres. At the October 1926 Central Committee plenum, Central Control Commission chairman E. M. Iaroslavskii spoke of the creation of Opposition committees,

59. Zinoviev's 18 Dec. 1925 editorial in *Leningradskaia pravda*, quoted from Deutscher, *The Prophet Unarmed*, 248.
60. Economic plans were being reviewed on the eve of the Congress. See Rykov's opening speech, *XIV s''ezd*, 2.
61. RGASPI 17/2/276/73. In the course of the economic year investment was allowed to rise to 1,068 million rubles. Carr and Davies, *Foundations*, i/1. 278 n.

bureaus, and other 'underground' organizations. He called it 'an attempt to create another party within the All-Union Communist Party'.[62]

Local party officials did not need any pressure from above to take action against the Opposition. They had no sympathy for the protests of the Opposition against violations of intra-party democracy. Stalin was able to use this lack of sympathy to silence the leaders of the Left. At the July 1926 Central Committee plenum, the Left 'Platform of the Thirteen' was declared a 'fractional' document.[63] By October, irritation with the Left had reached the point where Stalin was able to have Trotsky and Kamenev removed from the Politburo by a vote of the Central Committee.[64]

As the leaders of the United Opposition were finally purged, the party was moving to the left, increasingly uncomfortable with NEP compromises. There was a growing confidence that the planned economy would prove its superiority to the quasi-capitalist order of the NEP. Industrial regions were desperate for the new investment it promised and agricultural regions were interested in taking control of the grain supply away from the 'kulak'. Heightened international tensions, culminating in the severance of diplomatic relations with Great Britain and the war scare of 1927, convinced many that there was no choice but to accelerate the modernization of the country. As the projected tempos of the first Five-Year Plan increased, and ever more punitive action was taken against the 'kulak' (or, more accurately, those who resisted Soviet policy in the countryside), Nikolai Bukharin and those around him expressed their concern that social, political, and economic stability was being put at risk. In the autumn of 1928 Bukharin published his 'Notes of an Economist' in *Pravda*, warning of the potential dangers to economic equilibrium presented by the current projections for investment and production.[65] He warned of an imminent crisis that would be provoked by overambitious plans, but his predictions were premature. The attack on capitalist elements and promotion of more ambitious plan targets only seemed to accelerate plans for the construction of a socialist society. Stalin seemed once again to have the measure of party opinion. His calls for iron unity in the party and the retreat from party democracy continued to have

62. RGASPI 17/2/254/9.
63. RGASPI 17/2/238/1.
64. The vote was 182 for and 6 against with 5 abstentions. RGASPI 17/2/248/1.
65. *Pravda* (30 Sept. 1928).

resonance. Bukharin and his supporters were labelled 'cowards' and 'deviationists', and left to twist in the wind. At the same time, it was becoming ever clearer that to express doubts about the party line would not further a career in the party. Stalin could not be certain how many leading officials supported him only because they were afraid to speak out.

Stalin's own explanation of his rise to power is instructive. Almost two decades after he had defeated his main rivals, Stalin recounted to his inner circle how in 1927, 720,000 rank and file members of the party voted in favour of the 'Central Committee line' which he had authored; 4,000–6,000 voted for Trotsky, and a further 20,000 abstained. What is interesting in Stalin's comments is what is left unsaid. His praise of the party masses would seem to hint at a softness in his support in the highest echelons of the party.[66] Potentially, there were thousands of senior party members who continued to harbour sympathies for Stalin's opponents. More worrying still, OGPU surveillance of the oppositionists suggested that those sympathizers might coalesce into an underground organization bent on unseating him. Only days after the members of the United opposition had been expelled from the Central Committee, OGPU chairman Viacheslav Menzhinskii warned Stalin that unnamed former Left oppositionists planned to murder Soviet leaders in a coup d'état timed to coincide with the celebrations of the tenth anniversary of the revolution in November 1927. He observed that Opposition propaganda in the Army was threatening to undermine its loyalty to the regime—in the midst of the war scare—and that top secret information about activities and decisions at the highest levels was being leaked to foreign powers by the 'Opposition and its agents'.[67]

We have little direct evidence of the work of the OGPU 'cells' set up among oppositionists, but we know that the OGPU arrested hundreds of oppositionists in the course of 1928. The information Stalin received on the activities of oppositionists provoked him to write a further letter—a memorandum to the members of the Politburo—in which he argued that the Opposition had completed a transformation 'from an underground anti-party group into an underground anti-Soviet organization'. The letter was later published as a *Pravda* editorial under

66. RGASPI 558/11/1122/165.

67. Michal Reiman, *The Birth of Stalinism* (Bloomington, Ind., 1987), appendices.

the title 'They Have Sunk to This'.[68] Stalin had reason to believe that Trotsky had been able to control this subversive organization despite the effort to isolate him in Alma Ata, and so the decision was taken to expel him from the Soviet Union. Trotsky's interviews in the western press after his arrival in Turkey in February 1929, collected by the Soviet telegraph agency (TASS), immediately indicated that the fact of exile would have little effect. Western journalists, sensing a dramatic story, widely reported Trotsky's assertions that he would maintain contact with his underground network in the USSR and the danger that his network posed to the Soviet leadership. The interviews and reports painted a picture of Trotsky's substantial support in the party, the Red Army, and foreign communist parties, and hinted that Trotsky's struggle against Stalin would have the support of capitalist governments.[69]

The defeat of the Right Opposition later that year provoked less immediate cause for concern, but no fewer nagging doubts. Well aware of the GPU surveillance, Bukharin kept a low profile and accepted his demotion down the party ranks, but the economic crisis he had predicted in 1928 finally came to pass in the course of 1930. Stalin had vilified the Bukharin and the 'Right deviationists' for cowardice in the face of the colossally high plan targets of the first Five-Year Plan. In late 1929, he had famously insisted that 'there were no fortresses that Bolsheviks could not storm',[70] but in the face of shortages, bottlenecks, and a desperately strained transportation infrastructure Bukharin's earlier words of warning hung heavily in the air. There are no statistics on the number of party members who supported Bukharin in the late 1920s. The experience of the Left had established a powerful disincentive to openly declaring one's views. Stalin's campaign against the Right danger had made it clear that to question the realism of the plan was an offence against the party. But as it became clear that few of the plan targets could be achieved, who was not—privately—a 'Right deviationist'? Stalin did not back down, declaring that there were 'no objective reasons' for failing to fulfil the plan. No excuses would be accepted. Many thousands of party and state officials at all levels understood that they risked losing their jobs if they did not do what was to all intents and purposes impossible. Certainly many shared Stalin's

68. Stalin, *Sochineniia*, xi. 313–17; *Pravda* (24 Jan. 1929); Tucker, *Stalin in Power*, 126.

69. Copies of these TASS bulletins are in Anastas Mikoian's personal archive. RGASPI 84/1/135/3–51.

70. Stalin, *Sochineniia*, xii. 118–35; *Pravda* (7 Nov. 1929).

confidence in the superiority of central planning, but many must have regretted contributing to Stalin's now unchallenged grip on power. It is in this light that we must understand Stalin's apparent overreaction to those few officials who were prepared to criticize policy in the early 1930s. Objectively, Stalin's dictatorship was assured when Bukharin was expelled from the Politburo in 1929, but he had reason to worry that his position was not yet secure. Trotsky's activities abroad reinforced the impression that he was running a network of agents in the USSR. The constant stream of anti-Stalin invective he published from exile seemed evidence enough that Trotsky would do what he could to unseat the dictator. And the potential for a broader conspiracy of officialdom could not be dismissed.

4

The great break

NEP had driven an impressively rapid recovery of the Soviet economy in the aftermath of the Civil War, so the decision to abandon it was gradual and hesitant. Despite the obvious contradiction between the quasi-capitalist nature of NEP and state planning as it was emerging in the second half of the 1920s, Stalin did not at first openly favour one over the other. But between 1926 and 1929, the central pillars of NEP were knocked down one by one. The logic was clear enough. Central planning was at once the realization of a dream, an imposition of necessity, and blatantly populist politics. Neither the party nor the working class had ever been comfortable with NEP's reliance on the capitalist 'kulak' and 'NEPman'. Bukharin's theories defending NEP as the foundation of a transition to socialism were good economics, but bad politics. State planning, while not intrinsically Marxist, had the advantage of ending the reliance on 'capitalist elements' and driving a rapid transition to socialism. As the first Five-Year Plan took shape under Stalin's direction, industrial growth and new construction exceeded expectations and supported an enthusiasm for ever higher targets rooted more in fantasy than in reality. 'There are no fortresses which Bolsheviks cannot storm' was an apt slogan for the day, for it conveyed not only the exceptional optimism of the moment, but also its violence. Stalin was a stern and implacable general on the attack, but when the fortress storming inevitably failed, the ensuing crisis concerned more than just a shortfall from plan targets. He began to worry about his very grip on power.

NEP had done a brilliant job of bringing war-damaged, existing factories back into use, but by the mid-1920s it was clear that, for growth to continue, new factories would have to be built. Where would the investment come from? Bukharin's first reaction was to admit that growth rates would have to slow, but his image of 'riding into socialism on a peasant nag' was politically disastrous for him, and Stalin immediately disassociated himself from it. By contrast, he argued that investment could be found by imposing cost savings on existing factories, and then out of the efficiency of new plants. His optimistic views made bad economics, but good politics. The war scare in 1927, and the 1928 trial of the Shakhty engineers, accused of sabotaging Soviet industrialization plans on behalf of foreign interests, heightened the sense that a slowdown was unacceptable. At the November Central Committee plenum, Stalin asked delegates:

> Is it possible to get by without demanding (economic) plans? Is it possible to work with slower tempos in more 'calm' conditions? Can we explain the rapid tempos for the development of industry in terms of the restless character of the members of the Politburo and Sovnarkom? Of course not! They are calm and sober people in the Politburo and Sovnarkom. Speaking abstractly, ignoring internal and external circumstances, we could, of course, move at a slower pace. But we can't lose sight of external and internal circumstances, and we must admit that these circumstances dictate the necessity of the rapid development of industry . . . We are surrounded by capitalist countries with a much more technically developed industry. So we have the more advanced political system, but with an extremely backward industrial base. Can we achieve the decisive victory of socialism given that contradiction? . . . In order to achieve the decisive victory of socialism in our country, we must catch up to and overtake these countries technologically. Either we do that or they will wipe us out (*nas zatrut*).[1]

When the peasants brought a significantly lower percentage of the 1927 harvest to market, threatening investment plans and industrial growth, Stalin accused the 'kulak' of deliberately undermining Soviet policy, and demanded grain be seized as an 'extraordinary measure'. The move was fraught with danger for Stalin, because this frontal challenge to the logic of NEP and its trade between town and countryside could fail and expose the frailty of his optimism. He needed seizures to succeed if he was to carry party opinion with him. Anticipating a measure of resistance to grain seizures among regional officials, he took the unusual step of travelling to Siberia to justify the assault on the kulak. Viacheslav Molotov did the same for the Urals region and

1. Stalin, 'Ob industrializatsii strany i o pravom uklone v VKP(b)' (19 Nov. 1928), *Sochineniia*, xi. 246–7.

together with regional party secretaries they delivered a system of forced grain collections that made good the shortfall.

The success encouraged planners to raise capital investment by almost a quarter against the previous year.[2] Bukharin had long since disavowed the pessimism inherent in his 'nag' comments, but he felt compelled publicly to question the realism of some of the projections for industrial construction: 'If there are not enough bricks, and if, for technical reasons, no more than a certain quantity can be produced during the current season, then we must not draw up a building programme that exceeds this limit and create a demand that cannot be met. For no matter how much you force building activities, you cannot build factories out of air.'[3] Just as Stalin's 'extraordinary measures' had divided opinion in the state and party apparatus, there were many who agreed with Bukharin that construction and production plans had gone too far. And though it is impossible to measure precisely, there were arguably even more who shared the growing faith that, by ending the 'chaos' of the capitalist market, 'socialist' state planning had colossal unrealized potential. The faith was reinforced by material interest insofar as many officials both in the centre and in the regions were desperate to attract to their institutions the new investment and construction promised in the ever more ambitious plans. For some of them, the plans were not ambitious enough.[4] The tensions could be seen between the two central organizations most immediately responsible for the plan: the State Planning Commission (Gosplan) and the Supreme Economic Council (VSNKh). Less than two weeks after Bukharin's critique was published in *Pravda*, Gosplan chairman Gleb Krzhizhanovskii accused VSNKh planning officials of having 'lost their feeling for reality'. VSNKh officials responded with criticism of Gosplan's 'vulgar realism'.[5]

By mid-October, probably on Stalin's initiative, the press began to print articles warning of a 'Right deviation' in the party. At the November 1928 Central Committee plenum, Sovnarkom chairman A. I. Rykov attempted to smooth over differences of opinion in his

2. From 1.32 to 1.66 billion rubles. See A. I. Rykov's speech 'On the Control Figures for 1928/29' to Nov. 1928 Central Committee plenum. RGASPI 17/2/377/19–20.
3. N. Bukharin, 'Notes of an Economist', *Pravda* (30 Sept. 1928).
4. Harris, *The Great Urals*, ch. 3.
5. Quoted from E. H. Carr and R. W. Davies, *Foundations of a Planned Economy* (London, 1969), i/1. 321–2.

speech. He admitted that the control figures had left a 'huge mass of unsatisfied demands', but he argued against 'creating a fetish for tempos. The economy could not sustain a consistent increase in rate of economic growth, or even maintain the existing rate. He agreed that the 'Right deviation' in the party constituted cowardice before the tasks presented in the plan, but he insisted that it was necessary to struggle with it 'on an ideological level' and not by means of expulsion from the party.[6] Nevertheless, many delegates both from the regions and from the centre insisted on both higher tempos and a much harder line on the 'Right danger'. They took to the podium with criticism of inadequate funding for projects under their jurisdiction: tempos had to be raised, and those who opposed them removed from the party.[7] The Central Committee issued a compromise resolution:

> While leading a decisive struggle against all deviations, particularly underlining the necessity of an ideological struggle with the Right danger at the current moment...the Central Committee plenum draws the attention of the whole Party to the necessity of a thoughtful, and not clamorous, discussion of the issues of economic construction, which will demand a sober Bolshevik analysis of the whole situation, without any smoothing over of difficulties or...panicked exaggeration of dangers.[8]

Stalin could not simply remove the defenders of moderation, but his campaign against the 'Right danger' continued to embolden the enthusiasts of accelerated growth and made it increasingly difficult to defend restraint. In the course of 1929, officials from the centre and regions proposed ever more ambitious targets for investment and construction in the Five-Year Plan, while aggressively attacking those who opposed them. In his keynote speech to the April 1929 Central Committee plenum on 'inner-Party issues', G. I. Petrovskii accused Politburo members Bukharin, Rykov, and Tomsky of opposition to the Central Committee line, and of 'violations of party discipline'. The three meanwhile argued that they had been the objects of a campaign of rumours and 'unprincipled persecution' by the rest of the Politburo.[9] But the key issue was the perception of the Politburo 'Right' that the

6. RGASPI 17/2/377/23-24, 63–4.
7. RGASPI 17/2/381. See e.g. the speeches of R. I. Eikhe (Siberia), part 1, p. 15; F. I. Goloshchekin (Kazakhstan), part 1, pp. 25–6; V. Ia. Chubar′ (Ukraine), part 2, p. 54; S. I. Syrtsov (Siberia), ch. 2, p. 128; M. M. Khataevich (Middle Volga), ch. 2, p. 148.
8. *KPSS v rezoliutsiiakh*, iv. 382–3.
9. RGASPI 17/2/399, vol. 1/13–19, 45, 61–2 (Petrovskii); 17/2/400/11–30 (Tomsky).

current tempos were unrealistic and would create an economic crisis. In their speeches, a large number of Central Committee members insisted that the actions of the Right 'disorganized' the economy and slowed the tempo of industrialization.[10] A few weeks later at the Sixteenth Party Conference, regional delegates specifically linked cuts to proposed projects with the leaders of the 'Right Opposition'. N. B. Riazanov of the Institute of Marx and Engels joked that 'every speaker ends his presentation with "Give us a factory in the Urals and to hell with the Right!" "Build us a power station and to hell with the Right!"'.[11] Senior officials not only accepted Stalin's campaign against the Right, they encouraged it.

The Five-Year Plan was formally approved by the Fifth Congress of Soviets in May, but its projections were soon swept aside by those proposed in the course of the discussions of targets for investment, construction, and production (the 'control figures') for 1929/30. In August, the Presidium of VSNKh set the preliminary control figures at 3.1 billion rubles: 30 per cent higher than the target set by the Congress of Soviets, and 80 per cent higher than the figure for 1928/29.[12] In turn, Five-Year Plan targets were revised through the autumn. By October, the target for crude oil production in 1932/33 had been raised from 22 to 40 million tons. The projected output of the coal industry jumped to 140 million tons from the 75 million ton target set in May. The target for pig iron was raised from 10 million to 17 million tons.[13] The enthusiasts of high tempos were ascendant and the defenders of restraint in full retreat. On 7 November, the twelfth anniversary of the October Revolution, Stalin declared that 1929 had been the year of the 'Great Break'. The statement did not constitute an explicit break from NEP, but rather a break from the constraints imposed by the logic of capitalist relations of production. It was a powerful statement of faith in the power of 'socialist' central planning to deliver unprecedented rates of production and new construction. But state planning alone was not enough. The new targets could be achieved only if party and state officials at all levels fought for them with enthusiasm. In this

10. RGASPI 17/2/399, vol. 1/58; 17/2/400, vol. 2/71; 17/2/401, vol. 3/129.
11. *Shestnadtsataia konferentsiia VKP(b), 23–29 aprelia 1929g. Stenograficheskii otchet* (Moscow, 1929), 102.
12. RGAE, 3429/1/5134/743; Davies, *Soviet Economy in Turmoil*, 179–80.
13. Ibid. 195, 199.

context, Stalin considered scepticism about the targets 'the vilest form of wrecking', and encouraged the persecution of sceptics.[14]

He was also well aware that the new industrial plans would place exceptional new burdens on agriculture. The regime could not afford to step back from the 'extraordinary measures'. Indeed, the successful application of force in grain collections encouraged regional officials to take more permanent control of the grain supply by driving peasants into collective farms. The collectivization of agriculture had been a long-term goal of the regime since the revolution. The dominance of small-scale private agriculture in Russia inhibited the application of modern farming techniques and technologies. Large-scale collective farming promised not only to increase productivity, but to free up the excess rural labour for work in industry. For regional officials who had grown accustomed to an annual battle to get the peasants to part with the harvest, a growing collective farm sector had the added bonus of extending state control and simplifying collections. In the summer of 1928, less than 2 per cent of peasant households were in collective farms. By the autumn of 1929 that figure had risen to 7.5 per cent, with a few of the main grain-growing regions approaching 20 per cent.

Stalin understood that many of these existing collectives were created by force and poorly organized, but the potential of wholesale collectivization both to increase productivity and to take control of the grain supply made it too attractive a prospect to pass up. In both the centre and regions, officials with responsibility for agriculture were divided about how fast the pace of collectivization could be driven, but once again Stalin threw his weight behind the maximalists. In the first half of December, a special commission drew up a draft collectivization decree that reflected both the contemporary enthusiasm and caution. Stalin declared the draft 'unsuitable', and radically simplified it to reflect the views of the radicals—those who proposed to complete the collectivization of the main grain-growing regions by the end of the year. He essentially dropped the detail about the organization of collectives in favour of encouraging their 'spontaneous' development. The publication of the decree on 5 January 1930 launched what can only be described as a civil war in the countryside. The overwhelming majority of peasants objected to collectivization not only because the

14. David Priestland, *Stalinism and the Politics of Mobilization: Ideas, Power and Terror in Inter-War Russia* (Oxford, 2007), 199–200.

state was laying a claim to their land, livestock, equipment, and other property, but also because collectivization attacked centuries-old traditions of peasant self-administration. Many destroyed their equipment and sold or slaughtered their livestock rather than see it passed to the collective farm. By February and March resistance increasingly took the form of assaults and murder of local officials.[15] The regime's response to resistance was to assert that it was inspired and organized by the kulak, and to call for the 'elimination of the kulak as a class'. 'Dekulakization' quickly became the central instrument for forcing the pace of collectivization. Local officials were empowered to exile to the Gulag anyone who resisted.

Over a half a million peasants were exiled to the Gulag in the winter and spring of 1929–30. The furious violence on both sides, and the lack of attention to the organizational detail, quickly presented a direct threat to spring sowing. Unless the hostilities were calmed, there would be substantially less grain to harvest in the summer and autumn. In an article in the party's main newspaper *Pravda* on 2 March 1930, Stalin called a temporary halt to the campaign. He claimed that 'a radical turn of the countryside towards socialism may be considered as already achieved' and this was only one of a series of disingenuous claims. More strikingly, he insisted that 'collective farms must not be established by force'. He condemned local officials who collectivized too quickly and failed to pay sufficient attention to organizational issues.

On the surface of things it appears to be an act of breathtaking cynicism to blame others for implementing policy that he, more than any other, had shaped. And yet he appears genuinely to have believed that the failure of this first collectivization drive followed from the shortcomings of local officials, though at the same time he knew that the senior party and state officials who had advocated caution in December would blame him for ignoring their warnings. He made it clear in the article that these events should not 'provide grist to the mill of Right opportunism'. It was a thinly veiled warning against potential critics of central policy. Stalin could not quite so easily contain peasant reactions though. Hundreds of thousands quit the collectives, reducing the overall level of collectivization from 52.7 per cent of households in

15. Viola, *Peasant Rebels*, ch. 4.

February to 37.3 per cent at the beginning of April.[16] The reprieve was short-lived. Stalin had not surrendered his conviction that rapid collectivization was the way forward. The process resumed once the grain was ripening in the fields, and yet again, hundreds of thousands of peasants paid for their resistance with long sentences in the Gulag. The peasantry justifiably viewed collective agriculture as the imposition of a 'second serfdom', not least because the harvest had once again ceased to be theirs to distribute. The state had taken control of it because grain exports were essential to fund the process of industrialization. In the course of the next two years, grain collections were so high as to leave peasants without enough to eat. The famine of 1932–3 took the lives of millions. The peasantry—still the overwhelming majority of the population—had never particularly supported the Bolsheviks, but Stalin's policies ensured their simmering hostility for generations.

By contrast, the working class had broadly supported Stalin's Great Break. They had no great fondness for the petty traders of the NEP and the high prices they charged. They blamed NEP for the high unemployment that lingered despite the rapid recovery of industry. Workers were susceptible to state propaganda in the late 1920s promising a new revolutionary breakthrough that would hasten the arrival of socialism. Newspapers were full of reports of new achievements and new records broken. The expansion of existing plants and new construction the length and breadth of the country presented further, physical evidence of the promised new world coming into being. It inspired workers to join in the struggle against resistance. When the regime had called for vigilance against the wrecking activities of the 'bourgeois specialists' after the Shakhty Affair, and whipped up suspicion of 'class aliens' generally, they responded with almost worrying enthusiasm, attacking all 'bosses' instead of just the 'bourgeois' ones. Workers generally, and especially the younger generation, were willing to make sacrifices to build socialism, but in the longer term, those sacrifices proved to be greater than many could readily tolerate. The plan had always squeezed 'internal reserves' for new investment, demanding ever greater cost savings. It was inevitable that significant reserves were found at the expense of workers' standards of living. In fact, by 1932–3, workers' real wages had fallen to less than half of their

16. Lynne Viola et al. (eds), *The War Against the Peasantry, 1927–1930* (New Haven, 2005), 264.

1928 level.[17] The press made much of the fact that money wages were rising, but they said nothing about the fact that prices were rising much faster. The millions of peasants and others joining the proletariat in the course of the 1930s felt this drop less acutely than those who had been on the job for longer, but it was enough to sow seeds of disaffection. And mass migration into urban areas put an intolerable burden on the slow-growing housing stock, leaving hundreds of thousands living in overcrowded barracks, if not tent cities. By the time excessive grain collections had exhausted the peasantry and provoked a famine, food shortages in the cities provoked strikes, slowdowns, and 'hunger marches'.[18] For the millions of workers who retained close ties in the countryside, the regime's continuing war against the peasantry was itself a source of anger and resentment.

Concerns about the direction of central policy spread through the state and party apparatus too. Stalin's campaign against the 'Right danger' had succeeded through 1928 and 1929 because the crisis Bukharin predicted had not come to pass. Industrial production continued to rise, but mostly because of the relentless pressure to squeeze more production out of existing factories. The working day was shortened to seven hours, but only in order to make possible the continuous exploitation of machinery in three daily shifts. Experience seemed to indicate that those who had pressed for ever higher targets were justified in their confidence of the potential of state planning. But only months after Bukharin was expelled from the Politburo, the signs of crisis mounted. The disastrous course of the collectivization campaign in early 1930 was the first of them, but as the year wore on, it became clear that other major plan targets were not being met. Industrial production not only slowed in the summer of 1930, it began to contract. It would still be months and in many cases years before new factories and plants would drive the expansion of industrial production. The industrial economy could not continue indefinitely to squeeze more out of existing enterprises. Rapid growth meant that the persistent unemployment of NEP had been exchanged for labour shortages. New workers were pouring into the cities by their hundreds of thousands,

17. See Sarah Davies, *Popular Opinion in Stalin's Russia: Terror, Propaganda and Dissent, 1934–1941* (Cambridge, 1997), 24.
18. Jeffrey J. Rossman, 'A Workers' Strike in Stalin's Russia: The Vichuga Uprising, 1930', in Lynne Viola (ed.), *Contending with Stalinism: Soviet Power and Popular Resistance in the 1930s* (Ithaca, NY, 2002), 46.

but it was no simple matter to put them to work effectively. They needed to be trained, and where that training was incomplete or ineffective, new workers could do as much harm as good, damaging expensive new equipment or producing defective goods. Consequently, labour productivity began to fall. It fell even for experienced workers, with emerging shortages of consumer goods and food. Declines in the production of fuels and metals had knock-on effects for hundreds of other enterprises.

Stalin would not retreat on the industrial front. He had called a temporary halt to collectivization because the chaos in the countryside threatened a catastrophic failure of the whole sector. He saw no such necessity in industry. In the same way that he blamed local officials for the failure of the first collectivization drive, Stalin blamed officials in industry for the contraction of industrial production. There are no documents in his personal archive, no private letter or note, to suggest that he even considered the possibility that Bukharin had been right to question the realism of plan targets. Indeed, both publicly and privately, Stalin insisted that there were 'colossal reserves in the economy waiting to be exploited'. Existing plans could be achieved, and any failure to do so was the responsibility of officialdom: 'the party does not simply adapt to objective conditions. The party has the power to influence them, to change them, to find itself a more advantageous combination of objective conditions.'[19]

The formulation did not leave leading officials with much flexibility in the way they could deal with the exceptionally great demands inherent in central directives, and even less so given that they were told it was their responsibility to 'prove the correctness of Party policy in practice'! Stalin and the party press repeatedly asserted that central policy was correct a priori:

> The [political] line of our party is clearly the uniquely correct line. Its correctness is obvious and indisputable... The party must, as ever, watch its own ranks with unwavering attention... [The party] must defend itself against all those who attack its line, the correctness of which is being proven by experience every day. This is why deviationists rarely risk coming out in the open.

19. Peredovaia, 'Iskusstvo partiinogo rukovodstva', *Bolshevik*, 5 (1930), 10. See also Peredovaia, 'Na dva fronta', *Bolshevik*, 6 (1930); Peredovaia, 'Industrializatsiia SSSR k XVI s"ezdu VKP(b)', *Bolshevik*, 9 (1930); Em. Iaroslavskii, 'Bor'ba protiv opportunizma v period mezhdu XV i XVI s"ezdami VKP(b)', *Bolshevik*, 9 (1930), 11–18.

Now they are more inclined to support the party line verbally (in public), in order to make it easier to undermine it in practice.[20]

Stalin was convinced that plan targets could be met, but that to do so, it was necessary to mobilize and direct 'the enthusiasm of the masses', to ensure the effective use of existing resources, to have energetic leadership and strict verification of the fulfilment of directives, to sustain momentum, and to be intolerant of anything less than total commitment. Stalin watched the beginning of 1930 grain collections closely and he did not like what he saw. A Politburo resolution of 5 September on the first phase of the collections declared that they were 'absolutely unsatisfactory', characterized by complacency, inadequate measures against the kulak and anti-collective farm (*kolkhoz*) sentiment, and not enough work to strengthen the kolkhoz organizationally and to create new collectives. Stalin ordered that 'leading regional officials' should be brought back from vacation and set to work.[21] A week later, the regional party first secretaries were called to Moscow to discuss the plan for collections. Molotov subsequently wrote to Stalin, who himself was on vacation at the time, that he told the secretaries that '[we need] a merciless struggle against those with hesitations about whether the plan can be fulfilled. Any thought that the plan cannot be fulfilled would be the purest opportunism.'[22] He told Stalin that 'for the first time' no one complained about the plan for collections, though this was not entirely true. A few party secretaries were brave or foolish enough to express their doubts, but Molotov chose not to relay these to Stalin.[23]

Stalin continued to watch the situation in industry too. In early September, a letter to local organizations 'from the Central Committee', but almost certainly composed by Stalin himself, insisted that officials could only blame themselves for failures:

The most important reasons for the underfulfilment of production tasks of industry especially in its main branches are the lack of the necessary energy and initiative in the mobilization of internal resources; insufficient use of existing equipment; poor application of the shift system; lack of energy in overcoming bottlenecks; frequent idle time of equipment due to breakdowns and the poor organization of material-technical supply; many accidents due to a

20. Stalin, 'Politicheskii otchet', *Sochineniia,* xii. 357–61; 'S"ezd razvernutogo sotsialisticheskogo nastupleniia', *Bolshevik,* 13 (1930), 4–5.
21. *Tragediia sovetskoi derevni,* ii. 599–600.
22. Ibid. 627.
23. Ibid. 628–9.

criminal lack of care and poor technical oversight; the lack of systematic rationalization and thoroughly unsatisfactory in-factory planning.

Stalin was not in a mood to let officials evade the plan targets they had been set. Rather than surrender to those who hinted that the plan was unrealistic, the letter called for the party to help 'overcome technical conservatism'.[24] Three weeks later Stalin proposed to Molotov the creation of a 'Fulfilment Commission of the Council of People's Commissars exclusively charged with the systematic verification of the decisions of the centre, with the power quickly and directly to prosecute party and non-party officials for bureaucratism, non-fulfilment or the evasion of central decisions'. Stalin suggested that the commission should have direct access to the services of the RKI, OGPU, the Procuracy, and the press. 'Without such an authoritative and fast-acting commission, we will not break the wall of bureaucratism and the shoddy work of our apparatus. Without such a reform, our directives will remain unrealized everywhere.'[25] The 'reform' was directly linked to the ongoing purge of the state apparatus, with the power to remove those officials with a poor record of plan fulfilment.[26]

The relentless pressure exerted from the Kremlin to meet impossible targets had knock-on effects Stalin could not entirely anticipate. If, as they were told, underfulfilment could only be explained in terms of shortcomings in the organization of labour and production, officials could only blame one another. The director of the machine-building plant might want to blame the supply of metals from the foundry. The foundry director might want to blame the supply of ores. And the director of the mine might want to blame the machine-building plant. And yet, if the plans were realistic, as the central press so persistently asserted, perhaps there were hidden wreckers responsible for undermining the plan. Particularly since the Shakhty Affair, the press had warned officials to be vigilant about the wrecking activities of bourgeois specialists. Technical specialists did tend to be suspicious of plan targets and that made them an even more obvious target for arrest. According to a rapporteur at a 1931 conference of economic managers, 'up to one half of all engineers at the Donbas coal mines had been

24. *KPSS v rezoliutsiiakh*, v. 198–207; *Pravda* (3 Sept. 1930).
25. L. Kosheleva et al. (eds), *Pis'ma Stalina Molotovu*, 222–3.
26. E. L. Kiseleva, 'Chistka gosudarstvennogo apparata, 1929–1932 gg.', *Rossiiskaia istoriia*, 1 (2009).

sentenced to . . . forced labour'.[27] And specialists were not alone. When poorly trained peasants inadvertently damaged expensive imported equipment, they stood a good chance of being accused of sabotage. Train wrecks, fires, and other consequences of an overburdened infrastructure further heightened the sense that enemies of the state were at work. In 1931 alone, the OGPU arrested 15,670 people for terrorist activity.[28]

Many officials must have realized that they were vulnerable to denunciation. Most officials with targets to meet had no choice but to manage the flow of information to their bosses and to fulfilment checkers. They consistently exaggerated their need for inputs and underreported capacity in their annual plans. They degraded output quality in order to maximize quantity and shipped incomplete production.[29] In short, there was a widespread engagement in a mild form of 'anti-state activity'. Where they took the step of discussing their doubts about the plan even with close colleagues and friends, it was more serious. They risked being denounced for having 'Trotskyist' or 'Rightist' conversations.

For the time being, Stalin was content to let the purge commissions deal with such cases, because he was receiving intelligence of a far more worrying nature. Since the Shakhty trial in 1928, the OGPU had continued to investigate the foreign links of 'bourgeois' specialists, periodically relaying to Stalin 'evidence' of the efforts of capitalist states to undermine Soviet industrialization plans. In the summer of 1930, in the midst of the contraction of industrial production, Stalin was directing the investigation and prosecution of several 'counter-revolutionary conspiracies', including what became known as the Industrial Party, the Toiling Peasants' Party (TPP), and the Metro-Vickers Affair. The continuous flow of 'confessions' to his office encouraged him to think that the current problems of plan fulfilment were not attributable solely to 'Right deviationism', 'bureaucratism', and incompetence. Rather, he

27. Stalin, 'Novaia obstanovka—novye zadachi khoziaistennogo stroite'stva' (23 June 1931), *Sochineniia*, esp. 80; RGASPI 17/165/27/2–3 (Molotov), 14 (Kuibyshev); Oleg Khlevniuk, *In Stalin's Shadow: The Career of 'Sergo' Ordzhonikidze* (Armonk, NY, 1995), 47; See also O. V. Khlevniuk et al. (eds), *Stalin i Kaganovich: Perepiska. 1931–1936 gg.* (Moscow, 2001), 66, 68, 72, 711.

28. *Istoriia Sovetskikh organov gosudarstvennoi bezopasnosti* (Moscow, 1977), 226–7, 243–4; O. B. Mozokhin, 'Iz istorii bor'by organov VChK-OGPU s terrorizmom', *Voenno-istoricheskii zhurnal*, 5 (2002), 14–19.

29. Joseph Berliner, *Factory and Manager in the USSR* (Cambridge, Mass., 1957), chs 6–10.

was given cause to worry that capitalist states were organizing sabotage in an effort to undermine Soviet industrialization efforts in advance of an invasion. In October 1930, Stalin wrote to the head of the OGPU:

> Comrade Menzhinskii!
> [I] received your letter and accompanying materials of 2 October. The testimony of (engineer L. K.) Ramzin is very interesting. In my opinion the most interesting point concerns the intervention [i.e. invasion, JH] generally and its timing specifically. It looks as though they proposed to invade in 1930, but put it off until 1931 or even 1932. That is very probable and important...

Rather than wait to see if the testimony of others reinforced Ramzin's, he encouraged the OGPU to make the other's testimony conform: 'Run Messrs. Kondratiev, Iurovskii, Chaianov etc [i.e. the other accused, JH] through the mill; they have cleverly tried to evade [the charge of having a] tendency towards intervention but are (indisputably!) interventionist.' In the letter, Stalin also dictated to Menzhinskii, without reference to any further evidence, which of the figures abroad—the wealthiest émigrés and capitalists with contacts in the British and French governments—were 'directing' the accused specialists in the Soviet Union: 'It might seem as if the "TPP" or the "Promparty" or Miliukov's "party" represents the main force. But that's not true. The main force is the Riabushinskii-Denisov-Nobel group and the like—that is, Torgprom. The TPP, the Promparty, and Miliukov's "party" are errand boys for Torgprom.'

It was entirely characteristic of Stalin to rely on his 'revolutionary instincts', rather than on strong material evidence, to identify the enemies of the regime. Ramzin's testimony conformed to his image of leading capitalists directing their governments towards an invasion of the USSR. Stalin told Menzhinskii: 'If Ramzin's testimonies are confirmed and corroborated in the depositions of other persons accused...that will be a serious victory for the OGPU...[allowing us] to upset plans for an invasion in the next year or two which is very significant for us.'[30] The supposed foreign links of Soviet engineers were widely reported in the Soviet press together with allegations that the British intelligence service was using the engineers of the Metro-Vickers company to conduct sabotage in the USSR. But Stalin was just as concerned with the domestic connections of these 'conspirators'.

30. *Kommunist*, 11 (1990), 99–100. Lars Lih et al. (eds), *Stalin's Letters*, 195–6.

Whenever the political police passed him 'evidence' of wrecking activity or counter-revolutionary conspiracy, Stalin first wanted to know about links to foreign powers, but his second order of priority was to know about domestic links: who knew about these activities and failed to report them? Who might have encouraged them? In every case, the OGPU obliged, and beat 'confessions' out of conspirators. In the case of the Toiling Peasant Party and the Industrial Party, the confessions worryingly pointed to links with senior figures from the party, the state apparatus, and the army. Some of these purported links Stalin dismissed out of hand, such as those with the head of the Central Executive Committee (TsIK) Mikhail Kalinin, whom he viewed as essentially non-political, bumbling, and harmless. Links to the former Right Opposition and specifically Alexei Rykov, chairman of the Council of People's Commissars (SNK), he took as a given: 'of course he helped them,' Stalin wrote to Molotov in a private letter. A few days later he told Molotov that Bukharin must also be involved: 'Although he's not there in the case documents, he is, doubtlessly, the main instigator and campaigner against the Party.'[31] Rykov was quickly removed from his post and Bukharin placed under ever greater surveillance. The supposed links to the army gave Stalin pause for thought. Menzhinskii had drawn a picture of a military conspiracy led by Mikhail Tukhachevskii, with plans to kill Stalin and establish a military dictatorship. Stalin had the OGPU question Tukhachevskii and his immediate colleagues. Upon receiving the resulting transcripts, he wrote to Molotov that Tukhachevskii 'turned out to be 100% clean', but he concluded that others in the military were not. He ordered a substantial purge of the military to remove those elements who had, apparently, discussed with (unnamed) 'Rightists' plans for a military coup.[32] According to Stalin, the conspirators considered a coup necessary in order to 'get rid of the Central Committee, collective farms and Bolshevik tempos of industrial development'.[33]

And that was not the only embryonic coup plot reported to Stalin in the autumn of 1930. He was also given to believe that a colleague in the Politburo was conspiring against him. At the end of August 1930,

31. L. Kosheleva et al. (eds), *Pis'ma Stalina Molotovu*, 211, 220.
32. The relevant intelligence reports either remain in secret archives or have been destroyed.
33. Oleg Khlevniuk, *Politbiuro: Mekhanizmy politicheskoi vlasti v 1930-e gody* (Moscow, 1995), 37.

S. I. Syrtsov, chairman of the Council of People's Commissars of the Russian Federation and a candidate member of the Politburo, had delivered a major speech on the economy that was subsequently published in a pamphlet with a circulation of 10,000. While he praised the broad thrust of central policy, he also raised serious concerns about flaws in planning and the coordination of plan targets that subtly cut against the grain of Stalin's insistence that the plan was entirely realistic. Syrtsov faced no public rebuke in the summer, but as the economic crisis deepened, he was conscious of being isolated from policy discussions to which he felt he had much to contribute. In October he made the cardinal mistake of expressing his anger to a group of colleagues, one of whom, B. Reznikov, denounced him. The letter of denunciation accused Syrtsov of asserting that the party was turning against the regime, and that the crisis could encourage some members of the Politburo, supported by regional leaders, to attempt to remove Stalin. Syrtsov did not deny the meeting, or his disaffection, but he insisted that the talk of a coup was 'nonsense'. The few others present that day attempted to deny the meeting altogether, which only confirmed for Stalin the worst of his suspicions: 'It's unimaginably vile,' he wrote to Molotov. 'All the evidence suggests that Reznikov's version of events is true. They played at organizing a coup. They played at being an (alternative) Politburo.'[34] Stalin's tone suggests that he felt no immediate threat, but if Reznikov was right, he had good reason to watch his back.

It was not the first time, nor would it be the last that matters seemed more difficult and worrying than they need have done. The war scare of 1927 had been a chimera. Neither Britain, nor Poland, nor France had any plans for the invasion of the USSR, but Stalin's intelligence told them that they did. The Shakhty engineers and other bourgeois specialists were (quite sensibly) sceptical of Soviet industrialization plans, but it is highly unlikely that they were conspiring to undermine the Five-Year Plan on behalf of foreign governments and former owners. Stalin's intelligence nevertheless told him that they were, and he was not alone in finding the intelligence credible. The perceived threat made rapid industrialization that much more urgent, and with it, the collectivization of agriculture. Stalin shared a belief with many senior Bolsheviks that central planning was superior to capitalism and would

34. L. Kosheleva et al. (eds), *Pis'ma Stalina Molotovu*, 231; Khlevniuk, *Politbiuro*, 96–7.

make possible extraordinary achievements. The onset of the Great Depression in the west only reinforced their faith in the potential of the Great Break. He acknowledged that plan targets presented a great challenge to officialdom, but the very public persecution of sceptics both in the show trials of specialists and in the purge of 1929–31 skewed the flow of information to his desk. He had made it impossible to report 'objective' obstacles to fulfilment. Instead, the reports he received stressed the role of wrecking, 'Rightist sentiments', 'kulak sympathies', and plain incompetence in the emerging economic crisis of 1930.

He felt justified in blaming local officials for the failure of the collectivization drive. Too many had simply forced peasants to form collectives at gun-point, though the legislation he had authored made this sort of behaviour inevitable. As the collectivization drive continued in the autumn, Stalin continued to be insensitive to realities on the ground. He failed to grasp that the new collectives were organizationally too weak to support the grain collection targets they faced. As peasants or kolkhoz officials hid grain to ensure that there was enough to eat, Stalin saw evidence of 'kulak' designs to undermine the new order in the countryside. He sent Kaganovich to Ukraine and told him to 'take all measures to break the current mood of officials, isolate the whingers and rotten diplomats (no matter who!) and ensure genuinely Bolshevik decisions'.[35] His intransigence meant that appeals by regional and local officials to reduce collection targets were muted, and reports of mass starvation were slow to reach Moscow. Stalin did ultimately reduce collection targets, but only after loss of life on a colossal scale was inevitable. The peasantry, still the majority of the population, would resent the regime for generations.

His approach to industry was fundamentally similar. His unwillingness to accept that targets were unrealistic directly contributed to the crisis in industry. The squeeze on resources left the working class increasingly disaffected by the steady decline in their living standards. Shortages, bottlenecks, and overstrained infrastructure meant that less was achieved in the first Five-Year Plan than might have been possible. His unwillingness to accept that plan targets were unrealistic meant that the information he received and read excluded that possibility, and more sinister explanations of failures were found. Stalin and the party press repeatedly asserted that central policy was correct a priori:

35. O.V. Khlevniuk et al. (eds), *Stalin i Kaganovich: Perpepiska*, 205–10.

The [political] line of our party is clearly the uniquely correct line. Its correctness is obvious and indisputable... The party must, as ever, watch its own ranks with unwavering attention, exposing and target all manifestations of both Rightist and Trotskyist deviations... [The party] must defend itself against all those who attack its line, the correctness of which is being proven by experience every day. This is why deviationists rarely risk coming out in the open. Now they are more inclined to support the party line verbally (in public), in order to make it easier to undermine it in practice.[36]

That left a poisonous legacy that permanently damaged Stalin's relationship with officialdom generally. Not only were they afraid to pass on the sort of information necessary to effective decision-making at the top, but also because they had to meet impossible targets to keep their jobs, they had little choice but to lie to the centre, hide capacity, exaggerate the need for supplies, and engage in other behaviours that looked to the centre like a form of wrecking. This was what Stalin meant by praising central policy in public, while working to undermine it in private. The common term for it was *dvurushnichestvo*, literally being two-faced. It was a phenomenon that was doomed to spread.

Even before Bukharin had faced the onslaught of the campaign against the 'Right deviation', he wrote to Stalin about what he perceived to be a growing fear of expressing opinions frankly:

(About the procurements) campaign for the autumn we have neither a (political) line, nor a common opinion. Does that not worry you? We have stopped speaking on these issues: people are afraid to speak, to criticize. If the central intellectual laboratory has been destroyed, if we can't discuss the most important political questions openly and without fear, then the country is in danger. The economy is not an executive director. You can't shout at it and threaten to arrest it. We are not thinking things through enough. Self-criticism and so on—and the lack of communication about ideas [the phrase *otsutstvie ideinoi sviazi* can also mean 'lack of ideological coherence'] in the leadership—is a paradox of paradoxes, which is extremely dangerous.

As you know, I wrote the draft resolution on grain collections (for the July plenum). I didn't object when it was modified after it had been confirmed by the Politburo. I did not orchestrate any 'blocs' (at the plenum). I restricted my comments to the minimum of what I considered correct (though I was deeply upset by the people who clearly lied about the state of affairs in the localities, and 'sniffed the air' instead of speaking the truth).[37]

36. Stalin, 'Politicheskii otchet', *Sochineniia*, xii. 357–61; 'S″ezd razvernutogo sotsialisticheskogo nastupleniia', *Bolshevik*, 13 (1930), 4–5.
37. Kvashonkin et al. (eds), *Sovetskoe rukovodstvo*, 38–9.

The tendency to 'sniff the air' and hide one's deeper concerns only grew from there and in time it affected the Politburo itself. Bukharin's concerns for the intellectual apparatus of the state were prescient, and were ignored by Stalin out of hand. There is nothing in his personal archive to suggest that he paused for reflection, and contemplated the extent to which the economic crisis of 1930, or the famine of 1932–33, was the product not of 'bureaucratism', or 'kulak sympathies', or wrecking, but rather of unrealistic targets. Neither he nor those around him considered the consequences of telling leading officials that they could no longer explain their shortcomings in terms of 'objective conditions'. Stalin did not see that was closing down channels of communication between himself and his leading officials. Rather, he proceeded to break them down even further by demonizing those who questioned central policy.

In the days of the leadership struggle in the 1920s, from his position as General Secretary of the party, Stalin had generally been helpful, understanding, and at least cordial in his relations with the leaders of the republics and provinces. They came to him with their concerns and problems and he helped them. Now that they had helped him defeat the 'Oppositions', they were being told to meet their plans 'without discussion' or risk losing their jobs. This was neither as cynical a move on Stalin's part as it may seem, nor as sharp a transition. He did not pander to them just to get their support and then turn on them as soon as he no longer needed them. Stalin had always taken a hard line on the fulfilment of central directives, but this had been much easier to do in the context of the quasi-market economy of the NEP. The vagaries of the market could be blamed for problems. Under central planning, officials had no such figleaf behind which to hide. With the whole of the economy supposedly under their control, the buck stopped with them. If plans were not met, they had to answer for it. Under the Five-Year Plan not only were targets monumentally more ambitious, but the perceived need to fulfil them was greater—at least as far as Stalin was concerned. The existence of wreckers worried Stalin and the party leadership, but not as much as the 'spirit of opportunism': the questioning of the realism of the plan, the lack of will to rise to the challenges ahead. Meeting plan targets required an 'iron will' and 'iron discipline' from the top-down. Doubt and hesitation were intolerable in Stalin's view, and it was a short step from expressing doubt to conspiring against the regime. The party press warned that 'anyone who challenges the iron will of the Party will be crushed'.[38] When Syrstov and others like him chose to swim against the current and express their doubts about the direction of central policy, Stalin responded ferociously. He did not see that Syrtsov merely wanted a full-blooded role in the Politburo. Syrtsov felt he had a duty to raise his concerns about the sources of the crisis of policy. He was annoyed at being isolated from the policy discussions, and when he expressed that annoyance to the wrong people, he was denounced. He may well have believed, or have wanted to believe, that the crisis of 1930 would bring a change of leadership, but he was not in any direct sense organizing a coup. Stalin knew that Syrtsov did not present any immediate threat to him, but the disaffection of the peasantry, the wavering sentiments of the working class, the unreliable behaviour of broader officialdom, and hints of disloyalty near the top could not but have made him nervous. The Great Fear was beginning to coalesce.

38. See e.g. S. Shpilev, 'Dvurushnichestvo i Pravo-"Levyi" Blok', *Partiinoe Stroitel'stvo,* 21 (1930); Peredovaia, *Partiinoe Stroitel'stvo,* 22 (1930).

5

Relaxation?

The period of the first Five-Year Plan was characterized by colossal leaps in plan targets and intense pressure to fulfil them. Nothing short of total success was acceptable and any attempt to question the targets or challenge central policy, even in the face of economic crisis, was punished severely. Throughout, Stalin's public and private assessments of the crisis remained consistent. He blamed problems on the resistance of anti-Soviet elements, and the indiscipline, weakness, and incompetence of officialdom. 'Opportunism' and 'bureaucratism' were his preferred terms. At no stage did he consider the possibility that plan targets were unrealistic, or that enforcing them violently was counter-productive of both political and economic stability. And yet his faith in the almost limitless potential of central planning and his determination to enforce discipline was not without a measure of flexibility. For Stalin, planning for economic growth involved more than merely setting ever higher targets and enforcing them ruthlessly. Especially in conditions of general backwardness, material incentives to production would continue to play a role. And while Stalin drove the violent enforcement of targets, he was willing to accept that enforcers occasionally made mistakes, and needed disciplining themselves. However, one must guard against over-interpreting examples of this sort of flexibility. That Stalin saw a role for material incentives to production does not mean that he ever contemplated even a partial return to the quasi-capitalism of NEP. That Stalin occasionally restrained the political police and other such institutions does not mean that he questioned the necessity of the strict enforcement of central directives or the hunt for enemies of the revolution. The period from 1932 to 1934 is characterized by episodes of both ruthless repression and political moderation.

Examples of this flexibility can be seen even as the economy was descending into crisis in the spring and summer of 1931. Since the Shakhty trial in the spring of 1928, the central leadership had sustained a campaign of persecution against technical specialists as a group prone to resist the plan. At the very height of the economic crisis, in mid-July 1931, Stalin issued a directive limiting the power of the OGPU to arrest specialists on their own authority. In doing so, he acknowledged that, all too often, the political police were arresting innocent and capable workers: 'There's no need to allow policemen to be industrial technical experts. There's no need to allow a special OGPU office in a factory with a plaque, where they're sitting and waiting to be given work to do—and if there isn't any, they'll make some up.'[1] Stalin did not draw this conclusion suddenly or in isolation. For months, the chairman of the Supreme Council of the National Economy Sergo Ordzhonikidze had brought specific incidents of the harassment of specialists to Stalin's attention. Ordzhonikidze had warned against 'specialist-baiting' in his public speeches, and Stalin's line had notably softened through the spring. But there were others trying to influence Stalin on this matter. Since the end of the Civil War, the Commissariat of Justice had warned party leaders of the 'excesses' of the political police, not merely in terms of specific incidents, but more broadly in terms of their cavalier attitude to the most elementary standards of justice. They had tried time and again to convince Stalin that they should have some form of judicial oversight of OGPU operations, but with limited success. The OGPU had managed to defend its unlimited powers by arguing that such oversight would only hamper their struggle against the enemies of the revolution. Sensing once again that the Commissariat of Justice might get the upper hand in the aftermath of Stalin's decision on specialists, OGPU chairman Genrikh Iagoda issued a statement to all his officials criticizing, in particular, the use of torture to obtain confessions. The statement insisted that these 'excesses' were rare, and that there must not be any 'weakening of the struggle against counter-revolution in the sense of laxity or weakness in the face a determined and vigorous enemy'.[2] The statement was enough to convince Stalin that OGPU powers should remain intact, but his call for restraint had a powerful effect. Arrests for terrorist activity fell from

1. Khlevniuk, *Master of the House*, 61.
2. *Istoriia sovetskikh organov*, 234–5; *Lubianka: Stalin, 1922–1936*, 277–9.

15,670 in 1931 to 8,544 in 1932. Arrests for counter-revolutionary activity fell from 343,734 in 1931 to 195,540 in 1932 and 90,417 in 1933.[3]

The flexibility in Stalin's thinking can also be seen in economic policy, though it took longer for a coherent programme of action to emerge. The initial reaction to the economic crisis in the summer of 1931 was a heightened criticism of those who would question the realism of the plan and a renewed pressure on officials to meet the plan or face the sack. In July, Stalin insisted that the plan 'is realistic because its realization depends exclusively on ourselves, on our ability and our will to use the very rich possibilities we have'.[4] Through the autumn and winter, the telegrams traded between Moscow and the regions showed none of the cordial collegiality that had characterized them in the 1920s. Moscow sent sharply worded demands for total fulfilment, and regional leaders pleaded for plan reductions and other forms of special assistance. Stalin seethed with anger at what he perceived to be a determined resistance to central directives both in industry and in agriculture. The tension infected the Politburo itself. Stalin felt the need to reprimand both Ordzhonikidze and Mikoian (Commissar of Supply) for surrendering to the demands of institutions under their purview. Both proposed to resign, but they were ordered to remain in post.

Nevertheless, the unremitting tension encouraged Stalin to move beyond his dogged attacks on 'opportunism' and consider new ways of encouraging plan fulfilment. Through the winter and spring of 1932, the leadership warmed to the idea that, at least in agriculture, enterprises (i.e. collective and state farms) should be allowed to sell on the open market all production that remained after plan targets had been met. In one sense, the move only condoned what was happening anyway, but the official sanction hinted at a new openness to material incentives to labour reminiscent of the beginning of NEP, when grain seizures were replaced with a tax-in-kind. Grain collection targets were substantially reduced, and measures were taken to improve the supply of consumer goods to the countryside so that collective farmers would have something to buy with their profits.

The reform was both radical and extremely short-lived. A commitment to material incentives would have transformed the emerging

3. Mozokhin, 'Iz istorii bor'by', 19–20; Robert Thurston, *Life and Terror in Stalin's Russia, 1934–1941* (New Haven, 1996), 10.
4. Stalin, *Sochineniia*, xiii. 80.

command economy before it had become properly entrenched. And yet the commitment was not entirely solid. While collection targets were reduced, they were reduced only to the real level of collections from the previous year, which suggests that the leadership remained convinced that the kulaks were hiding agricultural output and that the promise of profit would flush more of it into the open. And because in reality the prospect of surpluses above plan targets remained remote, the material incentive to production was meagre. Rather than producing an acceleration of collections, they fell further still. The (reduced) July grain collection targets were only met by half. By early August 1932, the press once again blamed poor collections on the kulaks, and the infamous 7 August law on socialist property ensured that coercion and violence would drive the collection of the harvest like never before. The descent into a devastating famine was now inevitable.[5]

The weak commitment to the reform and the skittishness indicated by the promotion and sudden retraction of radical policies has several sources. It did not help the cause of reform in agriculture that the situation in industry took a turn for the worse in the summer of 1932. A sharp rise in costs was causing havoc with the construction plan and labour productivity was in sharp decline, but other factors, including the international situation, played a larger role in the decision to abandon the reform. Stalin and his intelligence agencies could sensibly have concluded that the onset of the Great Depression had improved the security situation. The economic crisis had a devastating impact on the ability of the capitalist economies to wage war. Nevertheless, Stalin saw the Depression as a crisis of overproduction, and following the logic of Lenin's theory of imperialism, he argued that conflicts over markets, sources of primary production, the export of capital, and colonies would only increase. The Depression, he argued, brought war closer and not further away. The only industry unaffected by Depression, he argued, was the armaments industry: bourgeois governments arm and rearm themselves. Why? 'Not for negotiation (*ne dlia razgovora*), but for war'. And war against the Soviet Union would solve many of their problems, not least by providing new markets for excess production and getting rid of the evil of communism exacerbating class tensions at home.[6]

5. The best source on the mini-reform is Davies, *Crisis and Progress*, 209–29.
6. I.V. Stalin, 'Politicheskii otchet TsK XVI s″ezdu VKP(b)', *Sochineniia*, xii. 247–56.

In the early 1930s, the Soviet leadership watched the political events in Europe with concern. The collapse of the Grand Coalition in Weimar Germany brought a sharp shift of politics to the right under Heinrich Bruning and the onset of emergency rule. They interpreted the rise of the Lapua movement and the fall of the Social Democratic government of Finland in June 1930 as a fascist coup.[7] They had similar concerns about the rise of the far right in Austria and Romania.[8] According to the party journal *Bolshevik*, the Depression was deepening the dependence of Poland, Finland, and the Baltic states on the imperialist powers and making them a solid base for their aggressive plans against the USSR.[9] The 'bloc' appeared to be getting bigger, and more aggressive. Following a flurry of Polish diplomatic activity in the Baltic states through the late summer of 1930, Stalin wrote to Molotov that the Poles 'were establishing (if they haven't already established) a bloc of Baltic states (Estonia, Latvia Finland) with the goal of waging war on the USSR. I don't think they'll attempt anything without the bloc, but as soon as they have it they'll go to war.'[10]

To them, the threat of war increased more sharply still when, on 18 September 1931, the Japanese launched an invasion of Manchuria. Stalin immediately concluded that the Japanese would not have acted without consulting the other capitalist powers and agreeing some kind of division of China. He thought that some of the Chinese warlords had to be involved as well, making further attacks on the Chinese Far Eastern Railway (KVZhD) likely.[11] As the invasion progressed, Stalin's predictions grew more pessimistic. At the end of November he wrote to Voroshilov:

Japan plans to seize not only Manchuria but also Beijing. It's not impossible and even likely that they will try to seize the Soviet Far East and even Mongolia to soothe the feelings of the Chinese clients with land captured at our expense. It is not likely to attack this winter, but it might try next year.

7. Anti-communist demonstrations had followed news of the suffering of ethnic Finns in collectivization. The significance of the 12,000-strong 'peasant' march on Helsinki and the adoption of anti-communist legislation called the Protection of the Republic Act was exaggerated in Moscow. Adibekov et al. (eds), *Politbiuro i Komintern*, 234–41.
8. Ibid. 604–5.
9. V. Mitskevich-Kapsukas, 'Ekonomicheskii krizis, Pol'sha i limitrofy', *Bolshevik*, 13 (15 July 1930), 105–24.
10. Kosheleva et al. (eds), *Pis'ma Stalina Molotovu*, 209–10.
11. RGASPI 558/11/76/76–76ob; Adibekov et al. (eds), *Politbiuro i Komintern*, 645–6; Kvashonkin et al. (eds), *Sovetskoe rukovodstvo*, 116–17.

Japan is driven by the desire to safeguard Manchuria, which it can only do if it turns the USSR against China.[12]

His suspicions were confirmed by intelligence he received in the middle of December 1931. A letter from Yukio Kasahara, the Japanese military attaché to the General Staff in Tokyo, intercepted by the OGPU, advocated a war against the USSR and the annexation of the Soviet Far East and Western Siberia essentially for the reasons Stalin had expected. It was not clear how much influence the attaché had in the General Staff, or how much influence the General Staff had in the government, but Stalin did know that Kasahara was not a lone voice in the military, and that many others outside the military were also advocating this sort of war of aggression. To make matters worse, Kasahara observed that 'the countries on Soviet western borders (i.e. at a minimum Poland and Romania) are in a position to act with us'.[13] A month later, Voroshilov wrote to his deputy Ian Gamarnik informing him of further (unconfirmed) reports to the effect that the Japanese

were in the midst of intensive preparations for war this spring. We also have evidence of the preparations of the Whiteguards, who boast that they can contribute 130,000 troops to an invasion force. They are proposing the creation of a 'Russian' government in the Far East and other such nonsense. All this is for now just rumour, but symptomatic (of the general situation). We must get working and in a Bolshevik manner in order to make up for lost time.[14]

Stalin continued to receive intelligence which indicated the imminence of a war on two fronts. At the end of February 1932 he received a further (intercepted) letter of Kasahara to the Japanese General Staff asserting that 'if we were to attack the USSR, Poland, Romania and the Baltic states would join (but not immediately), supported actively by the French and the not inconsiderable force of white Russians along the borderlands. Other powers would remain favourable.'[15] Had an anti-Soviet bloc emerged this time? The gist of that Japanese letter was 'confirmed' from the Polish side two weeks later when the OGPU passed Stalin the report of a conversation between a trusted source and the chief of the Polish General Staff. Plans for an attack were apparently well developed, and the French and Poles were trying to convince

12. Kvashonkin et al. (eds), *Sovetskoe rukovodstvo*, 161–2.
13. RGASPI 558/11/185/1–9.
14. Kvashonkin et al. (eds), *Sovetskoe rukovodstvo*, 167–8.
15. Khaustov et al. (eds), *Lubianka: Stalin, 1922–1936*, 298–308, 807.

the British to take an active part in the attack. The Romanians were preparing slowly, but there was still time. The invasion was planned for harvest time in order maximally to complicate the process of conscription and to take advantage of peasant hostility to the regime.[16] The 'evidence' of an active anti-Soviet bloc must have seemed compelling to Stalin, but it certainly does not conform to what we now know about British and French plans at the very least. It is quite possible that Kasahara and his Polish counterparts were engaging in some wishful thinking, if not outright fabrications, but it is also not inconceivable that the OGPU was creatively translating the materials it had in order to exaggerate the danger of war.

Reports from the Commissariat of Foreign Affairs also suggested that the situation was not quite as bad as the OGPU intelligence suggested. They observed that Japan was restrained by the war in China, and by reports of the strengthening of Soviet defences in the Far East, and that Poland was unlikely to fight the USSR while the revanchist far right in Germany was gaining strength.[17] Officials in the Commissariat did not, however, dismiss the threat of war, and events in the spring and summer of 1932 were far from reinforcing their relative optimism. TASS summaries of the far right press in Japan indicated that Britain had agreed to join France and Poland in a war against the USSR, and that certain unnamed American businessmen had agreed to help finance the war.[18] Japanese and pro-Japanese forces along the borders of the Far East appeared to be trying to provoke a conflict with border skirmishes and violations of Soviet airspace. Stalin gave strict orders not to respond to such 'provocations'. Stalin and Kaganovich agreed that the groups which favoured war with the USSR would blame any confrontation on Soviet 'aggression'. General Bliukher, head of the Far Eastern Military District, was raked over the coals by Stalin after shots were fired at Japanese planes entering Soviet airspace.[19] These 'provocations' reached a new height in June when these same groups were apparently threatening to topple the pro-Soviet government of Mongolia. Stalin was not prepared to risk sending in

16. RGASPI 558/11/185/65–70.
17. *Dokumenty vneshnei politiki SSSR (DVP SSSR)* (Moscow, 1957–77), xv. 214–17.
18. RGASPI 558/11/206/39–41.
19. RGASPI 558/11/43/116; Kvashonkin et al. (eds), *Sovetskoe rukovodstvo*, 135, 141, 220–1.

Soviet armed forces, though pro-Soviet forces were kept well supplied.[20]

Fears of invasion were played out against a background of growing labour unrest. In the late winter and spring of 1932, a growing number of workers from Ukraine to Siberia were protesting against shortages and cuts in rations. In the Ivanovo industrial region alone over 16,000 workers took part in a wave of strikes that were only quelled by a trainload of troops led by Lazar Kaganovich.[21] The reforms implemented in the spring and summer were, in part, a response to the unrest, in so far as it was hoped that they would encourage production and reduce shortages. However, they not only failed to increase production, they were also accompanied by sharp increases in prices and corresponding declines in living standards. In short, they made things worse, not better. Party leaders both in Moscow and in the provinces blamed the unrest on 'counter-revolutionaries', 'Trotskyite elements', and 'class aliens'. This was not a code, or a smokescreen for covering up policy failures. They genuinely believed that their enemies were exploiting 'temporary difficulties' in an effort to bring down the regime. The Politburo met in mid-April to discuss attacks on food depots and warehouses storing consumer goods across the USSR. They recommended holding five to ten show trials in which the 'enemies of the people' organizing these mass thefts would be publicly sentenced to death.[22] The unrest even threatened to infect the armed forces. At the end of May the OGPU informed Stalin that they had uncovered a plot by sailors aboard the cruiser *Marat* on the Baltic Sea to organize a rebellion against Soviet power.

The danger of widespread rebellion at home sharpened concerns about the international situation, where things seemed to be going from bad to worse. The western press was publishing reports of a Franco-Japanese pact, and the Soviet embassy (*polpredstvo*) in Paris received information to the effect that France was supplying Japan with arms on a grand scale.[23] Elections in Germany brought further setbacks for the communists and signs of deepening nationalism and anti-communism. In particular, Stalin began to worry that German

20. Ibid. 173–4; Khlevniuk et al. (eds), *Stalin i Kaganovich: Perepiska*, 136, 143, 156–7.
21. Rossman, 'A Worker's Strike', 44–83.
22. Khaustov et al. (eds), *Lubianka: Stalin, 1922–1936*, 310–11.
23. Jonathan Haslam, *Soviet Foreign Policy, 1930–1933: The Impact of the Depression* (London, 1983), 98.

anti-communism was sufficient common ground for a rapprochement with Poland and participation in the war with the USSR.[24] A Franco-German rapprochement seemed already to be on its way. While the possibility of German participation in the anti-Soviet coalition hung in the air, Poland gave every indication that preparations were under way for an autumn invasion. Resistance to the grain collection targets in the Ukraine was encouraging the Poles to send many small groups across the border with the aim of organizing resistance and ultimately a broad peasant rebellion. The radical reforms that were taking shape in the spring of 1932 must be understood in this context. Not only were they failing to bring any improvement in grain collections, but as far as Stalin was concerned, the reduced targets were also encouraging enemies of the regime to think they could exploit weakness and indiscipline in the party. Stalin told Kaganovich in mid-August that the Ukrainian party and OGPU had to break resistance to the grain collections immediately:

> If we don't take measures to correct the situation, we could lose Ukraine. Keep in mind that [Josef] Pilsudski [the Polish leader] is not daydreaming and his agent network in Ukraine is much stronger than [S. F.] Redens [chief of the republican OGPU] or [S. V.] Kosior [First Secretary of the Ukrainian Party] think. Also keep in mind that the Ukrainian Communist Party (500,000 members, ha-ha) has many (yes, many!) rotten elements, conscious and unconscious Petliurovites and direct agents of Pilsudski. If things get worse, these elements will not hesitate to open a front inside (and outside) the party, against the party... Without... the economic and political strengthening of Ukraine, and its *border districts* in the first instance... I repeat, we could lose Ukraine.[25]

'Correcting the situation' meant the abandonment of the reforms, and the imposition of a hard line on collection targets and conducting a ruthless purge of those party members who hesitated to meet them in full. Any indiscipline or hesitation was perceived to be lending encouragement to the kulaks and Polish agents who would launch a rebellion. Underpinning the new hard line was the infamous law of 7 August 1932 making the theft of public property, including the harvest on collective farms, subject to the death penalty. Stalin was conscious that the existing law punished thefts with two to three years of prison, of

24. Oleg Ken, *Mobilizatsionnoe planirovanie i politicheskie resheniia, konets 1920-kh—seredina 1930-kh gg.* (Moscow, 2008), 286–9.
25. Khlevniuk et al. (eds), *Stalin i Kaganovich: Perepiska*, 274.

which those convicted would serve six to eight months. This situation, he observed, 'only encourages these class aliens (*gospoda*) to go on with their counter-revolutionary work'.[26] He thought that the law was necessary to instil discipline and prevent a Polish attack as part of an imminent war. He did not anticipate that the ruthless application of the law would deepen the famine that was taking hold across the country. Inevitably, largely because of the perceived threat from Poland, the Ukrainian peasantry would suffer disproportionately.

The decision to abandon the reforms and to take a hard line on plan fulfilment had other equally serious consequences for the regime. For many officials, the promise of reform had aroused hope in the spring, and return to repression in the summer provoked anger. In July, one Left Opposition group with connections in Gosplan smuggled an extended criticism of state economic policy abroad, where it was published in Trotsky's journal *Bulletin of the Opposition*. What made the episode particularly troubling for Stalin was that the document contained a wealth of statistical material that had been circulated among a relatively small number of leading economic officials. Not only did that reinforce his concerns about Trotskyists and other hidden enemies among leading officials, but it also meant that this secret information, which openly discussed the weaknesses of Soviet economic development, received wide circulation outside the USSR where it might—as Stalin saw it—encourage capitalist governments in their aggressive plans against the regime.

Worse was to follow. In mid-September, the OGPU obtained a copy of an even more vitriolic oppositionist document calling for the violent overthrow of the regime: 'The Politburo, the Central Control Commission and secretaries of the regional party organs have become a lying and cowardly band of unprincipled intriguers and fraudsters ... Stalin and his clique do not want to and will not voluntarily resign. Therefore, they must be removed by force.' It had been written by Martem'ian Riutin, a former candidate member of the Central Committee and member of the Presidium of the Supreme Council of the National Economy. Riutin had been purged from those posts in 1930 for earlier oppositionist activity, but had been allowed to take up a lesser post after he had apparently renounced his views. However, Riutin had not only held to his oppositionist views, he had also

26. Ibid. 235.

continued to discuss them with leading officials in the party and state apparatus. His immediate associates were arrested and interrogated, and the case put before the Central Control Commission, which concluded that the platform had passed 'from comrade to comrade, group to group, from city to city, calling for the publication of pamphlets and appeals, newspapers propagating (the group's) views, and the organization, where possible, of strikes and other forms of protest for the preparation of an attempt to oust Stalin and other leaders of the Party and Soviet government'.[27] How far had the platform (and other appeals) circulated before the group was betrayed to the political police? Stalin obsessively pursued the answer to this question, because it promised to provide the measure of the potential conspiracy against him and the regime. How many other former oppositionists had lied to the Central Control Commission when they had 'renounced' their old views? How many of the thousands of former oppositionists who had been returned to positions of authority after such false declarations were secretly working to overthrow the current regime? The Riutin platform had been circulated widely enough to generate a spirited discussion in government and diplomatic circles abroad, providing yet more damaging evidence of Stalin's weakness at home. Reliable evidence of the circulation of Riutin's 'platform' within the USSR was harder to come by. As ever, OGPU interrogators relied on confessions obtained through torture. The pressure to 'name names' under interrogation lent the impression that the platform had been circulated more widely than it probably had been in fact. Stalin thus was given 'evidence' to conclude not only that many former oppositionists secretly supported removing him by force, but also that the leaders of the oppositions, including Zinoviev and Kamenev, had read and sympathized with the platform. Bukharin was also implicated but less directly in that Stalin was told that the platform had circulated within the Institute of Red Professors, with which Bukharin had close ties.

The OGPU soon uncovered yet more anti-Stalin 'conspirators'. On the same day Riutin and his associates were sentenced to imprisonment and exile, the OGPU informed Stalin that it had seized a bundle of letters and articles written by Khristian Rakovskii, an old friend and collaborator with Trotsky. These writings sharply criticized the

27. A. Artizov et al., *Reabilitatsiia: Kak eto bylo*, ii. *Fevral' 1956-nachalo 80-kh godov. Dokumenty* (Moscow, 2003), 394–8.

leadership of Stalin. In his view, Stalin's incompetence and lack of theoretical insight were contributing not only to the 'bureaucratization' of Soviet power but also to a new revolutionary situation, as the disaffected working masses edged towards rebellion. He proposed that the time was right for 'revolutionary communists' to join forces and lead the masses to the restoration of Leninism.[28] According to Lev Sedov, Trotsky's son, a 'group' of former leaders of the Left Opposition continuing to occupy senior posts in the government, including I. N. Smirnov, E. A. Preobrazhenskii, and N. I. Ufimtsev, was broken up in October. Then, in late November two senior figures in the state apparatus, N. B. Eismont, the People' Commissar for Supply of the Russian Federation, and V. N. Tolmachev, head of the Road Transport Administration for the RSFSR, were arrested after being accused of involvement in a group sympathetic to the Right Opposition. As it was reported to Stalin, they had advocated his removal. Both denied making such statements when they were hauled before a hearing at the Central Control Commission, and both denied being in an active 'Right Oppositionist group'. But members of the Central Control Commission did not accept their denials. On the contrary, they were inclined to interpret the verb 'to remove' (*ubrat'*) in its colloquial meaning of 'to kill'.[29]

They need not have taken such an extreme view, of course. There was no shortage of hostility to the regime and to Stalin's leadership in particular, but none of these groups and individuals had any realistic chance of orchestrating any meaningful political change. And yet, taken in the broader context, Stalin appeared to have good reason to be worried by their anger and, for some, their ambition to depose him. His intelligence services were telling him that the USSR was in danger of invasion from east and west. It would be exceptionally difficult to raise an adequate defence when the country was to all intents and purposes already fighting a civil war with the peasantry and facing significant unrest from the working class. At the same time, Stalin no longer enjoyed the easy, collegial relationship he had with senior officialdom, including regional leaders and heads of central party and state institutions. Since the late 1920s, his interaction with them, a group that constituted the overwhelming majority of the Party Central

28. Khaustov et al. (eds), *Lubianka: Stalin, 1922–1936*, 326–34.
29. Davies, *Crisis and Progress*, 254; Getty and Naumov, *Road to Terror*, 75–6.

Committee, consisted largely of badgering and threats of dire consequences should they not meet plan targets. Back in 1930, Syrtsov had claimed that there were Central Committee members waiting for the opportunity to replace him. Stalin could only assume that, by 1932, their ranks had grown. The situation was reminiscent of the revolutionary underground. The Bolsheviks were, on the surface of things, a wholly committed band of revolutionaries. But the movement was littered with provocateurs in the pay of the Tsarist *Okhrana*, secretly plotting to destroy it from within. Riutin, Rakovskii, Eismont, and others were insignificant figures on their own, but Stalin could not assume that they were on their own. Rebellion or war, or possibly both, would surely bring his opponents together and out into the open.

Historians have long observed that this period marked a rapid development of Stalin's dictatorship. Having defeated Bukharin, the last of those who could make a reasonable claim to succeed Lenin as undisputed leader, Stalin continued his assault on the democratic traditions of the party to extend his personal control. The evidence is plain to see. In the 1920s, Party Congresses and Conferences had met every year so that party members could come to the capital to hear the reports of executive office holders and share their views on major policy initiatives. The smaller Central Committee, consisting of the top officials in Moscow and the provinces, met four or five times a year to discuss and shape policy. Between 1930 and 1939, there was only a single Party Congress. Through the 1930s, the Central Committee met with ever decreasing regularity, and only then to receive instructions from Stalin and his inner circle. Even the Politburo, the locus of executive power in the party, fell into disuse as decision-making was increasingly concentrated in Stalin's hands. Key decisions were made less and less by formal meetings of the group and increasingly by Stalin from his office in the Kremlin or his dacha on the outskirts of Moscow.[30]

This is sometimes portrayed as evidence of Stalin's lust for power and as the realization of an elaborate plan, but there is no evidence in Stalin's personal archive to suggest that such a plan ever existed. At times Stalin berated his inner circle for insisting that he approve their every decision even when he was on vacation. But why did he erode

30. For more detail see E. A. Rees, 'Leaders and their Institutions', in Paul R. Gregory (ed.), *Behind the Façade of Stalin's Command Economy* (Stanford, Calif., 2001), 35–60; Kvashonkin et al. (eds), *Stalinskoe Politbiuro*.

the 'democratic', or at least consultative, institutions that had played such an active role in decision-making in the 1920s? In the 1920s, Stalin had made no secret of his concerns about what was called 'intra-party democracy'. When Lenin assigned him the role of General Secretary of the party, one of his first tasks was to put an end to the power struggles and petty squabbling that were paralyzing party organizations up and down the country. He did so primarily by empowering the First Secretary of party organizations to remove those who challenged their power. In essence, Stalin created hundreds of little dictatorships, and dictators who understood that they owed the stability of their positions to Stalin. This proved to be an enormous asset to Stalin in the struggle for the Lenin succession. He portrayed his challengers as petty squabblers and as 'oppositions' rather than advocates of legitimate policy positions. When Trotsky, Zinoviev, and Bukharin in turn attempted to promote their views before the broader party membership, Stalin could generally rely on party secretaries to stifle discussion and remove 'oppositionists'. When Trotsky criticized Stalin's 'secretarial regime' and demanded a respect for party democracy, Stalin insisted that Trotsky was not supporting democracy but a 'freedom of group struggle':

> It is not the [Secretarial] regime that is to blame [for the necessity of the retreat from intra-party democracy], but rather the conditions in which we live, the conditions of the country... If we were to permit the existence of group struggle, we would destroy the party, turn it from a monolithic, united organization into an alliance of groups and factions. It would not be a party, but rather the destruction of the party... Not for one minute did Bolsheviks ever imagine the party as anything but a monolithic organization, cut from one piece, of one will... In the current conditions of capitalist encirclement, we need not only a united party, but a party of steel, capable of withstanding the onslaught of the enemies of the proletariat, capable of leading the workers into a decisive struggle.[31]

Nothing had changed in the intervening years to change Stalin's view of party democracy. The threat from capitalist countries appeared to be worse. The party had never been a monolithic, united organization, but under the pressure to fulfil plan targets and in the midst of economic crisis and social unrest it was less united than it had been at any

31. *Trinadtsataia konferentsiia Rossiiskoi Kommunisticheskoi Partii (Bolshevikov)* (Moscow, 1924), 100–1, 106–7.

time in the past. Stalin had every reason to believe that a frank and open exchange of views within the party would give his enemies the perfect opportunity to unseat him. Even meetings of the Central Committee were dangerous to him because they brought together leading party officials who shared similar grievances about his leadership and gave them the opportunity to plot against him.

Stalin's dictatorship was not a function of a lust for power, but of an instinct for survival. A decade later, he confessed to Winston Churchill that this period had been more stressful than the war against Nazi Germany.[32] In the autumn of 1932, he knew that something had to be done to reduce domestic tensions, but without giving in to his enemies or surrendering his strategic vision. One opportunity presented itself in the closing months of the first Five-Year Plan and the discussions surrounding the launch of the second, which was to begin in January 1933. Planners, senior finance officials, and leaders of the administration of industry had been arguing about investment and production targets for the second Five-Year Plan since the beginning of 1932. Early in the year, Stalin had firmly sided with the maximalists, sustaining the threat that critics of ambitious plans would be labelled 'opportunists'. However, the economic crisis in the summer and autumn ensured that the critics did not go away. They insisted that recent experience had demonstrated that continuing existing projections for investment and production would only deepen existing inflationary pressures and repeat plan underfulfilment. Stalin was no stranger to such arguments, and on many occasions he had insisted that plans could be achieved if the necessary will and energy was applied. But in November, in the midst of dealing with the run of 'factions' plotting his downfall, he agreed to reduced targets for 1933 and the rest of the second Five-Year Plan. The plan varied from industry to industry, but growth rates were to average 14 per cent across the five years in place of the 20 per cent discussed in earlier versions.[33] This was no radical reform like those put forward in the spring. There was no question of factories selling above-plan production. Despite the substantial reductions in plan targets, they would not be easy to achieve, and Stalin showed no hint of retreating from his tough line on the verification of fulfilment. The consequences of underfulfilment would be even more

32. Winston S. Churchill, *The Second World War* (New York, 1959), i. 271–2.
33. Davies, *Crisis and Progress*, 322.

severe. Nevertheless, the broader thrust of Stalin's 'concession' would not have been lost on senior officials. The plan targets would still be difficult to meet, but at least there was a real prospect of meeting them finally. Furthermore, at the joint plenum of the Central Committee and Central Control Commission in early January, Stalin heaped praise on their achievements in the first Five-Year Plan. This was a welcome and striking break from the constant withering criticisms of their shortcomings in the previous months and years. It appeared to be a new beginning. Stalin almost certainly intended it to undermine any conspiracy against him.

If there was a new beginning, it did not yet apply to agriculture, where on Stalin's strict instructions grossly exaggerated collection targets ferociously enforced were deepening the descent into famine. While Stalin praised industrial officials for their achievements, he continued to criticize those in charge of agriculture particularly for their failure to understand the 'tactics of the class enemy'.[34] He believed that it was necessary to enforce a tough line so as not to give the enemies of the regime the upper hand, but the approach was misconceived on many levels. Most importantly, Stalin did not have reliable and accurate figures on the actual size of the harvest. He was convinced that it was substantially greater than it was, and so he saw the poor collection results as the work of 'anti-social, anti-state elements, wreckers and opportunists'.[35] He knew that peasants were starving, but he thought enemies in the countryside were to blame. To back down from the struggle, to lower targets or seek outside aid, might have saved lives, but as far as Stalin understood it, this would have handed a victory to those who were organizing resistance and rebellion. He did gradually release grain from state reserves to mitigate the effects of famine, but it was far too little, far too late. Millions of peasants died of starvation.[36]

The reduced industrial targets, eventually extended to agriculture, were intended to help repair Stalin's relations with senior officialdom, but he could not yet be sure that the immediate danger of a coup had passed. The international situation continued to be extremely delicate. The Commissar of Foreign Affairs Maxim Litvinov had orchestrated non-aggression pacts with the Poles and the French, but Stalin was not

34. Stalin, *Sochineniia*, xiii. 320.
35. Ibid. 229–31; *KPSS v rezoliutsiiakh*, vi. 26–9.
36. R. W. Davies et al., 'Stalin, Grain Stocks and the Famine of 1932–1933', *Slavic Review*, 3 (1995), 642–57.

inclined to think such agreements held much weight. He found more confidence in the successes of investment in Soviet military capabilities in the later years of the first Five-Year Plan. He made much of them in his January 1933 speech on the results of the plan, deliberately exaggerating them, as he exaggerated achievements in agriculture and industry, as a signal to the capitalists that any invasion would be difficult and costly.[37] The mood was not upset even by the appointment of Hitler as German chancellor on 30 January. The instinct in Comintern was to interpret the success of the Nazis as further evidence of the crisis of German capitalism and the maturing of a revolutionary situation.[38] They did not, at first, take the Nazis especially seriously. Germany was too weak politically and economically for the Nazis' anti-communism to be converted into action. The situation in the Far East was more worrying. Military and other conservative circles in Japan continued to advocate war with the Soviet Union and Stalin's intelligence told him that the Japanese military build-up proceeded at an undiminished pace,[39] and that Japanese spies and saboteurs continued to operate on Soviet territory.[40] By March, the new Nazi government seemed to be pushing a rapprochement with the Poles with the aim of improving their mutual security at the expense of the Soviet Union.[41] The danger of a two-front war had not passed, and Stalin's internal enemies could still make use of an attack to unseat him.

Stalin needed further reassurances. At the January plenum, the praise of the plan achievements was immediately followed by a discussion of the Eismont-Tolmachev Affair. Stalin watched and listened as senior party officials took turns at the podium to express their indignation at those who would secretly criticize and conspire against the regime.[42] There is no evidence in his private correspondence to indicate his reaction or his sense of how many of them he could really trust. Three

37. Stalin, 'Itogi pervoi piatiletki', *Sochineniia*, xiii. 162–8, 182–5.
38. V.V. Dam'e et al. (eds), *Komintern protiv fashizma: Dokumenty* (Moscow, 1999), 291–7.
39. Among other things, Stalin received intercepted correspondence between the British ambassador in Tokyo and the Foreign Office in London, observing that the Japanese military build-up was too great to be directed solely at China. The ambassador speculated that this was probably evidence of preparations for war against the USSR. He went on to observe that Japanese military officers considered war with the USSR inevitable in the next few years. RGASPI 558/11/185/97–102.
40. See e.g. RGVA 9/39/5c/2–21, 76–82, 109–116.
41. S.V. Morozov, *Pol'sko-Chekhoslovatskie otnosheniia, 1933–1939* (Moscow, 2004), 27.
42. See Getty and Naumov, *Road to Terror*, ch. 2.

months later, he announced a general purge of the party. The party had grown substantially in the previous two years, so such a 'cleansing' of the ranks was well within the tradition. And yet, this purge was not directed against the usual 'passive', corrupt, or careerist elements. This purge was about enemies. The first four categories of targets for the purge consisted of:

> 1/ Class-alien and hostile elements who have pushed their way into the party through deception and who remain within it for the purpose of corrupting the ranks;
>
> 2/ Duplicitous elements who live by deceiving the party, who conceal from it their real aspirations, and who, under cover of a false oath of 'loyalty' to the party, seek in fact to undermine the party's policy;
>
> 3/ Open and secret violators of the iron discipline of the party and state who do not carry out the decisions and plans set by the party and government and who cast doubt on and discredit the decisions and plans set by the party by their idle talk about their 'unfeasibility' and 'unattainability';
>
> 4/ Degenerates who, having coalesced with bourgeois elements, do not want to fight our class enemies and who do not struggle against kulak elements, self-seekers, loafers, thieves or plunderers of public property...[43]

No mention was made of former oppositionists, but Stalin was dealing with them by other means. The OGPU had stepped up surveillance, and at the time of the purge announcement quietly arrested 150 former oppositionists in Moscow alone. Sensing the opportunity to break their spirit of resistance, Stalin then brought Zinoviev and Kamenev back from exile in the provinces where they had been sent for their complicity in the Riutin Affair. The price for their return was a further humiliating confession of their mistakes and declaration of loyalty to the General Secretary.

Stalin was an experienced political operator, and he had every reason to be pleased with the way he was turning things around from the dark days in the autumn and winter. Not only had he made it much more difficult to conspire against him, and to resist party policy, but also on a practical level, the country started to emerge from crisis. The first signs of recovery came from heavy industry. Then in the summer, it became clear that there would be an excellent harvest. The worst of the famine was over, and many more collective farmers would be in a position to bring excess production to market. As the food situation

43. Ibid. 126–7.

improved, there was a corresponding decline of unrest. To reinforce that shift, the regime invested more heavily in the production of consumer goods. In the countryside, Stalin called a halt to mass repression, elevating the role of the judiciary over the political police in the conduct of any further arrests. The shift towards moderate policies was striking and consistent.

The Seventeenth Party Congress in early 1934 sustained the general tone. Hailed as the 'Congress of Victors', it continued the celebration of achievements in the economy, society, and culture, including most importantly, the declaration that socialism had been achieved. The Congress was not without a serious discussion of policy. In his opening remarks about the international situation, Stalin warned that the capitalist powers continued to arm themselves and ponder an attack on the USSR. Then on the domestic situation, he returned to some familiar themes. He warned the audience of officials not to be complacent. There were many challenges ahead and victory was not certain. Without saying it, he was pointing out that targets had been reduced, but meeting them would require hard work. Most familiar was the refrain about personal responsibility: 'There is no excuse for appealing to so-called objective conditions (if you fail to meet plan targets) . . . Responsibility for our failures and shortcomings lies, in nine-tenths of cases, not in "objective" conditions, but on ourselves and only ourselves.' He warned them that more would be done to verify the fulfilment of decisions, and to hold them personally responsible for failures in their organizations. Those who came up short would be replaced, no matter what position they held and 'regardless of their services in the past'.[44]

In the months that followed, the apparatus for the verification of fulfilment was reformed and strengthened, but from the perspective of leading officials in Moscow and the provinces, not to a worrying extent. For them, the general trend was in the opposite direction. The heavy hand of the state was getting lighter. Only ten days after the conclusion of the Seventeenth Congress, Stalin set in motion a fundamental reorganization of the political police. Now that the years of crisis appeared to have passed, Stalin was willing to curtail the arbitrary powers of the OGPU. The political police would continue to investigate political cases, but the courts would now supervise sentencing.

44. Stalin, *Sochineniia*, xiii. 366–70.

Behind the scenes, there was considerable criticism of OGPU methods in the past and particularly 'excesses' in the application of the 7 August law. There was no move towards anything that resembled the first stages of the rule of law, but there was a desire to reassure the public, and the peasantry in particular, that that there would be no return to the arbitrary repression that had blighted the countryside since the beginning of collectivization five years before.

Stalin and his inner circle finally seemed to accept that their power was secure. They continued to amnesty former oppositionists. They were not unduly concerned when the international situation took another turn for the worse in the summer and autumn of 1934. At the end of June, Stalin received intelligence from a mole in the Polish Foreign Ministry to the effect that Polish leader Josef Pilsudski and his Foreign Minister Josef Beck had tried (unsuccessfully) to convince French Foreign Minister Louis Barthou of the benefits of joining a Polish–German alliance against the USSR, but Pilsudski and Beck did not think they had long to wait before a more conservative government replaced that of the radical, Daladier. Intelligence from the OGPU Foreign Department informed Stalin that well-placed conservatives Andre Tardieu (a former Prime Minister) and General Maxime Weygand advised the Poles that, following a change in government, France would join a military alliance against the USSR. They had apparently already canvassed senior figures in the British government who promised their support for an anti-Soviet war. The report went on to assert that the Poles and Germans were now more openly negotiating a military pact with the Japanese. The support of the Romanians was likely, and there were hopes that Italy, Austria, and Hungary might join. The report concluded that 'war against the Soviet Union was never as realistic a possibility as now'.[45]

Then on 1 December 1934, the candidate member of the Politburo and Leningrad regional party secretary Sergei Kirov was assassinated.

45. RGASPI 558/11/187/28–44.

6

Tensions mount

For decades, historians concluded that the assassin, Leonid Nikolaev, had acted directly or indirectly on the orders of Joseph Stalin. They argued that Kirov had come to represent a 'moderate' wing in the political leadership that presented a threat to Stalin's leadership and that his assassination marked the beginning of the Great Terror, a programme of political violence intended to eliminate all those whose loyalty to Stalin was in doubt and thus confirm the dictator's total grip on power.[1] In 1985, six years before the archives opened, Arch Getty argued that, if unreliable memoir evidence and other third-hand accounts were set aside, the balance of evidence indicated that Nikolaev was acting on his own.[2] The overwhelming weight of archival research since then has supported his view.[3]

Stalin was informed of the assassination almost immediately, and within twenty-four hours he brought a delegation to Leningrad to open the investigation. He talked to the doctors who had attended Kirov, to Kirov's bodyguard, the leaders of the Leningrad Party and political police, and to the assassin himself. On the basis of this active participation in and close monitoring of the investigation, Stalin briefly toyed with the idea that Nikolaev was acting on behalf of a foreign power before he unambiguously instructed the NKVD to 'look for the perpetrators among the Zinovievites'.[4] He appears never to have

1. Deutscher, *Stalin*; Alexander Orlov, *The Secret History of Stalin's Crimes* (New York, 1953); Conquest, *The Great Terror*; Roy Medvedev, *Let History Judge* (London, 1972).
2. Getty, *Origins of the Great Purges*, 207–10.
3. The most recent and authoritative account of the murder is Matthew E. Lenoe, *The Kirov Murder and Soviet History* (New Haven, 2010).
4. The quotation is from Nikolai Ezhov's concluding speech to the Feb.–Mar. 1937 Central Committee plenum. See 'O dele tak nazyvaemogo "Moskovskogo tsentra"', *Izvestiia TsK*, 7 (1989), 69.

considered the possibility that Nikolaev acted alone. Why? There was, as we have seen, a long history of terrorism and political assassination perpetrated against the USSR. The Socialist Revolutionaries had attempted to assassinate Lenin in August 1918. During and after the Civil War the Whites periodically sent small parties into Soviet territory with the express purpose of assassinating Soviet leaders.[5] In response to the threat of assassination Kremlin security was tightened in the mid-1920s, and Stalin was subsequently forbidden to walk Moscow streets without a security detail.[6] In the face of many groups both domestically and internationally determined to overthrow the revolution and unseat the current regime, Stalin considered it the height of naïveté to think that an assassin or saboteur could be working alone. In August 1934, Kaganovich reported to Stalin, who was on vacation at the time, that a certain A. S. Nakhaev, the commander of a division of Osoaviakhim in Moscow, roughly the equivalent of the Territorial Army, attempted to get his men to take arms against Soviet power. They didn't follow him and Nakhaev was arrested immediately. Kaganovich assumed he was suffering some kind of breakdown, but Stalin insisted that Nakhaev had to be a spy in the pay of a foreign power:

> Of course (of course!) he's not working alone. We have to hold him to the wall and force him to tell the whole truth—and then punish him severely. He must be a Polish–German agent (or Japanese). The Chekisty make a mockery of themselves when they discuss his 'political views' with him. (This is called an *interrogation*!) Hired thugs do not have their own political views, or else he wouldn't be an agent of a foreign power.[7]

Three weeks later, Stalin received his 'whole truth', when Nakhaev 'confessed' that he had been recruited by Estonian agents.[8] In essence,

5. Andrew Cook, *On His Majesty's Secret Service: Sidney Reilly Codename ST1* (London, 2002); John W. Long, 'Plot and Counterplot in Revolutionary Russia: Chronicling the Bruce Lockhart Conspiracy, 1918', *Intelligence and National Security*, 1 (1995), 122–43; A. L. Litvin (ed), *Boris Savinkov na Lubianke: Dokumenty* (Moscow, 2001). O. B. Mozokhin, 'Iz istorii bor'by organov VChK-OGPU s terrorizmom', *Voenno-istoricheskii zhurnal*, 5 (2002), 5. *Istoriia sovetskikh organov*, 159–60.
6. Some of the intelligence reports that Dzerzhinskii received and passed on to Stalin between late 1924 and the first half of 1926 can be found in RGASPI 76/3/331/1–3; 76/3/364/4–8, 12–13, 21–25, 58.
7. Khlevniuk et al. (eds), *Stalin i Kaganovich: Perepiska*, 429; *Lubianka: Stalin, 1922–1936*, 549, 818–19.
8. See the telegram of Ia. S. Agranov (First Deputy People's Commissar of Internal Affairs) to Stalin in Aug. 1934. RGASPI 558/11/50/46.

through Kaganovich, Stalin had ordered the NKVD to torture Nakhaev until he confessed along lines that suited his preconceptions. He simply did not consider it plausible that such crimes against the state were not political and linked to a wider network of enemies.

Why then did Stalin dismiss the possibility of a foreign connection to the Kirov assassination? He did not do so immediately. Over the phone from Moscow, before he had even travelled to Leningrad, he had asked if Nikolaev was carrying any foreign items. He would have quickly learned that Nikolaev's wife Milda Draule was Latvian. This was a sufficiently promising link for the NKVD to pursue the foreign link for three weeks after Stalin's unambiguous instruction. Indeed, in the days after the assassination, Nikolaev's interrogators had him admit to visiting both the Latvian and German consulates in Leningrad in the summer and autumn of 1934. From the latter, he apparently received Deutschmarks which he subsequently spent in a hard currency shop. By the end of December, after almost four weeks of interrogations, he 'confessed' that he asked the Latvian consul to help his counter-revolutionary 'group' get in contact with Trotsky. But Stalin remained unconvinced that Nikolaev was acting on behalf of hostile capitalist powers. There is a traceable logic to his conviction. While the international situation was not good, it was not at a critical phase where the assassination of Soviet leaders would help pave the way for a successful invasion. A right-wing government had been installed in Latvia in May with links to both the Poles and the Germans, but as far as Stalin could see it in late 1934, the latter two were in the midst of a complex negotiation to bring the French into an anti-Soviet coalition.[9] It was too early for such a political assassination to serve their interests. Besides which, employing an ex-party member such as Nikolaev would have been unprecedented. Foreign governments had long tended to use Whites to conduct acts of terrorism in the USSR. Rather, in Stalin's view the recruitment of disaffected party members—Nikolaev had been purged in April 1934—was the modus operandi of the former oppositions.

It is worth remembering that leaders of the Left Opposition were accused of organizing a coup d'état timed to coincide with the celebration of the tenth anniversary of the revolution in 1927.[10] S. I. Syrtsov

9. See e.g. RGASPI 17/162/17/75–6; 558/11/187/120–3.
10. See Ch. 3.

was accused of trying to organize another plot to remove Soviet leaders in 1930. Martem'ian Riutin was trying to gather support for his alternative 'platform' in the summer of 1932 and other Left Oppositionist groups accused of planning to unseat the current leadership had been broken up in the autumn.[11] Stalin had tried to deal with the threat with a combination of arrests, purges, and humiliating declarations of loyalty from Left Oppositionist leaders, but he had no reason to assume that he had dealt with the problem of internal hostility to his rule once and for all. It was reasonable for him to think that he had only succeeded in pushing that opposition further underground, and in that respect, Nikolaev's anger with local authorities for cutting his party career short and leaving him unemployed made him ripe for recruitment. Leningrad was, after all, Grigorii Zinoviev's old stronghold, where, as Party First Secretary, he had recruited hundreds of like-minded officials who by late 1934 must have long bottled their deeply held opposition to Stalin. Stalin could see that the assassination of a senior figure like Kirov would send a clear signal that the struggle was not over and could still be won.

He did not anticipate that the political police would inevitably find 'evidence' to support his preconceptions. And in this case, the NKVD had a particularly strong institutional self-interest in playing up the dimensions of a conspiracy. Policing reforms in the past year had severely curtailed their power to act as judge, jury, and executioner. In the immediate aftermath of the Kirov murder, the restrictions on them were lifted and they had every reason to want to ensure that they were not reinvoked. As early as 4 December, Nikolaev 'confessed' that his decision to assassinate Kirov had been influenced by Trotskyists in the Leningrad party organization.[12] Arrests soon spread to the Leningrad Komsomol, which had had strong ties to Zinoviev's Leningrad opposition: 843 'former Zinovievites' were arrested by the Leningrad NKVD alone in the ten weeks after the murder.[13] A picture of a widespread 'Trotskyist-Zinovievite' organization began to emerge with 'centres' in Moscow and Leningrad. By the end of December, the testimony of those under interrogation suggested that the

11. See Ch. 5.
12. *Lubianka: Stalin, 1922–1936*, 577–9, 819.
13. Zinoviev and Kamenev were arrested after only two weeks. 'O dele Leningradskoi kontrrevolutsionnoi zinov'evskoi gruppy Safarova, Zalutskogo i drugikh', *Izvestiia TsK KPSS*, 1 (1990), 39.

Trotskyist-Zinovievite group calculated that the Stalin leadership would not be able to cope if there was a war against the USSR, and that in such an event Kamenev and Zinoviev would inevitably come to power. After the trial of those supposedly directly involved in the murder, a further trial of those who had 'inspired' the murderers took place. It concluded that the 'Leningrad counter-revolutionary Zinovievite group was systematically cultivating a hatred of the party leadership and particularly Stalin, and bore a 'moral and political responsibility for the Kirov murder'.[14]

The 'evidence' of the NKVD investigation suggested to Stalin that Zinoviev and Kamenev were planning more serious crimes. In the weeks after the Kirov murder, Stalin had ordered a review of security in the Kremlin. This was entirely sensible given that the investigation in Leningrad appeared to have uncovered a large number of 'hostile elements'—not least Nikolaev—with access to party institutions and, consequently, party leaders. The review of the Kremlin, undertaken by Nikolai Ezhov, revealed that security vetting had been lax. At first, the investigation only uncovered evidence of conversations (among cleaners, couriers, and other minor personnel) critical of Soviet policy and of Stalin—the sort of private conversations that were taking place up and down the country. But in the now well-established pattern of the NKVD arrests and interrogations, the investigation inevitably produced the appearance of a 'Leftist' conspiracy to assassinate Soviet leaders.[15] Lev Kamenev was himself interrogated, and admitted that his brother had been in his flat at times when he and Zinoviev were having conversations critical of Soviet policy and of Stalin. He categorically denied any link to events in the Kremlin and any knowledge of the political views of his brother, but his protests were not entirely convincing. Yet again, Stalin was presented with circumstantial evidence that members of the former oppositions continued to conspire against his leadership.

That turn of events was not in itself a grave cause for concern, but it was not alone among his worries. For example, the threat of war and invasion had not significantly receded. Stalin's intelligence reports repeatedly told him that the Poles, Germans, and Japanese were in the

14. Ibid. 42–3.
15. *Lubianka: Stalin, 1922–1936*, 599–612, 617–19, 626–50. Kamenev denied any involvement.

midst of military and diplomatic preparations for a 1935 invasion.[16] Their plans also appeared to involve subversive activities to weaken Soviet defences and exacerbate disaffection with the regime. The Commissariat of Foreign Affairs ordered the Soviet embassies (*polpredstva*) in the Baltic states and eastern Europe to confirm reports that White Russians were being recruited in large numbers to organize sabotage in the Soviet Union in the event of war in the Far East.[17] Stalin received a long series of intercepted communications, particularly from the Japanese military attaché, on the importance of subversion to an invasion.[18] Nevertheless, the rapid rise in the arrests of foreign spies and saboteurs in this period probably reflected the pressure the Politburo exerted on the NKVD to find them rather than any real proliferation of subversives.

Other signals suggested that war was on the horizon. The British appeared to be openly encouraging the Germans' aggressive anti-communism.[19] Soviet overtures to the Germans were rejected without consideration. Meanwhile Stalin had been warned that the Japanese would use a dispute over the ownership of the KVZhD, on Soviet territory, to justify war on the Soviet Union, and while talks on the sale of the railroad to Japan made no progress, Manchurian forces continued to attack Soviet workers and blame the USSR for the tensions.[20] While the Japanese appeared to be preparing public opinion for war, Stalin was informed of a scandal whipping up anti-Soviet opinion in Poland. The Soviet military attaché in Poland was accused of trying to recruit spies. Stalin was informed that he was probably trying to do just that, but the treatment of the attaché and press coverage in Poland indicated to him that the incident was being used to provoke the

16. RGASPI 558/11/187/81, 111–17.
17. Arkhiv Vneshnei Politiki Rossiiskoi Federatsii (AVPRF) 05/14/101/93/23, 05/12/86/64/12.
18. *Lubianka: Stalin, 1922–1936*, 494–500, 501–5, 517–18, 520–1; RGASPI 558/11/186/118–27; 558/11/187/62–79.
19. Britain was actively engaging Germany at this time in an attempt to commit her to a series of multilateral pacts that would make aggression more difficult. Graham Ross, *The Great Powers and the Decline of the European States System, 1914–1945* (London, 1983), 88–9.
20. G. M. Adibekov et al. (eds), *Politbiuro VKP(b), Komintern i Iaponiia: dokumenty* (Moscow, 2004), 131–8, 143, 159–60; Khlevniuk et al. (eds), *Stalin i Kaganovich: Perepiska*, 448, 470, 506, 517; *DVP SSSR* xvii. 562–70, 624–8, 815–17.

USSR. On his orders, it was categorically denied that the attaché was involved in espionage.[21]

The gathering clouds seemed to have one silver lining. British appeasement and the Polish–German rapprochement had worrying implications for French security. While Soviet intelligence agencies were concerned that the French might join the two in a war against the USSR, they also calculated that Germany might want to expand west first, particularly in order to be in a position to use French heavy industry and raw materials production in a prolonged campaign of expansion. Soviet diplomats made the most of this vulnerability to sustain the relationship with France, and to convince the Daladier government and its successors to continue to put pressure on Poland and Germany to join an 'eastern pact'.[22] This strategy was realized on a broader scale when the Soviet Union agreed to join the League of Nations in September. However, hopes that sustained diplomatic pressure might forestall war received two serious blows later in the autumn. On 9 October 1934, French foreign minister, Louis Barthou, was assassinated together with King Alexander of Yugoslavia while on a visit to Croatia. The Soviets were convinced that this was the work of the Nazi secret police, intended not only to destabilize Yugoslavia, but to eliminate in Barthou a key figure sustaining the French relationship with the USSR.[23] A month later, Gaston Doumergue's government of national unity fell. No sustained turn to the right followed, but the instability of French politics made France a far from reliable partner. There were some hopeful signs. In November 1934, Stalin received intelligence to the effect that Hitler had proposed a non-aggression pact with the French, but had been rebuffed. Three weeks later, French and Soviet diplomats signed a protocol reopening the negotiation of an eastern pact, but only a short time later, Stalin was told that the French were once again flirting with the appeasement of Germany, including permission for significant German rearmament.[24] In this case, the intelligence was reasonably accurate.

21. RGASPI 17/162/17/54; 558/11/87/20–30, 558/11/51/37–8, 43.
22. See e.g. RGASPI 17/162/17/47. In late Sept. 1933, Stalin instructed Litvinov not to rush to sign an eastern pact that did not include Poland and Germany. The two had formally rejected the French offer of a pact only two weeks before, but that did not put an end to efforts to negotiate one.
23. Morozov, *Pol'sko-Chekhoslovatskie otnosheniia*, 165.
24. This constituted approval for a rearmament that was already in progress. RGASPI 558/11/187/120–3; Morozov, *Pol'sko-Chekhoslovatskie otnosheniia*, 179.

At the end of December, Stalin received further reports from the NKVD foreign department indicating that a Franco–German rapprochement was in the process of being negotiated. This could be, he was told, the beginning of the Franco–German–Polish bloc that Pilsudski had been pushing for so long. It now appeared to Stalin that the December protocol had been a tactical manoeuvre, and the British, who publicly supported an eastern pact, were privately pushing the French towards a rapprochement with Germany. Finland was being drawn into the bloc, as was Hungary, and the Germans apparently hoped that Romania and Italy would contribute. Joint Polish–German military preparations were supposed to be well under way and frequent meetings between German and Polish leaders were no longer kept secret.[25] The meetings, which Stalin interpreted as part of preparation for war, were indeed attempts by the Germans to draw the Poles into an anti-Soviet pact. What Stalin did not know was that the Poles consistently refused the German offers. Once again Stalin thought he faced an elaborate and extensive anti-Soviet bloc, where nothing of the sort existed.

But to be fair to Stalin, war was a constant subject of diplomatic rumour and newspaper editorial at the time and further Soviet intelligence seemed to confirm the most pessimistic assessments. At the beginning of 1935, the western press was reporting that the military was on high alert, and all leave was cancelled. Universal military conscription in Germany was announced in March, while the military build-up continued at a breakneck pace, now openly violating the restrictions set by the Versailles Treaty.[26] Intelligence from Japan was only slightly less bleak. The Japanese were also rapidly building up their own armed forces, though they were still substantially committed to fighting in China. In January, Japanese Foreign Minister Hirota announced to the Japanese parliament yet another effort to negotiate peace in China. The Soviet ambassador (*polpred*) in Britain sent Moscow a report of his conversation with the Nationalists' representative in London suggesting they would take the Japanese offer

25. RGASPI 558/11/188/31–51. On the British, see also AVPRF 010/10/48/8/30–38 for Soviet ambassador Ivan Maiskii's report of his conversation with Sir John Simon and Anthony Eden. On Goering's meeting with Beck, see AVPRF 05/15/109/67/5.

26. Soviet agents in Germany confirmed the substance of these reports. RGASPI 558/11/188/55–6; 558/11/446/130–44. The Soviet estimates of the size of the German army contained in this document were for public consumption.

seriously, not least because the British and Americans were hesitating to continue financing the purchase of arms, potentially leaving them unable fight.[27] American recognition of the Soviet Union did not help Soviet security in the Pacific. Not only did the Americans seem ready to starve the Nationalists of financing at a crucial moment, but Stalin received intelligence in January, confirmed by further intelligence in May, that the Japanese and Americans were in the process of negotiating a non-aggression pact that would have put Japan into a better position to fight the USSR.[28] Meanwhile links between east and west were growing. Soviet diplomats observed that the French bourgeoisie had started to invest heavily in Manchuria,[29] and that the Japanese were busy training the Finnish army.[30] The Commissariat of Foreign Affairs assumed that Japanese military advisers were at work elsewhere in eastern Europe and demanded that diplomats report on any such activity.[31]

And yet, in the midst of what seemed to be a determined march to war in spring 1935, things unexpectedly started heading the other way. Soviet intelligence reports suggested the German military build-up was worrying the British and French and leaving them hesitant about supporting an anti-Soviet bloc.[32] Anthony Eden's visit to Moscow (after seeing Hitler in Berlin) at the end of March reassured Stalin that Britain was nervous about the growth of German military might. The French had even more reason to be worried. If Germany and Poland managed to conquer the USSR with the help of Japan, they might well turn on France next and, with the heart of Soviet industry and its natural resources to back them up, they would pose a serious threat. Stalin believed his warnings to the French had finally fallen on fertile ground. This time, however, rather than push for a multilateral pact in which the inclusion of Germany and Poland would remain a sticking point, Stalin directed Litvinov to explore French interest in a bilateral mutual assistance pact. With unusual speed, the text of a pact was agreed and signed on 2 May 1935. Two weeks later, a similar pact was signed with

27. AVPRF 010/10/48/8/10–11. Maiskii nevertheless observed that rumours of an end to hostilities were premature, and indeed, the Americans continued the arms trade with the Nationalists.
28. *Lubianka: Stalin, 1922–1936*, 594–7, 661–2.
29. AVPRF 05/14/101/94/12.
30. Together with the Germans. AVPRF 05/14/101/93/34.
31. AVPRF 05/15/109/67/5/6.
32. This was something they never seriously considered in the first instance.

Czechoslovakia. Stalin thought this was enough to force Japan, Poland, and Germany once again to delay their plans for an invasion.

From his perspective, Soviet diplomacy had once again saved the USSR from imminent disaster. It was an important victory, but he could not be sure how long it would last. French politics was extremely unstable, and while Barthou's successor Pierre Laval had, contrary to expectation, demonstrated his willingness to work with the Soviet Union, there remained a suspicion that his commitment to collective security was superficial and that the pact was yet another bluff to secure a deal with Germany on French terms. Soviet intelligence gatherers suspected that the British similarly did not want to go to war, and would try to balance Germany against the USSR, but if Germany was intent on expanding, then a deal would be struck to let it expand to the east.[33] British actions in the coming years only reinforced the impression. There was little reason to assume that Germany (or Poland or Japan) had given up its ambitions for territorial expansion at the expense of the Soviet Union. The Kwantun army continue to harass and threaten the Soviets along the border with Mongolia. Attempted military coups in Japan indicated to the Soviet leadership that the Japanese army was trying to eliminate those political forces that resisted the idea of a war against the USSR.[34] Germany had signed a series of trade and credit agreements with the USSR in 1934 and 1935, and while Stalin saw them as a disincentive to war, he did not think they would prevent it. The National Socialists did not in any way tone down their anti-communist and anti-Soviet rhetoric, or (in Stalin's view) restrain their use of saboteurs and spies in the USSR. Stalin believed the same could be said of Poland and Japan. Once plans for a hot war had to be put on hold, it appeared as though efforts to subvert the USSR from within were increased. In the autumn of 1935, and through 1936, Stalin received a steady stream of reports from Genrikh Iagoda, head of the NKVD, of the terrorist and espionage activities of these three countries.[35] The regime also became convinced that the

33. In the spring of 1936, the Germans proposed a non-aggression pact with France and Belgium, but the French were still publicly expressing an interest in broader arrangements for guaranteeing peace in Europe. For an expression of Soviet scepticism that the French and others would resist such deals, see e.g. A. E. (sic), 'Diplomatiia voiny', *Bolshevik*, 10 (31 May 1935), 83–90.

34. AVPRF 05/16/115/6/16.

35. *Lubianka: Stalin, 1922–1936*, 671–2, 679–81, 693–8, 705–10, 712–14, 735–7.

system they had used to grant asylum to political refugees had been used by their enemies to settle large numbers of spies and subversives in the Soviet Union.[36] Yet again the war was being conducted by other means.

Stalin might at least have hoped that his relations with senior officials were on a more solid footing after plan targets for the second Five-Year Plan were reduced and the party purge had begun to remove those 'opportunist' officials with a history of resisting them. The fulfilment of plan targets did indeed increase, but so too did the centre's impatience with those who fell short. When Kaganovich reported on the rise in output of defective goods in the textile industry, blaming weak administration and poor organization of labour, Stalin insisted that 'the guilty parties be punished regardless of their "communist" rank'. To reports of corruption in the Urals regional organization, Stalin insisted that 'the accused should be sacked and punished'. His approach to sorting out problems on the railway network was to send threatening telegrams and to order the arrest of 'those guilty of upsetting traffic plans'.[37] In discussing the high accident rate on the railroad network around Khabarovsk, he told regional officials to 'purge the railroads of the nests of wreckers'. Any delay in doing so, he warned ominously, 'might end badly for you'.[38] The message was even more blatant in the grain collections campaign of the summer and autumn of 1934. Regional officials were told: 'Either fulfil the plan or you will be removed from your post.'[39] Stalin agreed with Molotov that resistance to the collections should be characterized as 'counter-revolutionary sabotage'.[40] Several local trials were organized and executions followed which were publicized in the press.[41] Lest there was any doubt about the centre's uncompromising attitude to the fulfilment of directives, the central party press repeatedly asserted the importance of 'iron discipline' in work, and relentlessly directed purge commissions to expel 'open and hidden violators' of it.[42]

36. William Chase, *Enemies within the Gates? The Comintern and the Stalinist Repression, 1934–1939* (New Haven, 2001), 163–74; *Lubianka: Stalin, 1922–1936*, 738–41.
37. RGASPI 56/1/143/73, 83–103; 56/1/144/2, 4, 5; 558/11/152/53, 68, 74–6.
38. RGASPI 558/11/49/94.
39. Khlevniuk et al. (eds), *Stalin i Kaganovich. Perepiska*, 480.
40. RGASPI 558/11/64/88–89ob.
41. Khlevniuk et al. (eds), *Stalin i Kaganovich. Perepiska*, 511.
42. See e.g. Peredovaia, 'Ovladet' bolshevistskim stilem organizatsionno-prakticheskogo rukovodstva', *Partiinoe stroitel'stvo*, 9 (1934), 1–8; A. Shcherbakov, 'Neudovletvoritel'noe

Plan targets had been reduced, but that had only brought them from the realm of the patently impossible to the exceptionally challenging. In such a context where Stalin was unwilling to accept any result short of 100 per cent plan fulfilment, officials had little choice but to continue secretly to engage in illicit coping mechanisms. They deliberately degraded the quality of output in order better to meet quantitative targets. They exaggerated their need for inputs and traded them on the black market to address shortages as they arose. They delivered incomplete or faulty goods if it helped them meet monthly or annual plans. The mechanisms were widespread and fuelled by corruption.[43] Bribes and threats for the most part left central authorities unclear about how bad the situation was and inclined to see enemies, class enemies, and saboteurs where they should have seen a desperation to meet the plan. Local officials were inclined to see the same. Mining enterprises might fail to meet the plan because they had received faulty or incomplete excavation equipment. Steel makers might fail to meet the plan and blame mining enterprises for delivering poor-quality ores and fuels. And the manufacturers of mining equipment might blame the steel makers for delivering inadequate or poor-quality metals. Everyone could do their best, keep their own corrupt practices quiet, and legitimately think the real problems lay just beyond their horizon. At the same time, the top regional and ministerial officials (i.e. in the Moscow commissariats) protected themselves by building tight leadership cliques that managed the flow of information to the organizations that monitored plan fulfilment. When things went wrong in their organization, they were then in a position to identify a scapegoat or scapegoats. These were sacked or arrested, depending on the seriousness of the problem, labelled as incompetent, or as wreckers or class aliens, and presented as the cause of fulfilment problems.

The state and party apparatus was consequently riven with tensions as officials blamed one another for problems in order to escape blame

rukovodstvo i ego rezul'taty', *Partiinoe stroitel'stvo*, 9 (1934), 2–7; Em. Iaroslavskii, 'Pervye itogi chistki partiinoi organizatsii', *Bolshevik*, 15 (1935), 9–23; M. Rubenshtein, 'Ne zaznavat'sia, ne uspokaivat'sia!', *Bolshevik*, 16 (1934), 18–35; Peredovaia, '17 let oktiabria i organizatsionnaia rabota partii', *Partiinoe stroitel'stvo*, 21 (1934); E. Sh., 'Bor'ba s narusheniiami partiinoi i gosudarstvennoi distsiplinoi', *Partiinoe stroitel'stvo*, 23 (1934), 11–15.

43. The first and best study of the phenomenon is Joseph Berliner, *Factory and Manager in the USSR* (Cambridge, 1957).

themselves.[44] Stalin was at least aware of these tensions. He received regular reports of leading officials taking repressive action against subordinates who criticized them, and of regional organizations so badly divided by infighting that normal work had become impossible.[45] And yet Stalin did not see the tensions and conflict as an inevitable consequence of the ambitious plans he was imposing. Rather, he saw the conflicts as a healthy and necessary process in which the 'Bolshevik' leaders should be encouraged to win out over the 'opportunists' and root out enemies.[46] He sometimes gave one side of a dispute a 'mandate' to arrest its opponents, but he increasingly found it necessary to intervene in order to restrain this sort of judicial violence as it got out of hand. The way the press described it, in such cases, 'administrative methods' were taking the place of proper 'Bolshevik' leadership.

As the conflicts deepened and violence worsened, Stalin remained blind to the fundamental causes. He had, after all, specifically prohibited officials from questioning the realism of the plan. He had prohibited them from mentioning this source of the problems. Rather than act to limit the conflict, Stalin introduced further initiatives that only exacerbated them. For example, the Stakhanovite movement was intended to encourage innovation in the organization of production, but in practice it was terribly disruptive.[47] Stakhanovite records were often achieved by concentrating resources in one shift, starving those that preceded and followed it. The movement drove up labour costs. It led to increases in damage to equipment, accidents, and defective production. It pitted non-Stakhanovites against Stakhanovites, and would-be Stakhanovites against managers holding them back. Little

44. These tensions have been discussed at length elsewhere, so won't be discussed here in any detail. See e.g. Rittersporn, *Stalinist Simplifications*; Getty, *Origins of the Great Purges*; Harris, *The Great Urals*, chs 5, 6.

45. See e.g. Kvashonkin et al. (eds), *Sovetskoe rukovodstvo*, 245, 248, 258; Khlevniuk et al. (eds), *Stalin i Kaganovich: Perepiska*, 317, 329, 361–2, 364–7, 389, 505. Regional party officials occasionally requested an audience with Stalin in order to discuss conflicts in their organizations. See e.g. RGASPI 558/11/64/109, 112; 558/11/150/120.

46. See e.g. Stalin, 'Speech at the Kremlin Palace at the Graduation Ceremony of Academics of the Red Army', *Works*, i (14) (Stanford, Calif., 1967), 56–64.

47. See Lewis Siegelbaum, *Stakhanovism and the Politics of Productivity in the USSR, 1935–1941* (Cambridge, 1988); Francesco Benventi, *Stakhanovism and Stalinism, 1934–1938*, CREES Discussion Papers, 30 (Birmingham, 1989); Robert Thurston, 'The Stakhanovite Movement: Background to the Great Terror in the Factories, 1935–1938', in J. Arch Getty and Roberta Manning (eds), *Stalinist Terror* (Cambridge, 1993), 142–60.

wonder that many managers did what they could quietly to subvert the movement.

This sort of resistance was more dangerous than ever. The Kirov murder and subsequent investigations had deepened Stalin's conviction that enemies of the regime were at work. Calls for vigilance got louder in 1935 and 1936. The so-called 'Verification' and 'Exchange' of party cards at this time ensured that every party organization was brought into the hunt for enemies. Organizations were told that finding two or three enemies per district was not enough. If that was all they got, they were clearly not 'taking to heart the many directives of the Central Committee and Comrade Stalin that as our successes grow, the class enemy resorts to ever more sophisticated methods of struggle, making use in the first instance of the opportunist complacency and daydreaming of communists'.[48] Local organizations nevertheless dragged their feet and resisted these campaigns because they posed a direct threat to the tight leadership cliques they had established.[49] If the wrong people were purged in these campaigns, and particularly the people who knew most about corrupt and other illicit practices, it would spell disaster for them.

Stalin's calls for vigilance did not let up. A secret Central Committee letter to regional organizations in July 1936 insisted that the 'single most important characteristic of every Bolshevik in the current situation ought to be his ability to recognize and identify enemies of the party no matter how well they have camouflaged their identity'.[50] This was Stalin's way of making it clear that no one was beyond suspicion. Stalin knew there were serious problems with the state and party administration but he did not fully understand their real sources. His pressurized plans, his demands for 100 per cent fulfilment without excuses, and his calls for vigilance had created a recalcitrant, secretive, and corrupt bureaucracy. Few officials could claim to embody Stalin's ideal of 'Bolshevik leadership' because it demanded the impossible. Who was not an 'opportunist', if an 'opportunist' was defined as one who attempted to shield himself from the regime's impossible demands? Who was not a 'Leftist' (or Trotskyist/Zinovievite) if a 'Leftist' was defined as one who lacked faith in the construction of Socialism? Who

48. A. Shcherbakov, 'Glavnoe—povyshenie bolshevistskoi bditel'nosti', *Partiinoe stroitel'stvo*, 1 (1936), 18. Though some organizations got into trouble for going too far.
49. Getty, *Origins of the Great Purges*, ch. 3.
50. Getty and Naumov, *Road to Terror*, 250–5.

was not a 'Rightist' if a Rightist wanted to slow the tempo of socialist construction? The apparat was full of officials who could be described as 'double-dealers' (*dvurushniki*), praising central policy in public, but trying to escape its nearly impossible demands in less public settings. The pressure to find enemies was extremely dangerous because it threatened to tear the party and state apparatus apart in a spiral of denunciation and counter-denunciation.

Stalin should have been encouraged by the broader state of the economy and society. The 1934 harvest was good, putting an end not only to famine in the countryside, but to food shortages in the cities. Improvements in the food supply combined with more moderate plan targets to generate more consistent and stable economic growth. Collective farmers continued to harbour profound resentments towards the regime, but as the new system of collective farming bedded in, the threat of rebellion receded dramatically. The threat of labour unrest receded too. The dramatic expansion of the economy created many thousands of new positions of responsibility and authority, and those who enjoyed the career advancement that came with it tended to become enthusiastic supporters of the new regime.[51] The regime's efforts to spread its values through its control over popular culture and the press met with considerable success, especially among youth, many of whom sought to remake themselves according to the ideals with which they were presented.[52] More significantly, living standards began to rise again after a precipitous decline in the period of the first Five-Year Plan.

The improvement was not enjoyed uniformly across the population. Stalin understood that improving living standards would play a key role in solidifying popular support, but his economic policy was driven by other considerations as well. Rises in agricultural and industrial production made it possible to improve the supply of goods to the population, but they also made it possible to phase out the inefficient rationing system of the early 1930s. The end of bread rationing at the beginning of 1935, and rationing for most other goods in the autumn, brought sharp rises in prices that provoked initial concern that the

51. Sheila Fitzpatrick, *Education and Social Mobility in the Soviet Union, 1921–1934* (Cambridge, 1979).
52. See e.g. Jochen Hellbeck, 'Fashioning the Stalinist Soul: The Diary of Stepan Podliubnyi, 1931–9', in Sheila Fitzpatrick (ed), *Stalinism: New Directions* (London, 2000), 77–116.

situation would get worse and not better. Indeed, for the lower paid workers, including the mass of the peasantry, or those with large families, living standards continued to stagnate. For those with more money to spend by virtue of their qualifications or position, especially those living in larger urban areas, in key industries and institutions, the improvement in the range of available and affordable foods and consumer goods was felt before long. Stalin was well aware of the political implications of that change. The regime quite deliberately prioritized the distribution system, both to reinforce support among the elite and to encourage productivity in a targeted manner. So for example, the military, the secret police, and the party elite benefited disproportionately.[53]

While Stalin was using the carrot of improvements to living standards to strengthen his popular support, he employed the stick of police repression to deal with popular resistance and other manifestations of hostility towards the regime. Recent research has revealed the critical role in this played by the passport system.[54] From the end of December 1932, the regime began to issue internal passports to residents of major urban areas. The main initial purpose of the system was to stem the tide of peasant migration to cities in the midst of famine. The influx of starving peasants threatened to bring famine and unrest into urban areas. The passports not only contained an official residence permit, thus simplifying the procedure for the deportation of migrant peasants, but also registered the class and social status of the holder (in categories such as 'worker', 'office worker', 'member of the intelligentsia'), ethnicity, employment status, and social origins (son/daughter of a worker, peasant, aristocrat, and so on). The latter information represented the leader's image of society more than they represented Soviet society itself, but the categories into which each individual fell

53. Elena Osokina, Our *Daily Bread: Socialist Distribution and the Art of Survival in Stalin's Russia, 1927–1941* (London, 2000). See also Oleg Khlevniuk and R. W. Davies, 'The End of Rationing in the Soviet Union, 1934–1935', *Europe-Asia Studies*, 4 (1999), 557–609.

54. Gijs Kessler, 'The Passport System and State Control over Population Flows in the Soviet Union, 1932–1940', *Cahiers du Monde Russe*, 42 (2001), 478–504; David Shearer, 'Elements Near and Alien: Passportization, Policing, and Identity in the Stalinist State, 1932–1952', *Journal of Modern History*, 4 (2004), 835–81; Paul Hagenloh, *Stalin's Police: Public Order and Mass Repression in the USSR, 1926–1941* (Baltimore, 2009); David Shearer, *Policing Stalin's Socialism: Repression and Social Order in the Soviet Union, 1924–1953* (New Haven, 2009).

on this official document had an enormous impact on life chances. Those who fitted the 'desirable' categories had an easier time getting good housing and could rise faster in their careers. 'Undesirables' could face much worse than merely problems in living conditions and career advancement.

By the end of 1934, the regime had issued over 27 million passports to the residents of Moscow, Leningrad, and other strategic areas, and it continued to issue them long after the threat of famine had passed. The primary object of 'passportization' shifted to social control. In the process of building a map of Soviet society that identified the specific locations of 'desirables' and 'undesirables', the regime had created the opportunity to round up the 'undesirables', or 'socially harmful elements' as they were called, and remove them from areas of strategic importance. In this way, they sought not only to lessen the threat of sabotage and counter-revolution, but also to reduce crime and indeed to fashion an ideal society, at least in the strategic areas. As early as the first half of 1933, already 400,000 people had been removed from the so-called 'regime areas', and further mass deportations followed.

The police sweeps created more problems than they solved, though Stalin did not see it that way. There was no sudden end to crime or to registered acts of sabotage and counter-revolution, but there was a massive accumulation of 'undesirable elements' in the Urals, Western Siberia, and other dumping grounds of deportees. These regions could not adequately house, employ, or even track this new population. At the same time, the deportations had intensified labour shortages in the regime areas. Inevitably, the undesirables began to filter back into the regime areas where enterprise managers were inclined to collude in masking those with an unfortunate identity in order to fill empty posts. Instead of renewing the regime's confidence in society, the passport regime had intensely concentrated the population of those individuals and groups it perceived to be most hostile to the revolution, and had deepened the fear of 'masked enemies' as undesirables re-entered strategically important areas.

The regime had a parallel concern about the loyalty of non-Russian nationalities.[55] In the years immediately after the revolution, the regime had encouraged the cultural development of non-Russian nationalities

55. See Terry Martin, 'The Origins of Soviet Ethnic Cleansing', *Journal of Modern History*, 4 (1998), 813–61.

in the Soviet Union (*korenizatsiia*). It was hoped that the many nationalities and ethnic groups would accept Soviet ideals more readily if they were given cultural autonomy. While the cultures flourished in the 1920s, the regime began to worry that the policy was backfiring by encouraging a sense of separateness, rather than loyalty to the revolutionary project and Soviet ideals. The traumas of the first Five-Year Plan crystallized many of these fears. The horrifying experience of collectivization and famine encouraged many nationalities and ethnic groups to envy their brothers on the other side of the Soviet border. Stalin interpreted much of the resistance to grain collection targets as rooted in specific national or ethnic agendas. At the same time, countries on the Soviet periphery from Finland, Poland, and Germany through China, Korea, and Japan responded not merely by supporting their beleaguered co-nationals, but at times by actively encouraging unrest in the USSR. Stalin and his intelligence services became convinced that hostile foreign powers were using the ethnic minorities to run substantial spy rings. Intercepted intelligence made it clear that the Japanese militarists proposed to employ disaffected non-Russian nationalities on a grand scale to topple the regime in the event of an invasion.[56] Meanwhile Stalin's secret police worked out only in the mid-1930s that for many years hostile capitalist powers had sent spies into the USSR under cover of 'political refugees'.[57]

In the early 1930s, the regime began to abandon *korenizatsiia* in favour of a partial russification. The shrinking of cultural autonomy and the dismantling of national institutions did not win them friends among the non-Russians. The negative reaction was then compounded by a series of mass deportations of 'suspect' nationalities from border regions. Thousands of Germans and Poles were removed from the western parts of Soviet Ukraine. Finns, Estonians, and Latvians were removed from Leningrad border regions. Koreans were removed from border regions in the Far East. The regime was using the new internal passports to include non-Russians in the police sweeps in order to 'secure' borderlands in the event of invasion. The effect of the mass deportations was not dissimilar to that of the police sweeps of other 'undesirables'. Concerns about 'strategic' areas were alleviated by the

56. RGASPI 558/11/185/76–9, 186/118, 187/60–1; RGVA 4/19/13/2–15, 25; 9/39/5/76–116, 211–20.

57. Chase, *Enemies within the Gates?*, ch. 3; Getty and Naumov, *Road to Terror*, 201.

removal of individuals and groups whose loyalty to the regime might have been uncertain. And yet once again the regime concentrated populations of suspect non-Russians in areas where they could not be adequately housed and employed, and then had to worry not only about their heightened disaffection in places of internal exile, but also about those who escaped and returned to regime areas.

The regime's efforts to reduce tensions in state and society were clearly unravelling. With the beginning of the second Five-Year Plan targets had been reduced. The reform of the political police had decisively lessened their scope for arbitrary repression. Mass repression in the countryside had ended and a series of good harvests promised a new stability in the agricultural economy. The industrial economy had also entered a period of stable growth and living standards were beginning to recover. And yet, as far as Stalin was concerned, the relaxation had failed in what was perhaps its central aim: to stabilize the political order and rally support behind the regime. He was not prepared to see the Kirov murder as the work of a disaffected and mentally unstable former party member acting on his own. He insisted that Nikolaev must have had the support and encouragement of Left Oppositionists and others determined to rally dissidents to a campaign of assassination and sabotage. He restored the arbitrary powers of the political police for the purposes of the investigation. Because the political police continued to rely on confessions obtained under torture, and because they had an institutional interest in preventing the reintroduction of limits on their powers, the discovery of further counter-revolutionary crimes was inevitable. Stalin's fear of conspiracy and planned coups d'état was further heightened by his perception of the international situation. The treaties of non-aggression and trade pacts achieved by Maxim Litvinov and the Commissariat of Foreign Affairs seemed to have delayed an invasion of the USSR, but Stalin was in no doubt that a war with the capitalist powers was inevitable and imminent.

Once the passport system had achieved its first purpose in preventing mass peasant migration to urban areas, it seemed prudent to use it to purge undesirables from border regions, major cities, and other strategic areas. The move promised to deal a blow to the enemies of the regime both at home and abroad and to secure Stalin's power. But the campaigns of vigilance that accompanied it—encouraging both officials and the population at large to identify and denounce hidden enemies—deepened tensions within the state and society, particularly in the context of the pressure to fulfil plan targets. Officials towards the top of the party and state hierarchies found a measure of protection in tight cliques that could control the flow of information to the centre and shift blame for problems on to subordinates or to hidden 'wreckers'. Stalin was dismayed and angered by what he perceived to be the arbitrary repression of regional leaders. Further down those hierarchies, down to the ordinary worker and peasant, the regime's vigilance campaigns were provoking the denunciation of 'bosses': of those who appeared to be arbitrarily abusing their power.

Tensions heightened sharply in 1935. As German rearmament was gathering pace and other 'capitalist' powers were building their military capacity to keep pace, Stalin had little choice but to join the arms race.[58] Instead of reducing investment in civilian production and accepting lower plan targets, he chose to press for significantly higher productivity per worker. The change marked a sudden suspension of 'moderation' in economic policy.[59] The leadership had been exploring ways of obtaining an 'intensification of labour' and they settled on widely promoting the achievements of specific individuals. At the end of August 1935, Aleksei Stakhanov was reported to have mined 102 tonnes of coal in a single shift, or fourteen times his work norm. In due course, other record-breakers were identified to broaden the campaign and encourage all workers to become 'Stakhanovites'. While the campaign does appear to have achieved some increase in labour productivity, it was profoundly disruptive. More often than not many shifts were needed to prepare the ground for such record-breaking. Interrupting the rhythm of production this way could reduce productivity rather than increase it. As plans became substantially more difficult to achieve, many senior managers and party officials tried quietly to slow or subvert the campaign. Some workers resented the increase in work norms that inevitably followed, while others complained that their efforts to join the ranks of the Stakhanovites were being frustrated. As the fear of war was growing, so too was the spectre of the 'double-dealing' official, the saboteur, and other hidden enemies.

58. See Joe Maiolo, *Cry Havoc: The Arms Race and the Second World War, 1931–1941* (London, 2010).
59. R. W. Davies and Oleg Khlevniuk, 'Stakhanovism and the Soviet Economy', *Europe-Asia Studies*, 6 (2002), 867–903.

7
The perfect storm

Mass repression under both Lenin and Stalin had been triggered by a sense of immediate threat to the revolution and to the survival of the Soviet state. What is commonly referred to as the 'Great Terror' of 1936–8 had precedents, most obviously in the Civil War of 1918–20, in which the political police had been empowered to arrest and execute, en masse and without limitation, individuals and groups perceived to pose a threat to the new regime. In that period, the threat was very real. Soviet power hung by a thread as the Red Army fought the combined forces of the Whites and foreign armies, while the political police dealt with attempts to subvert the revolution on the home front. The next major episode of mass repression, affecting hundreds of thousands of Soviet citizens, came with the struggle for control of the grain supply at the end of the 1920s. In this case, peasant resistance presented a danger not to the survival of the state, but rather to Stalin's vision of the revolution. In between these episodes of mass repression, the regime's fears for its security and survival did not disappear. The fear of invasion waxed and waned, but it never waned to the point where Stalin was comfortable that 'capitalist' powers were not conspiring against the Soviet Union and communists wherever they might be. He remained convinced that, despite huge expenditure and effort to secure Soviet borders, it remained all too easy for hostile states to send spies and saboteurs into the USSR. Rarely did a week pass when he did not receive reports of border incursions with the aim of committing acts of sabotage, assassination, or the recruitment of disaffected groups and individuals to do the same. Similarly, Stalin received a steady stream of reports compiled on the basis of the surveillance of former oppositionists, a flow of information that increased substantially after the investigation of the Kirov murder underpinned demands for vigilance. Further, Stalin continued to worry about corruption, incompetence, and outright resistance among officials from kolkhoz chairmen and factory managers up to regional first secretaries and People's Commissars. None of these fears alone was likely to provoke an episode of mass repression. Indeed, most of the fears were misplaced, in so far as Stalin's dictatorship was stronger and more secure in the mid-1930s than it had ever been. And yet, by late 1936, the leadership convinced itself that it could only survive if it resorted to the kind of terror it had unleashed in the Civil War.

The fear of war played a critical role in that process. Since the Civil War, Soviet foreign intelligence services had looked for signs of diplomatic and military activity that could be construed as evidence of preparation for war against the Soviet Union. At various stages—1924, 1927, 1932, and 1934—the regime saw what it (wrongly) perceived to be credible evidence of preparations for an invasion. Soviet leaders took it for granted that the 'capitalist' powers were anti-communist, but in each case, as Soviet intelligence agencies saw it, tensions among them inhibited the realization of a united force necessary to a successful campaign against the Soviet Union. In the mid-1930s, the threat from the east continued to be presented by Japan, where the militarists made no secret of their desire to seize Soviet lands east of the Urals. It was the threat from continental Europe that was changing fundamentally. In the previous decade and a half, again in the eyes of Soviet intelligence, Poland had been the linchpin of the perceived anti-communist coalition. Particularly since Josef Pilsudski had seized power in 1927, Soviet intelligence reported negotiations variously among England, France, Germany, Hungary, Romania, Finland, and the Baltic states, with Poland as the core or conduit of an invasion, but tensions particularly among England, France, and Germany had prevented the formation of the coalition. What had changed was first the rise of Hitler and the Nazis in Germany in 1933, and then, more significantly, the rapid progress of German rearmament under an unambiguous banner of anti-communism and expansionism.

The promise of the Franco-Soviet Mutual Assistance Pact (May 1935) to contain Germany faded quickly, not least because it appeared only to excite Nazi aggression and the speed of rearmament. Stalin was not alone among world leaders in thinking that another world war was on the horizon. But would the Nazis first expand to the east or to the west? From the summer of 1935, greater effort was placed in directing German expansionism than in further joint efforts to contain Germany and enforce the terms of the Versailles peace. While French Foreign Minister Pierre Laval was busy rebuilding diplomatic bridges with his German counterparts after the shock of the Franco-Soviet Pact, the Soviets could do little more than propose economic agreements that would discourage Nazi expansion to the east. It was not long before Stalin was presented with solid evidence that the Soviet position was by far the weaker, and that the German expansion would come at the expense of the USSR. In the autumn of 1935, for the first time, Germany was taking the lead in building the anti-communist coalition. The outlines of an anti-Soviet pact between Germany and Japan were negotiated by Joachim Von Ribbentrop and the Japanese military attaché in Berlin, General Oshima Hiroshi. As it was originally conceived, the pact was to include both Poland and Britain, the other traditional enemies of the USSR. Neither joined, as it came to pass, but the British government in particular publicly neither criticized the idea of a pact nor discouraged it. As far as Soviet leaders were concerned, the emerging British policy of appeasement indicated a specific encouragement to Germany, as long as it expanded east.

From Stalin's perspective, this war scare was different to the others that had preceded it. Until now, Poland had been the main obstacle to the success of anti-communist coalitions, with France, Germany, and Britain unable to agree on its future. Now, as Stalin's intelligence told him, with Britain's blessing, Poland was firmly allied with Germany, and the French were impotently standing on the sidelines. Unlike the first years of the Nazi regime, German preparations for war were now diplomatically and militarily less secret, more open, more confident, and more aggressive. As events unfolded in the following months, the threat of war looked ever more stark. The French failure to stop the remilitarization of the Rhineland in March 1936 made it clearer still that the Franco-Soviet Pact had little value in containing Germany. More significantly, shortly after the Spanish Civil War broke out in the summer of 1936, it quickly became a proxy war between the Nazis who supported the Nationalists and the Soviet Union, which backed the Republicans. As far as Stalin was concerned, the war that he had anticipated for the previous fifteen years had finally begun in earnest. The alignment of forces was as he anticipated. Italy stood firmly behind Germany while other powers, notably Britain and France, were not directly involved. He sensibly expected the same to happen in the event of a war against the USSR.

Stalin's foreign intelligence painted a deeply troubling picture of preparations for war against the Soviet Union, but they were more troubling still in the light of parallel events within the country. At the very same time, the Soviet leadership was facing up to the possibility that spies from Germany, Poland, and its other main enemies had infiltrated the USSR and were preparing a fifth column for the coming war. For years, the Soviet authorities had granted asylum to foreign communists who had faced political persecution at home. Particularly given their relatively high levels of education, these communist 'brothers' were often given prominent positions in industry, the party, the Comintern, and the intelligence agencies. In 1932, the regime had received the first signals that some political émigrés might not be what they claimed. The lax procedures for accepting émigrés created an opportunity for hostile foreign governments and other groups to plant their agents in the USSR with unfortunate ease. A verification process began in 1932, but there was no reliable test that could prove if a given émigré was real or not, so doubts lingered, but they grew sharper after the Kirov murder. In February 1935, the head of the Comintern Georgii Dmitrov called for a thorough purge of the émigré community. The calls intensified a few months later when the entire network of Soviet military intelligence in Poland was betrayed.[1] Given the importance of Poland to the anticipated invasion of the Soviet Union, this seemed concrete proof not only that well-placed foreign spies were at work, but also that they were preparing for war.

All political émigrés were to be reregistered and thoroughly investigated. Because no reliable information on the numbers of émigrés existed, the Executive Committee of the Comintern conducted a 'census' in early 1936 which concluded that, since 1920, in excess of 35,000 had taken up residence in the USSR, of whom approximately 2,600 were Germans and 2,000 were Poles. At the same time, they realized that reliable records had never been kept, such that hundreds if not thousands could escape the reregistration process. This raised the spectre of scores of foreign agents occupying sensitive senior posts in the state and party. The Comintern Cadres Department partly

1. E. A. Gorbunov, 'Voennaia razvedka, 1934–1939', *Svobodnaia mysl'*, 2 (1998), 98–109; 3 (1998), 54–61.

compensated for this appalling gaffe by compiling extensive lists of those with less than spotless records in the past: those with the wrong class origins, with links to opposition groups, those who had held posts in non-communist parties or movements, and so on.[2]

Stalin's worries did not end there. The investigation of the Kirov murder had, by the middle of 1935, painted a troubling picture of underground oppositionist activity. The arrests of 'Zinovievites' in Leningrad and the subsequent Kremlin Affair had renewed speculation that former oppositionists, including Lev Kamenev and Grigorii Zinoviev, had lied in their professions of loyalty to Stalin and his policies and continued to organize a resistance that extended to plans for the assassination of Soviet leaders and a fundamental change of political course. They denied involvement in any conspiracy, but many other, less prominent, former oppositionists remained deeply hostile to the Stalin regime, and were less careful about whom they met and with whom they discussed their views. Arrests appeared to reveal a common thrust in what they thought would remain private conversations: that the current leadership should be removed, by force if necessary, echoing statements Trotsky had expressed in exile. Given the solidity of Stalin's position, this in all probability expressed a hope, a longing, rather than some outline of a plan of action. And because they shared the common feeling that war was imminent, it was unsurprising that some may have speculated that a foreign invasion would unsettle Stalin's rule and provide an opportunity for a return to power. Of course NKVD interrogation techniques were such that there is almost certainly a gap between what former oppositionists did and thought, and what they confessed to. And yet there is no evidence to suggest that Stalin dictated the confessions as part of some carefully hatched plan to eliminate his erstwhile rivals and other old Bolsheviks. On the contrary, the contemporary documents are peppered with the leaders' expressions of surprise and disgust at what the NKVD interrogation transcripts told them.

The investigations reinvigorated not only the surveillance of former oppositionists within the USSR, but also interest in the activities of Lev Trotsky abroad. It was commonly accepted that he had a network of agents in the Soviet Union but it remained a mystery how big, how organized, and how active it was. In the summer of 1935, Stalin was not

2. Chase, *Enemies within the Gates*, 133.

entirely convinced that this lot posed a significant threat to him and to the revolution, but he agreed that the new party purge—the Verification of Party Documents—should incorporate measures for the exposure of oppositionist activity. While Stalin remained agnostic on the issue, there was a battle brewing behind the scenes between Genrikh Iagoda, the head of the NKVD, and Nikolai Ezhov, the head of the Central Committee Cadres Department.[3] The conflict had begun with the investigation of the Kirov murder in which both were heavily involved. The murder put Iagoda in an awkward position, having to explain how the Leningrad NKVD failed to anticipate that Kirov's life was at risk. He blamed the relative youth and inexperience of the cadres in the regional branch, but insisted that the ongoing purge of 'Zinovievites' in the Leningrad organization was a sufficient response. Ezhov, on the other hand, concluded that the NKVD as a whole—and not just in Leningrad—was not up to the task of defending Soviet leaders from similar attacks in the future. A review of NKVD personnel files indicated to him that the agent network had been recruited to fixed quotas and without adequate vetting, such that it was not only accumulating incompetent and corrupt people, but it was at serious risk of being penetrated by enemies of the regime. He told Stalin that he believed that Iagoda's current measures were not adequate, and that the lives of Soviet leaders remained at serious risk, not least from oppositionists who had not given up the struggle against Stalin's leadership. Six months later, the Kremlin Affair lent weight to Ezhov's criticisms of Iagoda by apparently exposing another plot by former oppositionists to assassinate Soviet leaders. In his keynote address on the issue at the June 1935 Central Committee plenum, Ezhov argued that the affair had established that Zinoviev and Kamenev were not merely 'morally complicit' in attempts to assassinate Soviet leaders by encouraging an atmosphere of dissent. He insisted that they were directly involved in both the Kirov assassination and the Kremlin plot. However, from the resolutions of the plenum it was clear that his arch-conspiratorial view did not carry the day, though he did land serious blows on Iagoda and the NKVD, who were warned against complacency in rooting out oppositionists and other enemies of the regime.[4]

3. Ibid. 146–205, from which the following analysis borrows heavily.
4. Getty and Naumov, *Yezhov*, ch. 9.

When the Verification of Party Cards began, Ezhov demanded that the verifiers keep a special watch out for hidden enemies of the regime. His speech to a conference of regional party secretaries in September made it clear that he had not stepped back from his vision of the conspiracy, but that, on the contrary, he now included in it both Trotskyists and foreign powers:

> One thing is clear beyond dispute: it seems to me that Trotskyists undoubtedly have a centre somewhere in the USSR. It is impossible for a Trotskyist centre from abroad, located relatively far from the USSR and poorly informed about our conditions—it is impossible, I say, for it to direct with such detail those Trotskyist organizations which have unfortunately held out in our country and which, we believed, had been crushed.
>
> Everywhere the same methods are practised by Trotskyists who have held out in our party. Trotskyists try at all costs to remain in the party. They strive by every device to infiltrate the party. Their first device is to remain at all costs within the party, to give voice everywhere to the general line, to speak out everywhere in its favour while in fact carrying on their subversive work. But nevertheless, it sometimes happens that a Trotskyist slips up and is caught, is expelled from the party, in which case he takes all measures to run off with his party card. He always has in reserve a registration card, approaches another organization, and is registered. Such people are expelled three or four or even five times each. They move from one organization to another—we have quite a few people like that. Trotskyists try at all costs to keep their party card...
>
> [T]here is no better cover for their espionage and subversive operations than a party card, and they relied on that fact. For this reason, it is necessary to hide behind a party card at whatever cost. And they used every means of deception in order to obtain a party card for a spy or for a saboteur. We can firmly assert that Poles, Finns, Czechs, and Germans have been openly gambling on this...[5]

Some of the 'evidence' underpinning Ezhov's assertions came from the Verification of Party Cards, though it was not straightforward. His demands for vigilance were meant to compel verifiers to 'unmask' spies, Trotskyists and Zinovievites, but as Ezhov himself was aware, the local party purge commissions did not always respond well to such demands. They were concerned to limit the damaging effect of purges on the coherence of their organizations generally, and particularly to protect the tightly knit leadership groups. Consequently, less than 3 per cent of those expelled in the Verification were the oppositionists Ezhov had directed them to unmask. And very few expellees were from the upper reaches of the party. Clearly, party grandees were able to divert

5. Getty and Naumov, *Road to Terror*, 200–1.

the force of the purge to the rank and file. Ezhov understood this, and complained to Stalin about it,[6] but he could afford to put off that battle for the time being. The related investigation tracking the whereabouts of 'suspicious' political émigrés, assisted by the Comintern, was providing him with a rich vein of material for his theories of conspiracy against the regime. As they were arrested and compelled to confess to crimes against the regime, Ezhov collected their stories and passed them to party leaders. Iagoda and the NKVD continued to insist that the conspiracy was small and more or less effectively contained. This only encouraged Ezhov's determination to prove him wrong, but he had not yet convinced Stalin of his case.

His breakthrough came at the beginning of January 1935. In the space of a few days, Stalin received reports of a 'Trotskyist' terrorist group in Moscow, and a separate 'Zinovievite' terrorist group in Leningrad. He was told that the former had planned to assassinate him on the anniversary of the October Revolution during the celebrations on Red Square. The latter was a hangover of the Kirov murder investigation, mopping up others like Nikolaev who were purported to have been influenced by Kotolynov to commit acts of terrorism, including the assassination of Soviet leaders.[7] In the same week, Stalin was informed of the arrest of V. P. Ol'berg. Ol'berg was one of the thousands of 'suspicious' political émigrés the Comintern was trying to track down. As a German communist subject to persecution by the Nazis, he had applied for and been granted political asylum in the USSR. It was symptomatic of the poor record keeping in the Soviet asylum process that his application was approved without reference to his Comintern file, which showed that he had been expelled from the German Communist Party (CP) in 1932. Significantly, a German CP investigation at the time had concluded that Ol'berg sustained an extensive correspondence with Trotsky and his son Sedov, had helped them contact their supporters in the Soviet Union and other countries, as well as taken part in the production and distribution of Trotsky's newspaper *Bulletin of the Opposition*.[8] Overlooking the file and accepting Ol'berg's asylum application was

6. Getty and Naumov, *Yezhov*, 167–70.
7. Several other terrorist groups purportedly organized by 'class aliens' and foreigners were reported to Stalin in the weeks preceding this. *Lubianka: Stalin, 1922–1936*, 712–22.
8. Chase, *Enemies within the Gates*, 134–5.

a gaffe for which the NKVD took much of the blame. But his arrest and interrogation was more damaging still. Ol'berg ultimately confessed that from his new home in the USSR he continued to take orders from Trotsky not least in preparation of an attempt on Stalin's life. Together, the three reports delivered a serious blow to Iagoda's contention that the NKVD was effectively containing threats to the regime. Ol'berg was only one of thousands of suspect political émigrés, most of whom had yet to be traced. But more significantly, the reports made Ezhov's arch-conspiratorial view seem less far-fetched. They made it seem more plausible that the Trotskyists, Zinovievites, and foreign agents were connected; that the conspiracy was more widespread than Iagoda had claimed; and that the Kirov murder was only a harbinger of a campaign to overthrow the Stalin regime. In the circumstances, it was not unreasonable for Stalin to renew the investigation of the old Left Opposition with Ezhov in charge.

It was a fateful move, because it gave Ezhov a freer rein to build 'evidence' of conspiracy, and new opportunities to advocate his theories at the highest level. Though there is no way of knowing for certain, Iagoda was probably right that threats to the regime were under control. There were threats, or course. Some of those who had requested political asylum probably were spying for foreign powers, or otherwise hiding hostile intentions towards the regime. We know from Trotsky's personal papers that he did, in fact, have a network of informants in the USSR.[9] Even without access to those papers it was clear enough that stories in his *Bulletin* and other writings would have been impossible without well-placed informants. We don't know who these informants were, but they almost certainly came from among the thousands of committed revolutionaries who had tied their fates to the oppositions in the 1920s. When the oppositions had been defeated, their followers were required to renounce their 'mistaken' views and sign professions of loyalty to Stalin's political line if they wanted to stay in the party. Many did, not because they thought Stalin was right, but because a life outside the party was inconceivable to them. Stalin meanwhile was not so naive as to think all these professions of loyalty were sincere, but he probably thought that they would severely constrain oppositionist activity. The very public changing of sides to

9. J. Arch Getty, 'Trotsky in Exile: The Founding of the Fourth International', *Soviet Studies*, 1 (1986), 24–35.

Stalin's majority in the late 1920s had sapped the oppositionists' will to fight, but the subsequent economic, political, and diplomatic crises encouraged many to think that they could, perhaps, unseat Stalin after all. But Iagoda was probably right that they were not in a position to realize that dream. That many met and held 'political' conversations seems likely. It is logical that they should have expressed their hostility to Stalin and traded information about what their old allies were up to. We might expect some to have discussed scenarios, such as the coming of war, which might unsettle the Stalin regime and open a path for the return to power. All Bolsheviks, both in power and in opposition, understood that the First World War had shaken the power of the autocracy and had created the context in which they were able to seize power. It was only natural that both should now consider the implications of imminent war for the Stalin regime. And because these revolutionaries had risked their lives and liberty in the struggle against a hated regime decades earlier, we cannot rule out that some of them might have planned some kind of concrete action.

In his first three months in charge of the investigation, Ezhov oversaw the arrest of 508 political émigrés and former oppositionists. As one might anticipate, the testimony of the accused obtained under torture tended to confirm Ezhov's arch-conspiratorial view. The accused confessed that the meetings were part of a larger effort to (re)build a political organization that could ultimately overthrow the regime. Under Ezhov's supervision, the conversations were then portrayed as programmatic efforts to draw into the organization those with doubts and hesitations about the party line and mobilize them to commit acts of terrorism and sabotage.[10] On the surface of it, this sounds like a simple, cynical manipulation of the evidence to build a scenario of conspiracy that suited Ezhov's purpose, but the narrative generated by interrogators and accused defies easy interpretation.

In 1935, Zinoviev and Kamenev had accepted 'moral complicity' in the murder of Kirov. They accepted the power of their ideas to motivate the action of others and to change the course of history. Bolsheviks shared a strong belief in the power of ideas. They had brought them to power; they had mobilized the working classes. The accused oppositionists found themselves in NKVD cells because they were committed to their ideas, and they often shared with their interrogators the

10. See e.g. *Lubianka: Stalin, 1922–1936*, 716–20; *Izvestiia TsK*, 8 (1989), 78–94.

sense that their 'political' conversations had a power to mobilize political action even if they were not themselves directly involved in orchestrating assassinations or acts of sabotage. They would not deny the power of ideas. At the same time, the fact of arrest left them in no doubt that their political lives were at an end. They remained passionately committed to revolution, or at least their vision of it, but they understood that they would no longer have the opportunity to explain their actions with any subtlety or nuance. The political struggle had always been the stuff of polemic. From the very beginning of the Lenin succession, the majority and opposition had mercilessly exaggerated and caricatured the other's views as anti-Leninist and harmful to the revolution. They knew they would be forced to sign 'confessions' and that these documents would almost certainly be the final record of their role in the revolution. It would not show that they had fought for their vision of the revolution, not Stalin's. That record would only show as 'for' (if they provided grovelling admission of errors and crimes) or 'against'. It mattered to some that they should not be remembered as counter-revolutionaries. For that matter, some may have had pangs of conscience as they were reminded that they were fighting the regime as it was preparing for a great confrontation with fascism. Some denied the existence of a conspiracy in any form, even when faced in a judicial confrontation (*ochnaia stavka*) with a friend or colleague insisting they had played an essential role. But it was beyond the strength of others to withstand NKVD torture, or the threat of torture, or threats to their families. Though signing a confession embellished by the interrogator guaranteed nothing, it offered an end, however temporarily, to their nightmare. In short, we do not really know how far the oppositionists took their resistance to the Stalin regime, or how they individually reacted to arrest and interrogation. We have a pretty good sense of the methods employed by the NKVD, but we know little about how they absorbed and processed the information they obtained under torture. It is clear enough, however, that the core of oppositionist conduct was explosive material in the hands of the arch-conspiracist Ezhov.

Ezhov regularly circulated to the Politburo the results of interrogations and judicial confrontations, including both confessions and denials. Politburo members were well aware of NKVD methods and their problematic results. In a conversation with the German writer Leon Feuchtwanger at the beginning of January 1937, Stalin defended the reliance on confession on the grounds that it was within the Anglo-Saxon legal tradition and that the regime was fighting 'experienced conspirators... [T]hey don't leave behind a trail of documents in their work. When exposed by their own people, face-to-face, they are forced to admit their guilt.'[11] More privately, he and his inner circle had criticized the political police for an over-reliance on forced confession. The source was not ideal, though necessary at times of crisis.[12] They had no system, no set method for measuring the reliability of confessions, only a trust in their 'revolutionary intuition' (*revoliutsionnoe chut'e*). For a while, Iagoda tried to convince Stalin that Ezhov was exaggerating the evidence,[13] but Stalin ignored him. His personal judgement—his revolutionary instinct—was telling him that Ezhov's portrait of conspiracy made sense and was worth pursuing, not just in the context of the reports of terrorist groups and assassination plots he had been receiving through the winter, but from his broader perspective: his perception of the actions and intentions of his domestic and foreign enemies across the last decade and more.

He was not alone. Politburo members shared their reactions to the transcripts of interrogations in the spring and summer of 1936. For them, under the orchestration of Ezhov, the output of the NKVD torture chambers was ringing true. For example, while Stalin was on his summer vacation, Kaganovich wrote to him from Moscow:

> I read the testimony of the scoundrels Dreitser and Pikel'. Although it was clear enough before, in this one they reveal in fine detail the true criminal face of the killers and provocateurs Trotsky, Zinoviev, Kamenev and Smirnov. It's now absolutely clear that the mercenary whore Trotsky was the gang leader. It's about time to declare him 'beyond the law', and shoot the other bastards we have here.

Of the same transcripts, Stalin wrote to Voroshilov:

> Did you read the testimony of Dreitser and Pikel'? What do you think of the bourgeois dogs (*burzhuaznye shchenki*) in the camp of Trotsky-Mrachkovskii-Zinoviev-Kamenev? They want to 'remove' all Politburo members, these, to put it mildly, shitheads (*zasrantsy*)! It's ridiculous, isn't it? The depths to which people can sink...

11. RGASPI 558/11/1120/15.
12. The issue did not arise for the first time in 1936. See e.g. Molotov's address to a conference of procurators in 1934. RGASPI 17/165/47/161–4.
13. Getty and Naumov, *Yezhov*, 191.

Voroshilov replied:

> They're beyond the pale... That poisonous, vile scum should be completely destroyed. It only bothers me that these Dreitsers and Pikels were well known gentlemen. We didn't pay enough attention and they dug themselves in... The NKVD now has to do some serious purging.[14]

By June 1936, the Politburo had decided in favour of a public trial of the accused oppositionists. At the end of July, they sent a secret letter to local organizations informing them of the decision to hold a trial, and of the more striking findings of the investigation. The letter noted that, while in 1935 Zinoviev and Kamenev had admitted 'moral complicity' for the Kirov murder, in that Nikolaev had been inspired by their oppositionist ideas, it had since become clear that they were in fact *directly* involved, and not only in the Kirov murder, but in building a network of terrorist organizations throughout the USSR with the fundamental aim of assassinating Soviet leaders including Stalin. Quoting from the interrogation transcript of S. V. Mrachkovskii, it went on to observe that in mid-1932 Left Oppositionist leaders Trotsky, Shatskin, and Lominadze had joined the Zinoviev-Kamenev group to form a united bloc. And quoting from the transcript of the Dreitser interrogation that had so taxed Kaganovich, Voroshilov, and Stalin, the letter noted that the Trotskyist-Zinovievist bloc had 'lost all feeling of squeamishness', and were using White Guards, foreign intelligence services, foreign secret police services (including the Gestapo), spies, and provocateurs to carry out their programme of terrorism.[15]

Because Stalin remained on vacation in Sochi through the summer, and continued to correspond with Kaganovich and Ezhov, we have a further record of their impressions of the trial itself. In their 20 August 1936 letter to Stalin they observed not only that the defendants confirmed the details of the pre-trial investigation, but that new and compelling evidence of their actions had emerged. They noted that Smirnov had tried to downplay his role in terrorist actions, but that the other defendants had 'exposed his lies' in the course of cross-examination. Further, and perhaps most significantly, they told Stalin that Reingold had implicated other former Left Oppositionists such as G. L. Piatakov (then deputy commissar of heavy industry), Karl

14. Kvashonkin et al. (eds), *Sovetskoe rukododstvo*, 333–4.
15. *Izvestiia TsK KPSS*, 8 (1989), 100–15. The document is translated in Getty and Naumov, *Road to Terror*, 250–5.

Radek (a senior foreign policy adviser to Stalin and member of the editorial board of the national newspaper *Izvestiia*), and the leaders of the old Right Opposition: Nikolai Bukharin, Alexei Rykov, and Mikhail Tomsky.

When the accusations were aired in the national press, Bukharin responded most decisively. He wrote a letter to Stalin and the other members of the Politburo protesting his complete innocence. It is a fascinating document that, like so many other sources of the period, poses as many questions as it answers. The gathering momentum of the investigations into the activities of the former Left Opposition must have been discomforting to anyone who had publicly opposed the Politburo majority in the 1920s. How far might the NKVD cast its net? Even before the trial, he was conscious that the shadow of suspicion that had followed him since the late 1920s was darkening.[16] In the letter, Bukharin forcefully reiterated a position he had expressed even before the trial that the leaders of the Left were guilty and deserved their punishment. He then proposed that his accusers on the Left named him

> 1/ In order to show . . . that 'they' were not alone.
>
> 2/ To improve their slim chances for a show of mercy as if by demonstrating their extreme honesty ('exposing' those outside the group affords the potential to hide some of one's own).
>
> 3/ A subsidiary aim: to avenge themselves on those who still somehow lead an active political life . . .

It was not particularly convincing. He then asserted his commitment to Stalin and the party line in terms so fulsome that they risked conjuring the memory of the criticisms he had expressed in the late 1920s:

> Only a fool (or a traitor) wouldn't grasp its triumphant landmarks: industrialization, collectivization, the destruction of the kulaks, two great five year plans, the concern for the common man, the mastery of technology and Stakhanovism, rising prosperity, the new constitution. Only a fool (or a traitor) wouldn't grasp that the country has made leonine leaps forward, inspired and directed by the iron hand of Stalin.

But the broader thrust of the letter and the greater weight of its content consisted in providing evidence that he had broken off relations

16. See RGASPI 558/11/710/124–31. In mid-June 1936, he complained to Stalin when a purge at the Academy of Sciences was directed at him and his team in the History of Science and Technology project.

with his old comrades on the Right and that he rarely met any of the former Left Oppositionists, such that he not only had no *desire* to act against the regime, he also had no *opportunity* to do so.

Bukharin was doing his best to avoid the fate of Zinoviev and Kamenev, and to preserve his place in 'political life' as he put it. We know he took three days to craft the message, and thus took the time to consider what tone and what approach would best serve his purpose in the circumstances. Might he have thought that Stalin had instructed the NKVD to set him up in order to destroy him politically, as so many historians have asserted? His deeper reaction to the accusations he faced are not knowable, though some measured speculation is possible. Bukharin's extensive correspondence with Stalin through the 1920s and 1930s was not without episodes of tension and anger, but it was for the most part business-like and occasionally, even in the 1930s, friendly.[17] On that basis, he had little reason to think that Stalin was doing anything more than reacting to the 'evidence' presented in the trial. A more private letter to his erstwhile friend, Politburo member Kliment Voroshilov, reinforces that impression, because Bukharin revealed his desperation simply to know if Stalin and the rest of the Politburo really believed the accusations against him.[18]

For that matter, did Bukharin believe that the members of the former Left Opposition had been conspiring against the regime? Again this cannot be determined with certainty, but one can weigh the possibilities. If he did not believe in the existence a conspiracy, he could not have said so publicly. Stalin and the other members of the Politburo would not have tolerated such a direct challenge to their actions, particularly in the immediate aftermath of the August 1936 trial. But one should not forget that he was still a Politburo member when the NKVD informed the leadership of the Left's plans to

17. RGASPI 558/11/710.

18. Arkhiv Prezidenta Rossiiskoi Federatsii (APRF) 58/1/6/10–13. Cited from www.istmat.info. Voroshilov's harsh reply mortified him. Voroshilov sent Bukharin's letter back, and sent a copy, with his reply, to Stalin. Voroshilov wanted to make a strong statement to Stalin of political (and personal) loyalty to him. He would have known well that associating with former oppositionists accused of conspiring against the regime was dangerous. And yet it does not follow from this that Voroshilov was thus afraid of Stalin. Rather, Bolshevik leaders understood that political loyalties took precedence over personal loyalties, and the cause of the revolution took precedence over personal preferences. While the regime and the revolution were perceived to be under threat, they demanded of one another clarity that those priorities were being observed.

orchestrate a coup d'état in autumn 1927. He was approached by Zinoviev in 1932 about forming a bloc to oppose Stalin. He received bulletins from the Soviet telegraph agency reserved for the top leadership, so he would have known about Trotsky's actions abroad. He knew plenty of people, more than he would probably have preferred, who despised Stalin and would have celebrated his downfall. It is entirely plausible that he would have shared with Stalin and his inner circle the sense that such a conspiracy could be real.[19] In turn, if even those under suspicion appeared to believe this, Ezhov's 'investigation' was bound to continue.

In the immediate aftermath of the August trial, the press was relatively restrained, implying that the main conspirators had been captured, though continued 'vigilance' was needed lest other enemies remained hidden. Behind the scenes though, Ezhov did not waste time extending his investigation to the associates of Piatakov, Radek, Rykov, Bukharin, and the others implicated in August. Kaganovich's reaction to a judicial confrontation of Rykov and Bukharin with G. Ia. Sokol'nikov in mid-September suggested that the members of the Politburo had not yet entirely made up their minds. In a letter to Stalin he wrote:

> Sokolnikov gives the impression of an embittered criminal bandit, laying out plans for assassination without the slightest shame and outlining their involvement in it. Rykov restrained himself, pressing as to whether he knew of his [Rykov's] involvement from Tomsky or someone else. Clearly, upon learning that he knew of Rykov's links with Zinoviev and Kamenev only from Tomsky and Kamenev [now both dead—JH] he calmed right down and went on the attack. But both Rykov and Bukharin concentrated on the last few years, avoiding anything related to 31–32–33 ... I am left with the impression that perhaps that there were no direct organizational links with the Trotskyist-Zinovievite bloc, but in 32–33, and maybe subsequently, they were informed about what Trotsky was up to. It would appear that, they, the Rightists, had their own organization that allowed sub-groups to act on their own (*dopuskaia edinstvo deistvii snizu*) ... We have to look for a Rightist underground

19. The reactions of many others implicated in the August trial shared some similarities. Privately and publicly they showed no hint of doubt that the conspiracy existed. They only denied their role in it. See e.g. Kvashonkin et al. (eds), *Sovetskoe rukovodstvo: Perepiska*, 335–6, 338–42. When Tomsky committed suicide after being implicated, it was commonly taken as evidence of guilt. Even Bukharin considered the possibility: 'Poor Tomsky! Maybe he was caught up in it—I don't know. I can't rule it out.' APRF 58/1/6/10–13. Cited from www.istmat.info.

organization. It's there. I think the role of Rykov, Bukharin, and Tomsky will be exposed.

At no stage did Kaganovich consider that Sokol'nikov's odd behaviour might be the product of pressure from his NKVD captors. More ambiguously, why did Rykov relax when told the information against him came from a dead man? If he did not conspire against the regime, did it matter? But then again, the NKVD torture chambers could generate all manner of testimony. Kaganovich's reaction yet again shows that party leaders did not question the validity of evidence obtained under torture. Stalin later observed that he was inclined to believe Rykov and Bukharin at the time of that judicial confrontation, but that the steady flow of testimony against them, delivered by Ezhov, of course, made it hard to trust their pleas of innocence. It did not help that, when their case was discussed at the December Central Committee plenum, Rykov had repeated bouts of what appeared to be a 'convenient' memory loss when certain suspicious episodes, particularly concerning his knowledge of the Riutin platform, were discussed. Bukharin's participation came across to many delegates as lawyerly and evasive. It left a bad impression that he admitted to taking two or three years to adjust to the party line after he renounced his oppositionist views. And his insistence in the summer that he had not met with colleagues and followers in the former Right Opposition since the early 1930s was more than partially retracted. As evidence of those meetings mounted, together with evidence that some of Bukharin's associates were virulently hostile to the Stalin regime, he contended that he had not reported them or their views to the Central Committee because he wanted to win them over to the party line.[20]

In the summer and into the autumn of 1936, Stalin and his inner circle had been prepared to believe that conspiracy against the regime had been, in the main, exposed. Newspaper commentary on the trial suggested that the former opposition had been 'crushed to bits' and was driven to acts of terrorism by its utter lack of support in the country. They 'have no social base in the country and cannot have any serious number of supporters'.[21] And yet the flow of new 'evidence' from Ezhov and the NKVD had discouraged them from bringing the

20. RGASPI 17/2/575; *Voprosy istorii*, 1 (1995). Translations of some speeches are in Getty and Naumov, *Road to Terror*, 304–22.
21. *Pravda* (13, 15 Aug. 1936).

investigation to a close. Rather than conclude that Ezhov's work was done, Stalin appointed him Commissar of Internal Affairs in place of Iagoda. As we have seen, this was not done as part of some plan to pave the way for the further destruction of Bukharin and other 'Old Bolsheviks', but because Ezhov had finally convinced Stalin in the process of the August trial and its aftermath that Iagoda could not be trusted to protect the regime from its enemies.[22]

Ezhov had wanted Iagoda's job for months, if not years, and he did not hesitate to assert his authority. He almost immediately set about replacing hundreds of senior NKVD officials with appointments he personally approved. To some extent, he was simply replacing Iagoda's appointees with those who would be more likely to be personally loyal to him, but it goes beyond that. Ezhov's career, now very much on the up, had taken a serious knock in the previous year because of shortcomings in the Verification and Exchange of Party Cards that he had been leading. He had demanded that the purge should target spies, saboteurs, and other enemies among the former oppositionists, but local organizations had consistently deflected the purge down the party hierarchy to protect their tight leadership groups. This had deeply irritated him then, and now, as head of the NKVD, he could replace all the regional NKVD chiefs who had defied him in 1935. The impact was devastating, in ways he may not have anticipated.

The analysis so far has noted that the pressure to meet economic plans had put appalling pressure on local leaders and economic officials. They had engaged in a wide variety of deceptive and corrupt practices to create the appearance of success and to contain the grave tensions that plan fulfilment generated. Tight leadership groups were absolutely necessary to sustain local power structures by deflecting blame for problems, and by managing the flow of information to the centre. Ezhov replaced the local NKVD chiefs in order to facilitate his ongoing investigation into the activities of former oppositionists. But this had the subsidiary effect of removing the linchpin of the leadership group. There is no evidence to suggest that Ezhov had foreseen the consequences.

22. In a collection of interviews conducted in the 1960s and 1970s, Molotov accused Iagoda (that 'dirty, quasi-party small-fry') of having been blind to the danger from oppositionists. Feliks Ivanovich Chuev, *Sto sorok besed s Molotovym: iz dnevnika F. Chueva* (Moscow, 1991), 394. See also RGASPI 17/36/981/50; 85/27/93 12–13. Getty and Naumov, *Road to Terror*, 277–80.

The work life of the Bolshevik official in the 1930s was rarely straightforward and was generally stressful, but rarely more stressful than for regional party elite. Stalin had told them to ensure the Five-Year Plan targets were met, or expect to be fired. They were held personally accountable. They were meant to anticipate problems and address them before they became serious. But because the fundamental root of problems rested in the excessive ambition of the plans, the leadership groups tended to close ranks and shift blame to those below them in order to escape blame themselves. They were drawn into, and encouraged the regime's talk of 'wreckers' and 'saboteurs' because it helped explain fires, explosions, train wrecks, spoiled output that were ultimately products of the strains imposed by pressurized plan targets.[23] At the same time, they subverted central directives when they saw that they threatened the group (as with the Verification and Exchange), or when they threatened to complicate plan fulfilment (as with the Stakhanovite movement).

Long before Ezhov's promotion in the autumn of 1936, regional party leaders were in trouble for letting repression get out of hand. In late 1935, I. L. Bulat, the deputy Commissar of Justice for the RSFSR, warned Stalin that cases involving 'counter-revolutionary agitation' (often little more than being critical of those in power) had doubled since the spring.[24] Local tensions had also caused the 1935 Verification and Exchange of Party Cards to spiral out of control. On average, less than 10 per cent of party members were excluded in the process of those campaigns, but an expulsion rate of 30 per cent was not uncommon, and in a few exceptions, it hit 50 per cent. Rather than reduce local tensions as one might assume, by eliminating dissenters, troublemakers, and perceived enemies, local repression tended to exacerbate them, particularly given that Stalin was critical of local 'excesses'.[25] The opportunity to appeal against purge or arrest perpetuated conflicts and deepened resentment against those in power. Ultimately, the leadership groups around party secretaries in republics, provinces, and districts were closed groups of 'insiders' with the power, and where there were

23. Harris, 'Resisting the Plan in the Urals', 201–27.
24. Kvashonkin et al. (eds), *Sovetskoe rukovodstvo*, 316.
25. The Politburo took action to curb arrests for 'counter-revolutionary agitation' in the spring of 1936. RGASPI 17/3/948/95. For Stalin's reaction to the purges and his proposed measures to 'improve' the appeals process, see RGASPI 558/11/1119/100–7.

'insiders' there were also 'outsiders' offended at their exclusion from power, or angered when they were victimized.

The August 1936 show trial and subsequent demands for 'vigilance' excited denunciation and counter-denunciation in the regions, more than the centre expected or wanted in so far as they reflected local tensions rather than the centre's agenda. When Piatakov, the deputy Commissar of Heavy Industry, was implicated, it provided a convenient *external* focus for denunciations. A round of budget cuts implemented by the Commissariat in the first half of 1936 had adversely affected the ability of many organizations and enterprises to meet plan targets. The notion of a Trotskyist-Zinovievite conspiracy at the heart of the Commissariat that had tortured them with impossible demands made perfectly good sense to many. On the back of their enthusiastic denunciations, the NKVD built a case that Piatakov and his co-accused had sought to overthrow the regime by weakening the Soviet economy in general, and military industry in particular, in advance of a foreign invasion.[26] The unfortunate consequence for Piatakov's accusers was that the direction of NKVD investigations would later bounce back to the regions as they looked for his accomplices. At the end of September, the Commissariat of Justice sent instructions to regional and local procurators: 'Reconsider all cases of technical safety and every explosion, accident, and fire, which have occurred in industry in the past three years.'[27] Over the next two months, the NKVD began linking these cases with former Trotskyists, and charged the defendants with wrecking and the murder of workers, with the aim of undermining Soviet power. The first of the accused were tried and convicted in November. The trial received wide coverage around the country, and the defendants' confessions of deliberate murder served to enrage workers who were already upset at dangerous working conditions in industry.[28]

When Ezhov began to replace the regional NKVD chiefs, party secretaries understood that they were in deep trouble. The NKVD chief was a linchpin of the leadership group, because control over the apparatus of repression protected the 'insiders' from the 'outsiders'. They knew that Ezhov's new men would be loyal to him and not to

26. William Chase, 'Stalin as Producer: The Moscow Trials and the Construction of Mortal Threats', in Davies and Harris (eds), *Stalin: A New History*, 239.
27. Gorsudarstvennyi Arkhiv Rossisskoi Federatsii (GARF) 8131/37/84/108.
28. Wendy Goldman, *Terror and Democracy in the Age of Stalin* (Cambridge, 2007), 7–8.

them. Ezhov's men would be looking for Zinovievites, Trotskyists, wreckers, and spies in the first instance, but they would ask awkward questions, and of the wrong people. Ezhov would want to know why regional organizations had deflected the 1935 purge towards the rank and file, and what the regional party elites had to hide. And they had a lot to hide. Stalin had made clear his special hostility to the *dvurushnik*, the official who publicly praised state policy and secretly worked to undermine it. He considered those who doubted the regime's ability to build socialism in the USSR as 'Leftists', and those who thought plan targets were too high as 'Rightists'. In short, the tightly knit, self-protecting leadership groups surrounding local party secretaries were products of a system that demanded personal accountability for the fulfilment of hyper-ambitious tasks in conditions of backwardness and shortage. They were also the antithesis of the sort of 'Bolshevik' leadership Stalin demanded.

Stalin was not ignorant of what the regional secretaries got up to. The Seventeenth Party Congress in 1934 was largely about celebrating the achievements of the first Five-Year Plan, but Stalin observed some ongoing problems, including 'officials with well-known services in the past . . . who think that Party and Soviet laws were written not for them, but for idiots'.[29] Stalin's speeches and the press subsequently criticized 'familyness' (*semeistvennost'*) which was their term for the habit of local elites to close themselves off from the 'party mass'. His criticism of the excessive purging of the party rank and file in the Verification and Exchange of Party Cards was an even more pointed expression of his irritation with their refusal to play by his rules.[30] He knew enough about the activities of regional elites to be irritated, but what he learned in the coming year would deeply disturb him.

Because the centre was turning up the heat on them just as Ezhov was expanding his investigation into the oppositionist conspiracies, regional elites asserted their loyalty to Stalin and to the regime by playing up their intolerance of opposition. Not only did they blame their problems and shortcomings on Piatakov, but they attacked Bukharin and Rykov at the December 1936 Central Committee plenum, repeatedly interrupting their speeches, heckling them, and

29. *XVII s"ezd Vsesoiuznoi Kommunisticheskoi Partii (bol'shevikov). Stenograficheskii otchet* (Moscow, 1934), 34–5.
30. Khlevniuk et al. (eds), *Stalin i Kaganovich: Perepiska*, 753.

pouring scorn on their efforts to explain their actions. It fell to Stalin and members of the Politburo occasionally to calm the hecklers and let Bukharin and Rykov speak. Regional leaders demanded that they be expelled from the party and arrested, but Stalin chose to pass the investigation back to the NKVD for further investigation. By the time of the next Central Committee plenum, which opened in late February 1937, Ezhov had convinced Stalin of the probability that Bukharin and Rykov were guilty of actively conspiring against the regime; that they were not merely aware of the conspiratorial activities of their followers in the former Right Opposition, but that they coordinated and led them, in conjunction with the Trotskyists and Zinovievites, with the aim of overthrowing the regime.[31]

At the February–March 1937 Central Committee plenum, Bukharin and Rykov were given their last, now futile, opportunity to defend themselves. As in December, delegates vigorously attacked them in an effort to appear more Catholic than the Pope. That first item on the plenum agenda was concluded with the arrest of the former leaders of the Right, but the second item turned the spotlight on the delegates themselves. On the surface of it the item seems innocuous: 'On party organizations' preparation of the new electoral system for elections to the USSR Supreme Soviet, and the corresponding restructuring of the party-political work'. Beneath the surface of it, the item was intended to increase the pressure on regional cliques ('family groups') to reveal their darker secrets. The new NKVD chiefs had begun to expose corruption and deceit, and the 'new electoral system' promised to make it even more difficult for them to control the flow of information to the centre.

Andrei Zhdanov's speech introducing the item noted that the party statutes required district and city committees to be re-elected every year, and regional and republican party committees every year and a half. The requirement had been ignored. Elections had been replaced

31. The 'evidence' that drew him in may not have been wholly the product of the imaginations of interrogators in NKVD torture chambers. Some followers of Bukharin and Rykov deeply despised the Stalin regime and were ready to sacrifice themselves in the cause of its destruction. We are unlikely ever to be able to tease apart the NKVD embellishments and exaggerations from the actions of the former oppositionists, but we know that Stalin did not expect the oppositionists to leave 'material evidence' of their actions, and that he accepted the validity of testimony obtained under torture. This helps explain how Ezhov was able to spin a rich tale of conspiracy out of a thin core of fact.

by 'cooptation'—that is, people had been appointed according to the preferences of the leadership group and not elected by the organization they led. According to Zhdanov, this led to the isolation of the leadership groups from the party masses, or worse, to suppression of criticism, and worse still, to a situation in which 'hostile elements' could worm their way into party organizations. The solution, he told them, was not only to end the practice of cooptation but to have contested elections to the leadership group.[32] As Stalin put it in his own speech on the issue: 'We should have two approaches to check on the work of officials: one from above, the boss checking the subordinate, and the other from below, oversight from below ... by means of the restoration the democratic, elective principle in our party, when party members have the right to reject any candidate, to raise whatever criticisms and compel leaders to account for themselves before the party mass.'[33]

In their speeches, regional leaders tried to put off elections, arguing that deadlines were too tight, that the elections would complicate spring agricultural campaigns, that election campaigns would give a platform to enemies of the regime.[34] They understood that the elections would send a further, clear message to 'outsiders' and would-be critics of the regional leadership groups (the 'insiders') that if they voiced their grievances and suspicions, they would have the protection of the centre. Given that the regions had, for a decade, been ruled with an iron fist and a ferocious intolerance of dissent, it took considerable encouragement to draw out the critics, but that came not only in the form of the plenum, but also a series of articles in the national press attacking the 'suppression of criticism' and concrete evidence that new NKVD chiefs would defend the critics and not the regional leaders.[35] Through the winter and into the spring of 1937, the drip of unfortunate details about regional leaders' activities was becoming a disturbing flow. One by one, the regional cliques fell in the spring and summer of 1937 until the overwhelming majority of that group, comprising the majority of the party's Central Committee, had been arrested. The

32. 'Materialy fevral'sko-martovskogo plenuma TsK VKP(b) 1937 goda', *Voprosy istorii*, 5 (1993), 1–10.
33. 'Materialy fevral'sko-martovskogo plenuma TsK VKP(b) 1937 goda', *Voprosy istorii*, 11–12 (1995), 15.
34. 'Materialy fevral'sko-martovskogo plenuma TsK VKP(b) 1937 goda', *Voprosy istorii*, 5 (1993), 11–27.
35. See *Pravda* articles on vigilance: 6, 10, 17 Mar. 1937.

downfall of each leadership group followed its own logic, and the process has been little studied, but take the leadership clique of I. D. Kabakov, First Secretary of Sverdlovsk oblast', for example.[36]

Through 1935 and 1936, non-ferrous metallurgy in the Urals had been in trouble for a high accident rate, hindering the spread of the Stakhanovite movement, and for persistently failing to meet production targets. Local investigations typically pinned the blame on 'wreckers' and 'former oppositionists', in no small part because they were not allowed to attribute problems to overambitious plans. Calls for vigilance in the aftermath of the August 1936 trial provoked a flurry of denunciation and counter-denunciation. The head of the labour department of the Kirovograd Copper Smelting Plant and his assistant were denounced for 'anti-Soviet actions' on the grounds that they had kept wages for engineering personnel at 450 rubles a month when less qualified workers, probably Stakhanovites, were making up to 750 rubles.[37] At the same factory, Stakhanovites denounced engineering personnel as Trotskyists for failing to promote Stakhanovite methods. In turn, they denounced the factory Party Committee for protecting the engineers.[38] At the Krasnoural Copper Smelting Plant, tensions between the district Party Committee and the factory Party Committee exploded into a war of denunciations. Each accused the other of protecting former oppositionists, as a result of which both organizations were purged and the district committee first secretary Chernetsov was arrested.[39] In the next few months, the circle of mutual denunciation spread wider and wider until the directors of the largest enterprises in the regional non-ferrous metals had been arrested. These included senior figures like the chairman of the Urals Non-ferrous

36. For an excellent study of the fall of the regional clique in Iaroslavl', see J. Arch Getty, 'The Rise and Fall of a Party First Secretary: Vainov of Iaroslavl'', in James Harris (ed.), *The Anatomy of Terror: Political Violence under Stalin* (Oxford, 2013), 66–84. For more detail on Kabakov and the fall of the Sverdlovsk clique, see Andrei Sushkov, 'Krakh "imperii tovarishcha Kabakova": Sverdlovskoe rukovodstvo v politicheskikh vodovorotakh 1937 goda', *Vesi*, 6 (2013), 46–84; Harris, *The Great Urals*, ch. 7.

37. Tsentr dokumentatsii obshchestvennykh organizatsii Sverdlovskoi oblasti (TsDOO SO), 4/14/138/38.

38. TsDOO SO, 4/14/138/36.

39. TsDOO SO, 4/14/138/59–67. Gosudarstvennyi Arkhiv Administrativykh Organov Sverdlovskoi oblasti (GAAO SO), 1/2/20017/1.

Metallurgy Trust, the chairman of the Urals Copper Mining Trust, and the chairman of the Middle Urals Copper-Chemical Combine.[40]

Parallel to events in the non-ferrous metals industry was a series of arrests in the Oblast' state apparatus. Investigations of individuals known to have been members of the Left Opposition in the 1920s led to F. I. Striganov, the head of the Oblast' administration of local industry. Striganov was known to have been personal friends with two oppositionists. In the autumn of 1936, Striganov had been forced to do public penance for these contacts, but following the arrival of the new NKVD chief Dmitriev, this was deemed insufficient and he was arrested. Striganov had been particularly vulnerable because of the persistent underfulfilment of the plan for local industry.[41] In a less charged situation, that might have been enough to seal his fate and close the case but the new NKVD man dug deeper. For the most part, the underfulfilment had been the result of underfunding, and that underfunding had created considerable anger among officials in local industry towards Oblast' economic organs. Included in the materials of the NKVD investigation is a 27-page, unsolicited denunciation of the entire Oblast' state administration written by V. A. Riabov, the assistant director of the food sector of the administration of local industry. Riabov's denunciation was remarkably detailed, and damaging. It contained copies of correspondence between the chairman of the Oblast' Planning Commission M. I. Fuks and the chairman of the Oblast' Executive Committee V. F. Golovin, reinforcing his argument that the two knew about problems in local industry and took no action. And it showed how the Oblast' Planning Commission deliberately exaggerated plans for local industry as a way of increasing financing from the centre.[42] The denunciation effectively served Dmitriev his first scalps from within the Sverdlovsk oblast' leadership group. And yet, this was not a simple matter of Ezhov's new men coming in to orchestrate the downfall of the regional cliques. They could not, and did not, anticipate how their arrival would trigger a wave of denunciations.

40. GAAO SO, f. 1/2/22947/52: 1/2/20017/131; RGAE, 8034/1/1015/18. Zharikov was arrested on 10 Oct. 1936. The precise dates of the arrests of the other two are unclear.

41. Overall production in Sverdlovsk oblast' local industry declined in 1936 versus 1935. GAAO SO 1/2/34606 (t. 2)/14. (The pages of this file are numbered, but in no recognizable order.)

42. TsDOO SO, 4/14/138/16.

The regional 'outsiders' had begun to attack the 'insiders', but Kabakov's clique was still ready to fight back. In the aftermath of the arrest of senior figures in the Oblast' state administration, R. D. Kravchuk, the director of a small factory in Sverdlovsk, made a speech to a meeting of the Oktiabr'skii district party *aktiv*, in which he questioned how it could be that Kabakov had worked so closely and over such a long period with 'enemies of the people'. Were there, perhaps, other enemies in the Oblast' party bureau? The ferocious reaction of those at the meeting and subsequently in the Oblast' administration made it clear that Kabakov was not without his allies. Kravchuk was accused from various quarters of spreading 'Trotskyist, counter-revolutionary slander'. But the timing was extremely unfortunate for Kabakov. The centre was only beginning its campaign against the suppression of criticism, and in mid-February 1937 the national party newspaper *Pravda* chose to illustrate its aims with reference to the Kravchuk case. Kabakov was forced to restore Kravchuk's party membership and publish in the provincial and district party newspapers articles explaining how lessons would be learned. At the February–March Central Committee plenum that opened less than two weeks later, Zhdanov again raised the Kravchuk case in his speech, and Stalin gently mocked Kabakov's attempts to defend himself.[43]

That would certainly have been uncomfortable for the Sverdlovsk First Secretary, but more seriously, the Kravchuk case was a clear indication to 'outsiders' that they could publicly vent their grievances against the leadership clique. Critical letters to the regional party newspaper (*signaly s mest*) rose from 2,400 in January to 3,300 in March.[44] As Kabakov's political star plummeted, some of those within the clique's web of corruption and deceit chose to denounce Kabakov in an effort to save themselves. By the end of May 1937, the majority of the Obkom had been arrested by the NKVD. Details of the regional misdeeds, including the faking of production reports, the distribution of corrupt payments to clique members, the subversion of central policy initiatives, as well as information on the cover-up of disastrous construction projects, the squandering of public funds, and general

43. 'Materialy fevral'sko-martovskogo plenuma TsK VKP(b) 1937 goda', *Voprosy istorii*, 5–6 (1995), 13.
44. Sushkov, 'Krakh "imperii"', 81.

economic incompetence was communicated via the NKVD to the central leadership.

The reaction to this material, coming not only from Sverdlovsk, but also from other besieged regional cliques, is striking. The pattern of deceit and corruption was common to all regions because all leadership groups faced the same terrible pressure to realize overambitious plan targets in conditions of shortage and general backwardness. The revelations streaming in to Moscow from across the USSR should have provoked Stalin and his inner circle to understand some of the serious flaws in the systems of planning and administration. But Stalin did not see it that way. Nor, for that matter, did the regional leaders themselves. They were not pure technocrats, trained to engineer, refine, and manage the complexities of the machine of economic planning. They were Bolsheviks, trained to 'storm fortresses'. They were meant, of course, to understand the complexities of the industrializing economy, but like the central leaders themselves, regional party secretaries were all too ready to equate problems with the work of 'wreckers', 'saboteurs', 'oppositionists', and other hostile forces. They had done so through the 1930s. In 1935, they were blaming problems of the local economy on 'Trotskyists' like Piatakov and 'Rightist' conspiracies, labelled as such often for no other reason than their desire to reduce overambitious plan targets. When Kabakov was arrested in May 1937, he was charged with corruption, faking results and undermining the implementation of central directives, but all of these charges were connected to what regional NKVD chief Dmitriev labelled the work of a 'Rightist' counter-revolutionary organization in Sverdlovsk oblast'.[45] In Moscow, Ezhov gathered the reports from his regional plenipotentiaries and wove it together with the material from the Moscow trials to build a picture of a colossal conspiracy against the regime.

Back in late 1934, Stalin had good reason to be worried when his fellow Politburo member was assassinated. It was not wholly unreasonable to think that further assassinations might follow, or that former oppositionists on the Left and Right might want to see that happen, and even contribute to them. But the conspiratorial mindset, not just of Stalin but of Bolsheviks generally, formed in decades of conspiracy against the old regime, was feeding itself in ever more dangerous ways. In the summer of 1936, Stalin thought the threat to him and to the

45. GAAO SO 1/2/17368 (t. 1).

revolution was limited to a disaffected band of political has-beens. In the summer of 1937, he seems to have concluded that the majority of the Party Central Committee—the heart of the party elite—was in on the conspiracy. And it was getting worse. On the very day Kabakov's arrest was announced in Sverdlovsk, the NKVD arrested Marshal Mikhail Tukhachevskii, head of the Red Army General Staff. Less than three weeks later, he and seven other senior military commanders were tried for treason. In the months that followed, thirteen of fifteen army commanders and fifty-seven of eighty-five corps commanders were shot, as were 110 of the 195 divisional commanders. In all, somewhere around a third of the Red Army officer corps were removed by the NKVD.[46]

Given the rising tide of the regime's fears about its enemies, some kind of purge of the military was likely.[47] The military had too many long-standing associations with perceived enemies for Ezhov to pass over them. Most obviously, it was Trotsky who had formed the Red Army in the Civil War period and who had been its first commander-in-chief. He had gathered and nurtured many of its senior officers almost two decades earlier. The army had generally stayed out of politics, but Trotsky's plans for a November 1927 coup d'état, as then OGPU chief Menzhinskii reported them to Stalin, were based on the calculation that he could carry the army with him.[48] It did not help that there was significant resistance within the military to reforms imposed by the party in the late 1920s and a deep disquiet about the effects of forced collectivization on an army made up overwhelmingly of peasant-soldiers. These concerns contributed to 'Operation Vesna' in 1930–1 in which thousands of military specialists and other Red Army officials were arrested and accused of conspiring with foreign enemies to overthrow the regime.[49]

46. John Erikson, *The Soviet High Command* (London, 1962).
47. For a detailed treatment of the background to the terror in the military, see Peter Whitewood, *The Red Army and the Great Terror: Stalin's Purge of the Soviet Military* (Lawrence, Kan., 2015).
48. Michal Reiman, *The Birth of Stalinism* (London, 1987), appendices.
49. Stephen J. Main, The Red Army and the Soviet Military and Political Leadership in the Late 1920s: The Case of Inner-Army Opposition of 1928, *Europe-Asia Studies*, 2 (1995), 337–55; Roger Reese, Red Army Opposition to Forced Collectivization, 1929–1930: The Army Wavers, *Slavic Review*, 1 (1996), 24–45; Nonna Tarkhova, *Krasnaia armiia i stalinskaia kollektivizatsiia, 1928–1933 gg.* (Moscow, 2010).

That was not all. Since 1922, the Red Army general staff had had a close working relationship with their counterparts in Germany following the Treaty of Rapallo. Both countries had emerged from the First World War as pariah states, such that a cooperative relationship made sense. The treaty provisions as they were publicized concerned economic relations, but secret military cooperation (forbidden under the terms of the Versailles Peace) emerged shortly afterwards.[50] The close military contacts were both an asset and a liability with the end of Weimar and the rise of the Nazis. The Soviet leaders hoped the history, and potential, of cooperation might play some role in discouraging an invasion of the USSR, but they were equally worried that the pattern of loyalty might work the other way. Concerns about the loyalty of the Red Army were exacerbated by the betrayal of a significant part of the Soviet military intelligence network in 1934.[51] Was there a mole or moles? And were the moles linked to the Trotskyists? In the subsequent Verification and Exchange of Party Cards (1935), 244 former 'Trotskyists and Zinovievites' among party members in the military were expelled, along with 555 others accused of 'Trotskyist and counter-revolutionary agitation', but Ezhov's investigations in 1936 and 1937 continued to find links between the military and the Trotskyist-Zinovievite conspiracy. At the February–March 1937 Central Committee plenum, Voroshilov portrayed them as isolated and uncharacteristic, but the momentum of the investigation was not in his favour.[52]

The steady stream of interrogation transcripts and other materials of the NKVD investigation was augmented by echoes of the regime's own disinformation from almost twenty years before. At the tail end of the Civil War, the newly created foreign department of the political police had tried to expose foreign threats to the regime by inventing counter-revolutionary groups seeking foreign assistance. Their greatest successes came from the promotion of a wholly fictitious military conspiracy led by General Mikhail Tukhachevskii. Foreign organizations and governments hostile to the USSR were attracted to the scenario because of Tukhachevskii's aristocratic origins, and because his senior

50. Aleksandr M. Nekrich, *Pariahs, Partners, Predators: German-Soviet Relations, 1922–1941* (New York, 1997).
51. Gorbunov, 'Voennaia razvedka', 54–61.
52. V. A. Lebedeva, 'Tragediia RKKA: M. N. Tukhachevskii i voenno-fashistskii zagovor', *Voenno-istoricheskii arkhiv*, 1 (1997), 149–256.

position in the Red Army suggested to them that a coup was not only possible, but had a good chance of succeeding. That such a conspiracy was an invention of the Soviet political police did not stop it churning through the rumour mill of the anti-communist west through the 1920s and 1930s to the point where Stalin and Ezhov were influenced by its echoes. Because so many in the capitalist west believed in, hoped for, and discussed a military conspiracy against the regime, the foreign chatter lent a further gloss of credibility to the 'confessions' the NKVD was beating out arrested army officers. But it was Reinhard Heydrich, the director of the Nazi security agency, the Siecherheitsdienst (SD), who saw the value to Germany of sowing distrust between the Soviet political leadership and its general staff. He invented stories of Tukhachevskii's work for the Nazi regime and channelled them to Stalin via the Czech leader Edvard Beneš.[53] In the spring and summer of 1937, as he was receiving regular reports detailing conspiracies to overthrow the regime, Stalin was particularly susceptible to Heydrich's ploy. At the beginning of June 1937, when he addressed a meeting of the top Soviet Military Council to confront commanders with evidence of the purported military conspiracy, Stalin emphasized the links with the Nazi regime, asserting that Tukhachevskii had betrayed the Soviet plan of operations (in the event of war) to the Reichswehr.[54] Heydrich had sealed Tukhachevskii's fate.

Almost certainly there was no military conspiracy against the regime. Nor was there a conspiracy among the oppositions beyond perhaps a small network passing information to Trotsky and a few hotheads who dreamed of removing the Stalin clique they so hated. The regional 'conspiracy' consisted of nothing more than the strategies employed by republican, provincial, and district leaders to survive the tremendous pressures of the Stalinist administrative system. That was corruption, not counter-revolution. And yet because the regime was extremely sensitive to internal and external threats; because the regime tended to believe the substance of confessions obtained under torture; because Stalin had promoted a committed conspiracy theorist to head the political police, the world's most powerful dictator had become

53. Igor Lukes, *Czechoslovakia between Stalin and Hitler: The Diplomacy of Edvard Beneš in the 1930s* (Oxford, 1996), 95.
54. We do not have copies of the notes Stalin received via Beneš, but the thrust of Stalin's speech suggests that the 'evidence' of treachery came from Germany. RGASPI 558/11/1120/28–43.

convinced that his regime and the revolution itself were in grave danger from a vast, interconnected conspiracy. Events in Europe and the Far East made it clear not only to Stalin but also to many contemporary observers around the world that a war of aggression against the USSR was imminent. Gutting the Red Army central command and officer corps made no sense in this context unless Stalin believed in a deep-seated military conspiracy.

The history of revolutionary movements in which the Bolsheviks were so well versed told them that counter-revolution tended to follow closely on the heels of revolution. As they approached the twentieth anniversary of the seizure of power, they felt they were living on borrowed time. Counter-revolutions tended to be bloody affairs. The 'white terror' in the Civil War showed the Bolsheviks at first hand that the bourgeoisie was ruthless in its determination to exterminate them. They felt that they had to be ruthless in defence of the revolution. Many innocent people might have to die in the process of prosecuting those acting to subvert the regime. At the June 1937 meeting of the Military Council, Stalin insisted that it was 'the duty of every party member ... every citizen of the USSR' to report anything that struck them as suspicious: 'if only 5 per cent of it is true, then that is fine (*to eto khleb*)'. Bukharin himself expressed a sympathy for this logic in his last letter to Stalin: 'that with the approach of war ... the purge encompasses a/ the guilty b/ the suspects c/ the potential suspects. Of course I had to be included ... *great* plans, *great* ideas and *great* interests trump everything and personal considerations are petty against the backdrop of the tasks of world-historical significance that rest on your shoulders.'[55] Of course, Bukharin was flattering Stalin in a vain, final effort to forestall his execution, but it remains that the logic of the appalling political violence unleashed by Stalin was not the logic of some lone, paranoid, bloodthirsty dictator. It was the logic of the Bolsheviks, and albeit in a more extreme form, the logic of Russian Tsars determined to preserve and protect the autocracy.

That logic also dictated that the political violence had not yet run its course. Far from it. The regime was convinced it had uncovered a conspiracy in the heart of the political and military elite, but it was far from certain that it had exposed all its participants. In the spring and summer of 1937, it ramped up calls for 'vigilance', in essence employing the

55. APRF 3/24/427/13–18. Cited from www.istmat.info.

colossal state propaganda machine to solicit denunciations. They flowed into the offices of the NKVD in an appalling abundance. The social dynamics of state repression in this period are still little understood and very controversial, particularly as historians debate the degree to which the regime lost control of the process of repression.[56] Defining 'control' is the problem. There is no reason to doubt that Stalin was in a position to accelerate or restrain state repression, but neither he nor the NKVD had an adequate system for judging the evidence of conspiracy and identifying its limits. They saw it in confessions obtained under torture. They saw it in official corruption, industrial accidents, plan underfulfilment, poor quality output, and other effects of pressurized plans. They saw it in doubts, hesitations, criticisms, and grumbling about the current state of affairs. Aggressively soliciting denunciations was bound to feed their fears. The flow of denunciations came not merely because the propaganda machine demanded the unmasking of hidden enemies. Many Soviet citizens similarly interpreted industrial accidents and poor workplace safety as evidence of 'wrecking'. They saw it in low wages, shortages of consumer goods, and the harsh treatment they received at the hands of their bosses. Factory officials saw it in funding cuts, the delivery of faulty inputs, and the shortcomings of their staff. Tensions in the workplace were such that many workers and officials wrote denunciations before being denounced themselves. Stalin had wanted 'criticism from below' to expose the shortcomings of officials, but he did not anticipate what would follow, and he was tragically primed to see conspiracy and to instruct the NKVD to prosecute it as such. Stalin did not lose control over the process of repression because he remained in a position to restrain it, but his interpretation of the 'evidence' it churned up ensured the spread of political violence from the political and military elite to the wider ranks of officialdom and the population as a whole.[57]

As the dimensions of the perceived conspiracy widened, the threat of invasion was looming ever larger. With the support of Nazi Germany, General Franco's Nationalist forces were gaining ground at the expense

56. J. Arch Getty, 'The Politics of Repression Revisited', in Getty and Manning (eds), *Stalinist Terror*, 49–62; E. A. Rees, 'Stalin: Architect of the Terror', in Harris (ed.), *Anatomy of Terror*, 49–65.

57. For a more detailed treatment of the social dynamics of repression, see Rittersporn, *Stalinist Simplifications*; Goldman, *Terror and Democracy*; Lynne Viola, 'The Question of the Perpetrator in Soviet History', *Slavic Review*, 1 (2013), 1–23.

of the Communist-backed Republicans.[58] Preparations for a broader European war gathered pace not least among the revisionist states led by the parties to the Anti-Comintern Pact. In May, Neville Chamberlain came to power in Britain, initiating a new phase of Anglo-German relations that sapped Soviet hopes for any form of collective security arrangements to contain German aggression. The thrust of British appeasement seemed to them to consist of a tolerance of German aggression as long as it was directed to the east. Meanwhile Soviet relations with Japan were worsening amidst border skirmishes in the Soviet Far East.[59] The spectre of an imminent two-front war heightened anxieties not only about counter-revolutionary conspiracies but also about the will of the Soviet people to fight when war came. The perceived weakness of elite power on the threshold of war naturally heightened insecurity about popular support for the regime, and specifically the danger that disaffected groups might collaborate with invading forces. These anxieties provoked a new and even more lethal phase of Stalinist political violence: the 'mass operations'. The victims of Stalin's 'Great Terror' were by no means limited to the political elite, or to broader Soviet officialdom. Only since the opening of the archives have we come to understand that the majority of those caught up in the maelstrom of state repression were ordinary Soviet citizens. The mass operations affected many groups, but the largest of these were so-called 'socially harmful elements' (such as kulaks and criminals and others perceived to be inherently hostile to the USSR), and national minorities with perceived links to potential invaders. In the second half of 1937 and through 1938, the regime addressed the danger they perceived these groups represented by means of summary execution, mass deportation, or exile to the labour camps of the Gulag.

Each of the mass operations had its own logic, developing and gaining momentum over the previous months and years, some of which has been discussed in previous chapters. Operations directed at 'socially harmful elements' had their deepest roots in the peculiar Soviet

58. Stalin's intelligence reports were attributing much of the disarray among the Republicans to Trotsky and his agents. William Chase, 'The Conspiratorial Worldview in 1936–1937: Did the Spanish Tail Wag the Soviet Dog?' (paper presented to AAASS Convention, 2010); Getty, 'Trotsky in Exile'.

59. B. N. Slavinskii, *SSSR i Iaponiia na puti k voine: Diplomaticheskaia istoriia, 1937–1945 gg.* (Moscow, 1999), ch. 1.

practices of fighting crime and maintaining social order.[60] All modern states monitor their populations with the aim of isolating dangers and distributing benefits, but perhaps more than any other, the Soviet state sought to engineer society through the 'politics of inclusion and exclusion'. In the 1920s, it created the first of what were referred to as 'regime cities'. Determining who could live in urban areas of particular economic, military, and political significance can be seen as a characteristic of a utopian programme of 'perfecting' society, but more prosaically, this was about using the full power of the state not merely to react to crime, but to anticipate and prevent it. The police began to gather information on every Soviet citizen, including data on social class, nationality, work record, and criminal record, in order to identify and manage what the regime perceived to be its natural 'friends' and 'enemies'. The system was augmented in the early 1930s with the issuance of internal 'passports'. The immediate impulse in this case was to inhibit the massive movement of peasants from rural to urban areas during the famine of 1932–3, but the new measure reinforced the general requirement that citizens should carry with them at all times a record that indicated not just neutral facts of identity, but markers used to identify 'friendliness' and 'hostility' to the regime.

The information the regime was gathering formed the basis for periodic police sweeps of regime cities and the deportation of tens of thousands of Soviet citizens to areas on the periphery. Harsher measures were not uncommon. Stalin was occasionally informed of incidents, for example, in which citizens with the wrong markers of class or nationality were stopped by the police far from their registered residence or workplace, but near a factory or other installation of significance to national security. In such cases arrest and summary execution was likely. The graver extremes of repression were curbed briefly around 1934 as we have seen, but several factors militated against restraint. The deportation of very large numbers of people to the periphery created an unsustainable situation in that people were being sent away from areas where work, housing, and food supply were concentrated. It should come as no surprise that many of those subject to deportation returned to the regime cities. Returnees to the regime

60. Paul Hagenloh, *Stalin's Police: Public Order and Mass Repression in the USSR, 1926–1941* (Baltimore, 2009); David Shearer, *Policing Stalin's Socialism: Repression and Social Order in the Soviet Union, 1924–1953* (New Haven, 2009).

cities were not the only concern. In the process of collectivization in the early 1930s, hundreds of thousands of peasants had been labelled as 'kulaks' and exiled to the labour camps of the Gulag. The expiry of their five-year terms was creating a serious problem for the regime. Having only recently brought some stability to the new collective farm order, they did not want that jeopardized by the return of those whom they believed were hostile to it. The further danger was that five years in the Gulag would have hardened the hostility of this group not just to the kolkhozy, but also to the regime more broadly. The perceived risk was that hundreds of thousands of angry 'kulaks' would return to their home villages and whip up anti-Soviet sentiment amongst a still wavering population and encourage a mass flight from collective agriculture, all on the eve of a new great war. That was unacceptable to the Soviet leadership, so peasants were released from the Gulag, but were prevented from return home. And yet that created the same problem as with the deportees. Without adequate food, housing, and work, and having been kept from their families for five years, many went home without permission.

In early 1937, the head of the West Siberian NKVD S. N. Mironov reported that local kulaks were forming insurrectionary organizations (*povstancheskie organizatsii*). Reports of similar organizations of kulaks, Cossacks, and returning Gulag inmates followed from other regions in the spring. For regional officials, the concern was not limited to insurrection. Since the new constitution was announced in 1936, and the prospect of contested elections loomed, they reported to the centre their concerns that 'anti-Soviet elements' would take advantage of the process. This found some resonance in the centre. In March, regional NKVD officials were warned by the centre to monitor the plans of church officials in advance of elections. A month later, a similar communication warned of the activization of former parties—Mensheviks, SRs, Trotskyists, and Rightists—apparently planning to use the elections as a platform for launching a campaign of insurrection.[61] It is not unlikely that the centre was, in effect, only compiling, collating, and summarising reports that they had been receiving from the regions. Regional leaders were concerned about the threat from 'anti-Soviet

61. V. N. Khaustov and Lennart Samuelson, *Stalin, NKVD i repressii, 1936–1938gg.* (Moscow, 2009), 261–4.

elements' but they were also generally hostile to the idea of contested elections and they would have been happy to see the idea shelved.[62]

The centre was not prepared to back down on the matter of elections, though it appears to have been more flexible on what to do with the 'anti-Soviet elements'. In early July, Stalin and Ezhov agreed the creation of extra-judicial 'troiki' (three-man teams empowered to act as judge, jury, and executioner) to deal with them. All kulak returnees were to be registered, and those engaged in hostile activities were to be arrested and executed.[63] Two weeks later, on 16 July, Ezhov convened a conference of regional NKVD chiefs to review the results of the previous two weeks. He criticized some for their slow progress, but he received requests from others that powers of arrest and interrogation be extended further still.[64] The meeting accelerated mass repression in the provinces. We have no archival access to the reports Ezhov was receiving from the provinces at this time, but it seems likely that such reports were deepening his conviction that insurrectionary organizations of anti-Soviet elements were forming across the USSR, and that they posed a grave threat to the revolution, particularly in the event of war.

On 30 July he submitted 'operational order 00447' for the approval of the Politburo. It proposed to further coordinate regional action in order to address the threat, in his words, 'once and for all':

> The results of investigations regarding anti-Soviet formations have established that a significant number of former kulaks who had earlier been subject to repressive measures and who had evaded them, who had escaped from camps, exile and labour settlements, have settled in the countryside. This includes many church officials and sectarians, and those who in the past were active participants in armed, anti-Soviet uprisings. Many members of anti-Soviet political parties (SRs, Georgian Mensheviks, Dashnaks, Mussavatists, Ittihadists), active participants in bandit uprisings, Whites, members of punitive expeditions, repatriates and others remain untouched and at large. Some of these above-mentioned elements, leaving the countryside for the cities, have infiltrated industrial enterprises, transport and construction sites. Additionally, many criminals are still entrenched in the countryside and urban areas... Inadequate efforts to combat these criminal groups have created a state of impunity that aids their criminal activity. We have established that all these

62. On the hostility of regional officials, see J. Arch Getty, 'Pre-Election Fever: The Origins of the 1937 Mass Operations', in Harris (ed), *Anatomy of Terror*, 224–7.
63. Getty, *Road to Terror*, 470–1.
64. Khaustov and Samuelson, *Stalin, NKVD i repressii*, 264–6.

anti-Soviet elements constitute the chief instigators of every kind of anti-Soviet crime and sabotage in collective and state farms as well as in transport and certain spheres of industry. The organs of state security are faced with the task of mercilessly crushing this entire gang of anti-Soviet elements, of defending the labouring Soviet people from their counter-revolutionary machinations, and, finally, of putting an end, once and for all, to their base efforts to undermine the foundations of the Soviet state.

On the surface of it, it might appear as though the centre was pushing the regions, but the reality was somewhat murkier. The order set colossal figures for arrest and execution. 'The most active... elements' were to be shot; the 'less active but nonetheless hostile elements' were to be sent to the Gulag for eight to ten years. In all, almost 300,000 were to be 'subject to repressive measures', of whom more than 72,000 were to be subject to summary execution. The directive stated that only the Politburo reserved the right to adjust the figures, but by mid-October, Stalin passed that power to Ezhov. Many local organizations asked to have their figures raised, and by autumn, Ezhov seems to have agreed all requests immediately. According to NKVD statistics, by the time the operation was brought to a close in 1938, 767,397 had been arrested, of whom 386,798 had been subject to summary execution. The figures for arrest had been exceeded by 150 per cent and for execution by over 400 per cent.

It is still not clear why the 00447 was so much more lethal than the original directive proposed.[65] Regional organizations had genuinely grave concerns about the return of kulaks, about crime and social instability, but that alone cannot explain the impulse to the summary execution of hundreds of thousands of Soviet citizens. One must remember that the party and state organizations directing the mass repression were themselves also under investigation. 'Vigilance' was the order of the day. Many officials were arrested for failing to expose enemies. In the autumn of 1937, few were in trouble for exposing too many. In June, Stalin had requested that cadres be judged not by their social origin or by black marks on their political records in the past. They should be judged by the vigour with which they fought enemies

65. Arch Getty emphasizes regional initiative in 'Excesses are Not Permitted', 113–38. For an emphasis on top-down control, see Khlevniuk, 'The Objectives of the Great Terror', in J. Cooper, M. Perrie, and E. A. Rees (eds), *Soviet History, 1917–1953: Essays in Honour of R. W. Davies* (London: 1993), 158–76, 165; Khaustov and Samuelson, *Stalin, NKVD i repressii*, 260–86.

of the revolution in the present.[66] As arrests were cutting a broad swath through republican, regional, and district organizations, arrests fuelled more arrests. At the same time, the regular regional reports on the 'progress' of mass repression were necessarily couched in terms of the 'exposure' of ever more counter-revolutionary and insurrectionary organizations. Week on week, as those reports arrived in the offices of the NKVD and as summaries were presented to Stalin, the centre lost any inclination it may have had to restrain the violence. Social and political tensions stoked by the impossible demands of pressurized plans, campaigns of vigilance, and the barrage of media reports of new conspiracies, large and small, all sustained the momentum of denunciations, arrests, exile, and summary execution.

00447 was by no means the only mass operation. The so-called 'national operations' targeted Germans, Poles, Finns, Koreans, and many other nationalities. The regime had long-standing concerns about the loyalty of 'foreign' populations, especially where those populations lived close to Soviet borders. Concerns were intensified by the experience of mass outmigration during the period of collectivization and famine, and reports that some incoming 'political refugees' were actually spies, assassins, and saboteurs acting on behalf of hostile states on Soviet borders.[67] It did not help that Soviet intelligence agencies intercepted correspondence from these states indicating the value they placed on Soviet ethnic tensions in the event of invasion. The regime had resettled some ethnic minorities in the 1920s, but by the mid-1930s, it was resorting to mass deportation from border regions. As the regime's sense of its political and military vulnerabilities intensified in the spring and summer of 1937, suspect national minorities were increasingly subject to deportation from urban areas and central regions far from the borders. As ever, arrests and investigations generated

66. See Hagenloh, *Stalin's Police*, 255–7.

67. For further detail on the national operations, see Terry Martin, 'The Origins of Soviet Ethnic Cleansing', *Journal of Modern History*, 4 (1998), 813–61; N. F. Bugai, *L.P. Beriia-I. V. Stalinu: 'Soglasno Vashemu ukazaniiu . . .'* (Moscow, 1995); James Morris, 'The Polish Terror: Spy Mania and Ethnic Cleansing in the Great Terror', *Europe-Asia Studies*, 5 (2004), 751–66; Chase, *Enemies at the Gates*; A. E. Gurianov (ed.), *Repressii protiv poliakov i pol'skikh grazhdan* (Moscow, 1997); I. L. Shcherbakov (ed.), *Nakazannyi narod: po materialam konferentsii 'Repressii protiv rossiiskikh nemtsev v Sovetskom Soiuze v kontekste sovetskoi natsionalnoi politiki'* (Moscow: 1999); Michael Gelb, '"Karelian Fever": The Finnish Immigrant Community during Stalin's Purges', *Europe-Asia Studies*, 6 (1993), 1091–1116; Michael Gelb, 'An Early Soviet Ethnic Deportation: The Far-Eastern Koreans', *Russian Review*, 3 (1995), 389–412.

'evidence' of further threats. On 20 July 1937, Stalin ordered Ezhov to arrest all Germans working in defence, electrical, chemical, and building industries.[68] Operational order 00438 (the 'German operation') was approved five days later.

On 9 August, operational order 00485 initiated the so-called Polish operation. The identification of targets became a model for subsequent national operations. In this case, the order directed the political police to arrest: active members of the Polish Military Organization (Polska Organizacja Wojskowa) already on NKVD lists; former prisoners of war from the Polish army remaining in the USSR; émigrés from Poland; former members of anti-Soviet political parties; and the most active anti-Soviet and nationalist elements in the Polish regions. It fell only slightly short of calling for the arrest of all Poles in the USSR. As in the German operation, Poles were to be removed from sensitive industries in the first instance. Only five weeks later, Ezhov reported to Stalin that 23,216 people suspected of spying for Poland had been arrested and scores of espionage organizations (*rezidentury*) and diversionist groups identified at defence plants. Stalin replied: 'To Com. Ezhov. Well done! Keep digging and sweeping out this Polish-spy filth. Destroy it in the interests of the USSR!' The same day, Ezhov sent out telegrams demanding that regions which had been relatively slow to track down Polish agents should pick up the pace immediately.[69]

In part under the pressure to conduct arrests, it was not long before the operations drew in not just the targeted nationalities, but those with whom they had contact. For example, D. M. Dmitriev, the head of the Sverdlovsk NKVD, reported to Ezhov that the German engineers and other specialists had recruited many agents in Urals military industry in the 1920s and early 1930s in the years of the German-Soviet Rapallo agreement. Dmitriev's investigation implicated the directors of many major plants supplying the Red Army.[70] By early 1938, as operation 00447 was being wound down, it was common for local NKVD officials to continue arrests of 'anti-Soviet elements' and blend them into the national operations. In March 1938, Ezhov's assistant M. I. Frinovskii raised objections, but neither Ezhov nor the Politburo chose to act.[71]

68. Hagenloh, *Stalin's Police*, 248.
69. Khaustov and Samuelson, *Stalin, NKVD i repressii*, 288–91.
70. Ibid. 288.
71. Ibid. 294–5.

According to NKVD statistics, a total of 335,513 people had been caught up in the national operations by the time they were firmly brought to a close in the autumn of 1938. Of these, 247,157 were executed. The combined figures for national operations and 00447 are hard to take in. Almost certainly, they resulted in the capture of some foreign agents and others who would have joined the enemy in the event of war, but they were unlikely to be anything but a vanishingly small percentage of the total number of victims. The overwhelming majority of them would surely have defended the regime had they lived to see the beginning of the war. The mass operations were the apotheosis of the Great Fear.

Conclusion

The end of the 'Terror' is very difficult to date. Official concerns about the impact of mass repression were expressed as early as January 1938, when the Central Committee plenum resolutions criticized 'excessive or false vigilance'.[1] There was a recognition not only that innocent people were being caught up in the hunt for enemies, but also that the wide-scale arrest and execution of party and state officials was at least occasionally counter-productive. This may seem appallingly obvious, but the transcripts of interrogations, foreign intelligence, and other reports crossing Stalin's desk and those of his inner circle indicated that the multiple, interlocking conspiracies against the regime continued unabated. Stalin was trying to strike a balance between rooting out conspirators on the one hand, and sustaining the effectiveness of political and economic institutions severely shaken by the repression. The extremely high incidence of arrest among officialdom left party secretaries, factory managers, and other officials paralysed with fear that their next decision would be their last. The protection of innocent people from state violence was a secondary consideration to Stalin when the future of the revolution was at stake, though he did get impatient when the backlog of judicial appeals was left to grow.

This ambiguous phase of terror and restraint continued for months. Repression in the army was curtailed in the spring of 1938, but the arrest and execution of regional party secretaries and other senior party figures continued through the summer. The Third Moscow trial

1. See 'Ob oshibkakh partorganizatsii pri iskliuchenii kommunistov iz partii, o formal'no-biurokraticheskom otnoshenii k appeliatsiiam iskliuchennykh is VKP(b) i o merakh po ustraneniiu etikh nedostatkov', *KPSS v rezoliutsiiakh* (Moscow, 1985), vii. 8–17.

in March was reported widely, reinforcing the impression that 'enemies of the people' were everywhere. Somewhat more quietly, district procurators were given more judicial oversight in cases of 'counter-revolutionary crimes'. The most portentous change came when Stalin assigned Lavrentii Beriia as Ezhov's assistant in August. Ezhov had done more than anyone else to shape Stalin's understanding of the threats facing the regime. He had convinced Stalin that Iagoda was not up to the job of fighting its enemies, and that he should take over as head of the political police. Ezhov played a pivotal role, perhaps *the* pivotal role, in orchestrating the mass repression of 1936–8. The appointment of Beriia as 'assistant' to Ezhov was immediately perceived by the latter as a blow to his authority, and a sign of Stalin's displeasure: 'I thought that his appointment was a step towards my dismissal', he later claimed.[2] But it did not mean that Stalin was coming to the conclusion that Ezhov had exaggerated the threat presented by enemies of the regime.

There were several reasons why Ezhov was removed as head of the NKVD in the autumn of 1938. He was, first and foremost, not coping with the tasks he faced, though he had a very strong reputation within the Bolshevik Party as a leader and administrator. It did not help that Stalin had appointed him People's Commissar of Water Transport in April, though this kind of dual responsibility was common in the highest echelons of power. More significantly, Ezhov's reach had exceeded his grasp as Commissar of Internal Affairs. His commitment to break the conspiracies against the regime and root out enemies was doomed to fail because the conspiracies and enemies were largely chimaeric products of a misguided reading of flawed intelligence. Accelerating the pattern of arrests, interrogations, execution, and exile deepened the appearance of conspiracy and enemy activity. Because the NKVD acted overwhelmingly on the content of denunciations or 'confessions' obtained under torture, and not on physical evidence of counter-revolutionary conduct, they could never get to the 'bottom' of conspiracy. Ezhov did not seek and thus would not find a logic for drawing the hunt for enemies to a close. There was no way of claiming some kind of final victory, but the devastation wrought by mass

2. Nikita Petrov and Mark Iansen, *Stalinskii pitomets—Nikolai Ezhov* (Moscow, 2008), 355–9. The overwhelming majority of Ezhov's private papers remain secret, but this book contains an excellent selection of materials relating to his fall.

repression continued. The Bolshevik leadership was largely inured to the immeasurable human cost. They were more sensitive to the damage that was being done to the party, the economy, and the army by wave upon wave of arrests and executions.

The concerns about NKVD excesses expressed from the beginning of 1938 did not particularly worry Ezhov at first. He loyally relayed criticisms down the NKVD chain of command. And yet these criticisms, reported in the press alongside articles on trials of counterrevolutionaries and conspiracies, contributed to a growing backlog of appeals against NKVD convictions. That constituted a source of vulnerability for Ezhov, but not enough to undermine him. The roots of his demise stretched further back. When he came to the NKVD in the autumn of 1936, he had wasted little time purging the organization not only of Iagoda loyalists, but of those who did not share his vision of the threats facing the regime. The tactic of thoroughly purging the old boss's allies and sympathizers, so common in Bolshevik political practice, tends to work only as long as the new leader is ascendant. Once his star began to wane, Ezhov could not stem the flow of largely anonymous critical letters, compromising materials, and attacks on his close colleagues. And a major knock to his reputation was delivered by the defection to Japan of the NKVD's Far Eastern bureau chief Genrikh Liushkov in June 1938. The problem this created for Ezhov was not merely that Liushkov leaked a huge amount of extremely sensitive information to the Japanese. Much more significantly, the defection signalled to Stalin and other members of the inner circle that—at a minimum—Ezhov had failed to identify an enemy of the people within his most senior staff. To the profoundly suspicious Bolshevik mind, this opened the possibility that the NKVD apparatus was harbouring other enemies. Did that not, after all, explain the excesses? Perhaps enemies in the NKVD were orchestrating the arrest and execution of large numbers of innocent people, provoking hostility to the regime and destabilizing party and state structures while protecting their own agents?

Ezhov knew that he could not survive politically with that cloud of suspicion hanging over him. The denunciations against him suggest that he was drinking heavily in the summer and autumn of 1938. He was letting the backlog of appeals against the NKVD grow as he tried to deal with the flow of denunciations against him and his senior team. This reinforced the broader impression that he might be using the

NKVD to condemn innocent people and protect enemies. In October 1938, for example, Beriia sent Stalin the transcript of an interrogation of a regional NKVD chief from the Urals. It suggested that the NKVD harboured a network of Rightists and Trotskyists hostile to the party line and determined to protect hives of their agents throughout the USSR.[3] One of the last denunciations delivered to Stalin before he dismissed Ezhov suggested that the head of the NKVD was destroying evidence of his misconduct, including evidence of payments to Ezhov and his wife from hostile foreign governments.

On 15 November 1938, twenty-four hours after the Stalin received the latter denunciation, the work of NKVD troikas was halted. This was an unmistakable signal that the political tide had turned against mass repression. The Great Terror was drawing to a close. On 17 November, a Politburo decision sent to all regional NKVD organizations proclaimed the 'successes' of the campaigns against terrorists, subversives, spies, and other enemies, but it announced the need for new methods, and particularly an emphasis on investigation, on material evidence to corroborate confessions. The Politburo acknowledged that mistakes had been made in the recent campaigns. Many innocent people had been arrested. And as he had done many times before, Stalin pinned the blame on others, in this case enemies who had wormed their way into the NKVD and encouraged mass, unjustified arrests.[4] Taken in isolation, such a statement sounds like cynical scapegoating, but the most private and secret of the leader's papers continued to indicate that the terror had been necessary and that the campaigns to root out and exterminate enemies had strengthened the Soviet state. Ezhov resigned on 23 November after a four-hour meeting with Stalin, Molotov, and Voroshilov.[5] His resignation letter, which was never intended for publication, said little about 'excesses'—about the arrest and execution of innocent people. Rather, the central theme of the letter is the presence of enemies of the people among Ezhov's closest associates in the organization he led. He resigned because he had failed to unmask them.[6] In this letter and in his subsequent correspondence with Stalin up to his execution he sought Stalin's praise for his successes

3. V. N. Khaustov et al. (eds), *Lubianka: Stalin i Glavnoe Upravlenie Gosbezopasnosti NKVD, 1937–1938* (hereafter *Lubianka: Stalin, 1937–1938*) (Moscow, 2004), 577–602.
4. Ibid. 533.
5. Getty and Naumov, *Road to Terror*, 537.
6. *Lubianka: Stalin, 1937–1938*, 552–4.

in the struggle against the enemies of the regime. The incidence of arrest and execution fell sharply in 1939 and never returned to the levels of 1936–8, but Stalin and the Soviet leadership continued to believe that the regime faced an array of foreign and domestic enemies bent on removing him and putting an end to Soviet power and the world revolution.

Fear and suspicion were built into the structure of Russian history. From the earliest beginnings of Slavic civilization, the population was vulnerable to attack from all sides. The relentless expansion of empire and the concentration of power in a narrow centre were both driven by insecurity. Palace coups, popular rebellions, foreign invasions, and latterly, revolutionary terrorism ultimately spawned a dictatorial police-state on a permanent watch for domestic and foreign threats to its existence. The Bolshevik state was at once wholly different and substantially the same. The Bolsheviks wanted to replace the ancient, religious, autocratic institutions with modern, scientific ones, led at least in the name of the masses. But they necessarily inherited the geo-political problems of their predecessors. They were attempting to gain control over an immense, extremely diverse, restive empire surrounded, indeed occupied, by hostile states. The concentration of political power in a narrow centre, and the exertion of repressive force could not be avoided if the revolution were to have any prospect of survival. And survival was very much on their minds.

The Bolsheviks were avid students of revolution. They wanted to know why previous revolutions had failed so that old mistakes would not be repeated. This study convinced them that the bourgeoisie would do everything in its power to overthrow a Marxist, proletarian revolution. They had to be prepared to recognize and combat those efforts. They needed to gather intelligence on the counter-revolutionary threat, and to be completely ruthless in the struggle against its manifestations, because a life and death struggle was inevitable. The ultimate victory of the proletariat was inevitable, but a successful counter-revolution would set back the cause by decades if not by centuries. The Bolsheviks felt they had a grave responsibility—to the working population of the world—not to fail.

The hyper-sensitivity to threats played a significant part in the decision to collectivize agriculture and industrialize the country at a breakneck pace. 'We are fifty or a hundred years behind the advanced countries. We must make good this distance in ten years. Either we do it or we shall go under,' Stalin had declared in 1931, almost exactly a decade before the German invasion. That was exceptionally prescient, but the broader analysis of threats to the regime and to the revolution tended to be well wide of the mark, feeding anxieties about foreign and domestic conspiracies, popular resistance, spies, and saboteurs. The drip-feed of foreign intelligence, surveillance material, and other reports crossing Stalin's desk presented a credible, compelling, and comprehensive picture of mortal danger, but it was profoundly misleading. The bulk of the analysis in this volume concerns the gathering and analysis of intelligence. It shows that the ways the information was gathered and processed served to exaggerate the threats the regime faced. Leaders were hesitant to accept that threats might recede and become insignificant. They over-relied on testimony obtained under torture, and on 'revolutionary instinct'. Information gatherers developed a professional and institutional interest in finding 'enemies', and in that process, the intelligence system came to echo and reinforce leaders' preconceptions. Through the 1920s and 1930s, the regime gained colossal economic, military, and political power, but at the same time became convinced that its enemies were everywhere, and conspiring to overthrow it. This was not a product of unstable, bloodthirsty minds, but rather of a misconceived information-gathering system that delivered a hugely detailed, nuanced, compelling—and substantially erroneous—image of the enemy.

The events of 1936–8 were by no means inevitable. The targets of the second Five-Year Plan were being met in the main. After the years of collectivization and famine, the Soviet order in the countryside was relatively stable. There was no plausible, real, or potential challenge to Stalin's rule. And yet the murder of Sergei Kirov unsettled the regime before it had the chance to gain confidence from these advances. The assassin was almost certainly acting alone, but the investigation churned up 'evidence' of further plots to assassinate Soviet leaders. The sharp deterioration of the international situation, with the rise of anti-communist right-wing dictatorships along Soviet borders led by the aggressive, expansionist Nazi regime, intensified fears of invasion, particularly after the emergence of the Anti-Comintern Pact and the beginning of the Spanish Civil War. Stalin and his colleagues believed that the revolution had to be defended at all costs, not merely so that they could continue to occupy their offices in the Kremlin but because the end of Soviet power would guarantee the worldwide ascendancy of the forces of capital over the working class for generations. In the autumn of 1936, the Politburo decided that political police chief Iagoda was not up to the task, and replaced him with the arch-conspiracy theorist Ezhov. From that moment, further 'evidence' of conspiracy was doomed to emerge given the methods of the NKVD at his disposal. Subsequent revelations of widespread corruption and 'double-dealing' within the upper reaches of officialdom, connections between former oppositionists and foreign powers, and treachery within the army, all fed the regime's insecurities and fears for the fate of the revolution. The heightened impression of disloyalty at the top reinforced the perceived need to neutralize the danger posed by those in the mass of the population who might not defend the regime in the event of war.

Stalin personally bears a heavy weight of responsibility for the deaths of hundreds of thousands, if not millions of Soviet citizens, but explanations of this mass murder focusing on his personal psychopathology are inadequate and unhelpful. Stalin was not paranoid, at least in the sense that it implies a clinical condition. Stalin did more than anyone else to shape the perverse information system and to direct the responses of the political police, but Stalin's actions and reactions were by no means unique. His inner circle shared his reaction to incoming intelligence. Many of those who opposed his rule also believed in the existence of foreign and domestic counter-revolutionary conspiracies, as did the population at large, fed as they were on a steady diet of campaigns of vigilance, news reports of conspiracies, and novels, plays, and films about wreckers and spies. It made perfect sense in the context of the pressurized plans of the 1930s. Most officials and workers did their best to meet work norms and fulfil the plan, but all too often it was impossible. To simplify slightly, in the closed production cycle of heavy industry, the producers of metals received substandard ores and fuels, and in inadequate quantities, so they produced substandard metals. Machine-builders then could not produce equipment of a suitable standard, and that made it difficult for mining industries to extract enough fuels and ores of an appropriate quality. In every sector of the economy and in the state system, roughly the same logic applied. The 'real' problem lay just beyond the horizon, just out of view. It made sense to people at all levels that there were wreckers and saboteurs at work. That seemed to explain the delivery of faulty goods, shortages, train crashes, fires, and other problems that were ultimately products of a planning system that demanded what could not be achieved. And when called upon to exercise vigilance and unmask the enemy, many were ready to do it.

It was in Stalin's power to initiate and intensify or restrain and stop campaigns of political violence, but he never recognized the fundamental flaws in the system of information gathering and analysis. Neither he nor many of his colleagues ever accepted that the root cause of official corruption and double-dealing, economic problems, 'anti-state conversations', and popular resistance lay in the system itself rather than the acts of agents of counter-revolution. Stalin never had a 'eureka moment' where he understood what had gone wrong, though he did grasp that at some stages of the campaigns of repression 'excesses' were being committed. He knew that radically simplified legal procedures and reliance on confession obtained under torture contributed to a situation in which very large numbers of innocent people were caught up in state repression. He tended to consider that a necessary cost in defence of the revolution. It is particularly striking that, as appeals against arbitrary arrest multiplied in 1938, and evidence of the appalling scale of 'excesses' accumulated, Stalin drew the conclusion that there must be enemy agents in the NKVD. That was not merely scapegoating. The political violence of this period was never just about protecting and extending the personal power of the leader, though Stalin did think he was uniquely capable of leading the world revolution. The violence of this period cannot be explained as the culmination of a drive to perfect a personal dictatorship. It had the opposite effect. The 'Great Fear' made the Soviet system almost ungovernable and left it much more vulnerable to foreign invasion.

Epilogue

The regime never again unleashed political violence on the scale of 1936–8. It remained a unique episode in Soviet history, but at the same time, neither Stalin nor his successors ever shook off the sense that the state faced a wide variety of existential threats from hostile foreign powers and domestic conspiracies. At no stage did either the leadership or the political police ever entirely come to terms with the terror, beyond acknowledging that 'excesses' had been committed. They never again reacted with such extraordinary violence, but the sense of threat remained. As the whole of Europe was arming itself at an ever accelerating rate in the late 1930s, Stalin had only Britain and France standing between the USSR and war with Japan and Germany. He then watched as Chamberlain followed a policy of concessions to Germany, including the infamous Munich pact, and as France turned again to the Right after the collapse of the Popular Front. Neither showed much interest in entering a mutual assistance pact with the Soviet Union, and there was not much in that to surprise Stalin. For most of the more than two decades since the October Revolution, Stalin's intelligence had told him that Britain and France were leaders and organizers of anti-Soviet coalitions. The common fear of Germany had drawn the French towards the USSR, but Stalin seems to have been inclined to assume that the primary motivation of the Franco-Soviet rapprochements was to convince Germany to agree to security arrangements set by France, if necessary at the expense of the USSR. Stalin continued to direct his diplomats to explore the potential of collective security, but a deal without a guarantee that Britain and France would come to the defence of the Soviet Union in the event of a German invasion was worse than no deal at all. It would not deter German expansion to the east. A non-aggression pact with Germany was more attractive than collective security, because if war was inevitable, it made more sense to push Hitler west than to rely on two enemies of long standing to come to the aid of the Soviet Union.

The Nazi–Soviet pact was signed on 23 August 1939. The pact did not indicate that Stalin trusted Hitler, or share plans for totalitarian world domination. Before and during the pact, he continued to receive reports of Nazi espionage and terrorist activities in the USSR.[7] Rather, signing the agreement was consistent with Stalin's determination to delay what he perceived to be an inevitable war as long as he could. In the summer of 1941, he discounted the many intelligence reports warning of imminent Nazi invasion not because he failed to grasp that Hitler might consider such a step, but because he found the intelligence indicating the contrary to be more credible. The Battle of Britain was still being fought. Surely Hitler would not ignore the lesson of the

7. See e.g. the FSB archival material cited in Petrov and Iansen, *Staliniskii pitomets*, 359–63. Many more examples can be found in V. N. Khaustov, V. P. Naumov, and N. S. Plotnikova (eds), *Lubianka: Stalin i NKVD-NKGB-GUKR 'Smersh', 1939-mart 1946* (Moscow, 2006).

First World War and draw himself into a war on two fronts? A Nazi invasion of the USSR was likely but surely not at the end of June when, in only a few short months, frosts and snow would immensely sharpen the challenge of supplying invading forces across the Russian steppe. Stalin seems to have had great faith in his ability to read the intelligence and set the correct course of action. Across the previous *two decades*, that intelligence had told him that the USSR was under almost continuous threat of invasion. As the intelligence services consistently exaggerated the threat the USSR was actually facing, Stalin developed an undue confidence in his ability to thwart the plans of the capitalists encircling the Soviet Union. The great irony of this is that, by launching Operation Barbarossa on 22 June 1941, Hitler established that Stalin was wrong in this specific instance, but the beginning in earnest of the inevitable war was solid evidence for Stalin that the general concept of 'capitalist encirclement' was correct; that the USSR had been under constant threat of invasion in the inter-war period and that the capitalist powers would never tolerate a successful communist state. Of course, Britain, America, and the USSR were allies for the duration of the war. Lend-Lease played a significant role in the ability of the Soviets to survive the Nazi onslaught, but it was not difficult to see that as a self-serving effort to tie down the Wehrmacht in the east. Similarly, the very long delay in opening the second front was seen as a calculated move to exhaust the Soviets.[8] And when it was opened, with Operation Overlord in June 1944, it had the gloss of an operation to stop the advance of Soviet troops into Europe.

It is beyond the ambition of this volume to provide a discussion of the origins and evolution of the Cold War, though this analysis of the origins of the Great Terror specifically, and Soviet images of counter-revolution generally, has implications for the decades that followed. Stalin's successor Nikita Khrushchev brought the political police apparatus firmly under party control and considered the possibility (at least initially) that capitalism and communism could peacefully coexist, but he was careful not to discredit the apparatus of political policing. He knew of the millions of arrests and executions in the late 1930s, but he only ever referred to the repression of the elite. Many of his colleagues

8. In fact, the Soviet intelligence agencies understood that, in 1942, the Germans were in contact with the Americans and British with the aim of negotiating a separate peace. Chebrikov (ed.), *Istoriia soverskikh organov*, 335.

in the Politburo remained convinced that, while Stalin had gone too far, the hunt for enemies had been necessary.[9]

Meanwhile, the Cold War presented a wealth of evidence to suggest that the capitalist west continued in their efforts to undermine Soviet power. The Americans' unwillingness to share the atom bomb with their erstwhile ally seemed to indicate not merely a lack of trust, but an anticipation of conflict. The Marshall Plan (1947) was seen as a challenge to Soviet influence in eastern Europe. The Truman doctrine (1947), the American efforts to break the Berlin blockade (1948), and the Korean and Vietnam conflicts were among the many further flashpoints that served to sustain the perceived relevance of Lenin's view that the confrontation of capitalism and communism was inevitable. Soviet intelligence agencies were also well aware that the CIA spent billions of dollars on spy satellites, on sophisticated listening devices, and on various forms of covert action not only to limit the spread of Soviet influence internationally, but to weaken domestic support and encourage dissent. They dropped tens of millions of pamphlets, delivered by balloon, across the USSR and attempted to support groups whose interests were not wholly consonant with those of the regime. They had meagre success in shifting popular attitudes to the regime, but the Soviet political police could not break the habit of looking for the hand of the CIA behind every act of dissent.[10]

It is not unreasonable to wonder if the chronic and exaggerated fear of enemies that characterized the Stalin era—and indeed pretty much the whole of Russian history—has extended to the present day. At the time Vladimir Putin entered the KGB in the latter part of the 1970s, his instructors were still presenting the history of the state security organs as an unbroken line of successes undermining and exposing the efforts of the capitalist powers to subvert the Soviet Union. The main history textbook presented the NKVD as a victim, rather than as a perpetrator of Stalin's terror. There is little in the book that Stalin would have criticized, and certainly no mention of the fundamental shortcomings of

9. Nikolia Vert, *Terror i besporiadok: Stalinizm kak sistema* (Moscow, 2010), 414–15, 434–5.
10. Vladislav Zubok and Constantine Pleshakov, *Inside the Kremlin's Cold War: From Stalin to Khrushchev* (Cambridge, Mass., 1996), ch. 2; David F. Rudgers, 'The Origins of Covert Action', *Journal of Contemporary History*, 2 (2000), 249–62; Loch K. Johnson, 'Spymasters in the Cold War', *Foreign Policy*, 105 (Winter 1996–7), 179–92; Loch K. Johnson, 'Covert Action and Accountability: Decision-Making for America's Secret Foreign Policy', *International Studies Quarterly*, 1 (1989), 81–109.

intelligence collection that led Soviet leaders to exaggerate the threats they faced.[11] On completion of his KGB training, Putin's work revolved around the sorts of tasks described at such length above: identifying the threats posed by enemy agents.[12] The quality of Russian intelligence may well have improved since then, but given that the exaggeration of threat has such deep roots in Russian history, it would be surprising if the echoes of the 'Great Fear' had wholly dissipated. Deep-seated habits of mind may have something to do with the current, severe restrictions on press freedom, on freedoms of assembly and speech in Russia, with the decision to close the offices of the British Council, to convict the members of the punk band Pussy Riot to terms of hard labour, and so on. As things stand, Putin's administration does not encourage the sort of research that would make it possible to address such a question, so it is likely to remain a matter of conjecture for some time.

11. Chebrikov (ed.), *Istoriia soverskikh organov*; For other evidence of continuities of thinking in the KGB, see the work of the director of Fifth Directorate (political counter-intelligence) in the 1970s and 1980s. F. D. Bobkov, *Kak borotsia s 'agentami vliianiia'* (Moscow, 2014). The bulk of the book concerns the struggle with enemies of the USSR during his time in office, but he concludes with advice to Putin on measures apparently needed now 'to preserve the integrity and sovereignty of our country'.
12. See e.g. Richard Sakwa, *Putin: Russia's Choice* (Abingdon, 2008).

Bibliography

ARCHIVES

Arkhiv Vneshnei Politiki Rossiiskoi Federatsii (AVPRF)
Gosudarstvennyi Arkhiv Rossiiskoi Federatsii (GARF)
Rossiiski Gosudarstvennyi Arkhiv Ekonomiki (RGAE)
Rossiiskii Gosudarstvennyi Arkhiv Sotsial'no-Politicheskoi Istorii (RGASPI)
Rossiiskii Gosudarstvennyi Voennyi Arkhiv (RGVA)
Gosudarstvennyi Arkhiv Administrativnykh Organizatsii Sverdlovskoi Oblasti (GAAO SO)
Gosudarstvennyi Arkhiv Obshchestvennykh Organizatsii Sverdlovskoi Oblasti (GAOO SO)

PUBLISHED PRIMARY SOURCES

Adibekov, G. M., Adibekova, Zh. G., Rogovaia, L. A., Shirinia K. K., eds, *Politbiuro TsK RKP(b)-VKP(b) i Komintern, 1919–1943: Dokumenty* (Moscow, 2004).

Artizov, A., Sigachev, Iu., Shevchuk, I., Khlopov, V., eds, *Reabilitatsiia: Kak eto bylo.* ii. *Fevral' 1956-nachalo 80-kh godov. Dokumenty* (Moscow, 2003).

Bobkov, F. D., *Kak borotsia s 'agentami vliianiia'* (Moscow, 2014).

Bol'shevik

Chase, William, *Enemies within the Gates? The Comintern and the Stalinist Repression, 1934–1939* (New Haven, 2001).

Chebrikov, V., ed., *Istoriia Sovetskikh organov gosudarstvennoi bezopasnosti* (Moscow, 1977).

Chetyrnadtsatyi s"ezd Vsesoiuznoi Kommunisticheskoi Partii (Bol'shevikov), 18–31 dekabria 1925 g. Stenograficheskii otchet (Moscow, 1926).

Churchill, Winston S., *The Second World War* (New York, 1959), i.

Dam'e, V.V., Komolova, N. P., and Petrova, N. L., eds, *Komintern protiv fashizma: Dokumenty* (Moscow, 1999).

Dvenadtsatyi s"ezd Rossiiskoi Kommunisticheskoi Partii (Bol'shevikov), 17–25 aprelia 1923 g. Stenograficheskii otchet (Moscow, 1923).

Dokumenty vneshnei politiki SSSR (21 vols. Moscow, 1957–77).

Getty, J. Arch, and Naumov, Oleg V., eds, *The Road to Terror: Stalin and the Self-Destruction of the Bolsheviks, 1932–1939* (New Haven, 1999).

Izvestiia TsK

Khaustov, V. N., Naumov, V. P., and Plotnikova, N. S., eds, *Lubianka: Stalin i VChK-GPU-OGPU-NKVD ianvar' 1922-dekabr' 1936: Dokumenty* (Moscow, 2003).

Khaustov, V. N., Naumov, V. P., and Plotnikova, N. S., eds, *Lubianka: Stalin i Glavnoe Upravlenie Gosbezopasnosti NKVD, 1937–1938* (Moscow, 2004).

Khaustov, V. N., Naumov, V. P., and Plotnikova, N. S., eds, *Lubianka: Stalin i NKVD-NKGB-GUKR 'Smersh', 1939-mart 1946* (Moscow, 2006).

Khlevniuk, O.V., Devis, R. U. [R. W. Davies], Kosheleva, L. P., Ris, E. A. [E. A. Rees], and Rogovaia, L. A., eds, *Stalin i Kaganovich: Perepiska. 1931–1936 gg.* (Moscow, 2001).

Khlevniuk, O.V., Kvashonkin, A.V., Kosheleva, L. P., and Rogovaia, L. A. eds, *Stalinskoe Politbiuro v 30-e gody* (Moscow, 1995).

Kommunist

Kommunisticheskaia Partiia Sovetskogo Soiuza v rezoliutsiiakh i resheniiakh s"ezdov, konferentsii i plenumov TsK (14 vols. Moscow, 1972–84).

Kosheleva, L. P., Lel'chuk, V., Naumov, V., Naumov, O.V., Rogovaia, L. A., and Khlevniuk, O.V., eds, *Pis'ma I. V. Stalina V. M. Molotovu, 1925–1936 gg.* (Moscow, 1995).

Kvashonkin, A. V., Kosheleva, L. P., Rogovaia, L. A., and Khlevniuk, O. V., eds, *Sovetskoe rukovodstvo: Perepiska, 1928–1941* (Moscow, 1999).

Kvashonkin, A.V., Livshin, A.V., and Khlevniuk O.V., eds, *Stalinskoe Politbiuro v 30-e gody. Sbornik dokumentov* (Moscow, 1995).

Latsis, M. I., *Krasnaia Kniga V. Ch. K.*, 2 vols. Reprint, ed. A. S. Belidov (Moscow, 1990).

Lenin, V. I., *Polnoe Sobranie Sochinenii* (52 vols. Moscow, 1959–69).

Lenoe, Matthew E., *The Kirov Murder and Soviet History* (New Haven, 2010).

Lih, Lars T., Naumov O.V., and Khlevniuk, O.V., eds, *Stalin's Letters to Molotov, 1925–1936* (New Haven, 1995).

Litvin, A. L., ed., *Boris Savinkov na Lubianke. Dokumenty* (Moscow, 2001).

Mikoian, Anastas, *V nachale dvatsatykh* (Moscow, 1975).

Orlov, Alexander, *The Secret History of Stalin's Crimes* (New York, 1953).

Partiinoe stroitel'stvo

Petrov, Nikita, and Iansen, Mark, *Stalinskii pitomets—Nikolai Ezhov* (Moscow, 2008).

Piatnadtsatyi s"ezd Vsesoiuznoi kommunisticheskoi partii (b). Stenograficheskii otchet (Moscow, 1928).

Plekhanov, A. A., and Plekhanov, A. M., *F. E. Dzerzhinskii: Predsedatel' VChK-OGPU, 1917–1926. Dokumenty* (Moscow, 2007).

Pravda

Shestnadtsataia konferentsiia VKP(b), 23–29 aprelia 1929 g. Stenograficheskii otchet (Moscow, 1929).

Stalin, I.V., *Sochineniia* (13 vols. Moscow, 1947–51).

Trinadtsataia konferentsiia Rossiiskoi Kommunisticheskoi Partii (Bolshevikov) (Moscow, 1924).

Trinadtsatyi s"ezd RKP(b), mai 1924 goda. Stenograficheskii otchet (Moscow, 1963).

Troinitskii, N. A., ed., *Pervaia vseobshchaia perepis' naseleniia Rossiiskoi Imperii* (St Petersburg, 1905)

Velikaia Oktiabr'skaia Sotsialisticheskaia Revoliutsiia: Entsiklopediia (Moscow, 1987).

Viola, Lynne, Danilov, V. P., Ivnitskii, N. A., and Kozlov, Denis, eds, *The War Against the Peasantry, 1927–1930* (New Haven, 2005).

SECONDARY SOURCES

Avrich, Paul, *Peasant Rebels, 1600–1800* (London, 1972).

Benvenuti, Francesco, *Stakhanovism and Stalinism, 1934–1938*, CREES discussion papers, 30 (Birmingham, 1989).

Berliner, Joseph, *Factory and Manager in the USSR* (Cambridge, Mass., 1957).

Carley, Michael Jabara, 'Down a Blind Alley: Anglo-French Soviet Relations: 1920–1939', *Canadian Journal of History*, 2 (1994), 147–72.

Carley, Michael Jabara, 'Episodes from the Early Cold War: Franco-Soviet Relations, 1917–1927', *Europe-Asia Studies* 7 (2000), 1275–1305.

Carley, Michael Jabara, 'Behind Stalin's Moustache: Pragmatism in Early Soviet Foreign Policy, 1917–41', *Diplomacy and Statecraft*, 3 (2001), 159–74.

Carr, E. H., *A History of the Bolshevik Revolution: The Bolshevik Revolution, 1917–1923* (London, 1950), i.

Carr, E. H., and Davies, R. W., *Foundations of a Planned Economy* (London, 1969), i/1.

Conquest, Robert, *The Great Terror* (London, 1967).

Cook, Andrew, *On His Majesty's Secret Service: Sidney Reilly Codename ST1* (London, 2002).

Daniels, Robert V., 'The Secretariat and the Local Organisations in the Russian Communist Party, 1921–1923', *American Slavic and East European Review*, 1 (1957), 32–49.

Daniels, Robert V., *Conscience of the Revolution: Communist Opposition in Soviet Russia* (Cambridge, Mass., 1960).

Daniels, Robert V., 'Stalin's Rise to Dictatorship', in Alexander Dallin and Alan Westin (eds), *Politics in the Soviet Union* (New York, 1966).

Daniels, Robert V., *Red October: The Bolshevik Revolution of 1917* (New York, 1967).

Davies, R. W., *Crisis and Progress in the Soviet Economy, 1931–1933* (Basingstoke, 1996).

Davies, R. W., and Khlevniuk, O. V., 'Stakhanovism and the Soviet Economy', *Europe-Asia Studies*, 6 (2002), 867–903.

Davies, R. W., Tauger, M. B., and Wheatcroft, S. G., 'Stalin, Grain Stocks and the Famine of 1932–1933', *Slavic Review*, 3 (1995), 642–57.

Davies, Sarah, *Popular Opinion in Stalin's Russia: Terror, Propaganda and Dissent, 1934–1941* (Cambridge, 1997).

Davies, Sarah, and Harris, James, *Stalin's World: Dictating the Soviet Order* (New Haven, 2014).

Deutscher, Isaac, *Stalin: A Political Biography* (Oxford, 1949).

Deutscher, Isaac, *The Prophet Unarmed, Trotsky: 1921–1929* (London, 1970).

Fitzpatrick, Sheila, *Education and Social Mobility in the Soviet Union, 1921–1934* (Cambridge, 1979).

Gellately, Robert, *Lenin, Stalin and Hitler: The Age of Social Catastrophe* (London, 2007).

Getty, J. Arch, *Origins of the Great Purges: The Soviet Communist Party Reconsidered, 1933–1938* (Cambridge, 1985).

Getty, J. Arch, 'The Politics of Repression Revisited', in J. Arch Getty and Roberta T. Manning (eds), *Stalinist Terror: New Perspectives* (Cambridge, 1993), 49–62.

Getty, J. Arch, '"Excesses are Not Permitted": Mass Terror and Stalinist Governance in the Late 1930s', *Russian Review*, 1 (2002), 113–38.

Getty, J. Arch, and Naumov, Oleg V., *Yezhov: The Rise of Stalin's Iron Fist* (New Haven, 2008).

Getty, J. Arch, 'Pre-Election Fever: The Origins of the 1937 Mass Operations', in James Harris (ed.), *Anatomy of Terror* (Oxford, 2013), 224–7.

Hagenloh, Paul, *Stalin's Police: Public Order and Mass Repression in the USSR, 1926–1941* (Baltimore, 2009).

Harris, James, *The Great Urals: Regionalism and the Evolution of the Soviet System* (Ithaca, NY, 1999).

Harris, James, 'The Purging of Local Cliques in the Urals Region, 1936–7', in Sheila Fitzpatrick (ed.), *Stalinism: New Directions* (London, 2000), 262–85.

Harris, James, 'Resisting the Plan in the Urals, 1928–1956: Or Why Regional Officials Needed "Wreckers" and "Saboteurs"', in Lynne Viola (ed.), *Contending with Stalinism: Soviet Power and Popular Resistance in the 1930s* (Ithaca, NY, 2002), 201–27.

Harris, James, 'Was Stalin a Weak Dictator?', *Journal of Modern History*, 2 (2003), 375–86.

Harris, James, 'Encircled by Enemies: Stalin's Perceptions of the Capitalist World, 1918–1941', *Journal of Strategic Studies*, 3 (2007), 513–45.

Harris, James, 'Intelligence and Threat Perception: Defending the Revolution, 1917–1937', in James Harris (ed.), *Anatomy of Terror: Political Violence under Stalin* (Oxford, 2013), 29–43.

Haslam, Jonathan, *Soviet Foreign Policy, 1930–1933: The Impact of the Depression* (London, 1983).

Hellbeck, Jochen, 'Fashioning the Stalinist Soul: The Diary of Stepan Podliubnyi, 1931–9', in Sheila Fitzpatrick (ed.), *Stalinism: New Directions* (London, 2000), 77–116.

Hingley, Ronald, *The Russian Secret Police: Muscovite, Imperial Russian and Soviet Political Security Operations, 1565–1970* (London, 1970).

Holquist, Peter, '"Conduct Merciless Mass Terror": Decossackization on the Don, 1919', *Cahiers du Monde Russe*, 1–2 (Jan.–June 1997), 127–62.

Holquist, Peter, *Making War, Forging Revolution: Russia's Continuum of Crisis, 1914–1921* (Cambridge, Mass., 2002).

Hosking, Geoffrey, *Russia and the Russians* (London, 2002).

Johnson, Loch K., 'Covert Action and Accountability: Decision-Making for America's Secret Foreign Policy', *International Studies Quarterly*, 1 (1989), 81–109.

Johnson, Loch K., 'Spymasters in the Cold War', *Foreign Policy*, 105 (Winter 1996–7), 179–92.

Ken, Oleg, *Mobilizatsionnoe planirovanie i politicheskie resheniia, konets 1920-kh–seredina 1930-kh gg.* (Moscow, 2008).

Kessler, Gijs, 'The Passport System and State Control over Population Flows in the Soviet Union, 1932–1940', *Cahiers du Monde Russe*, 42 (2001), 478–504.

Khaustov, V. N., and Samuelson, Lennart, *Stalin, NKVD i repressii, 1936–1938 gg.* (Moscow, 2009).

Khlevniuk, O. V., *In Stalin's Shadow: The Career of 'Sergo' Ordzhonikidze* (Armonk, NY, 1995).

Khlevniuk, O. V., *Politbiuro: Mekhanizmy politicheskoi vlasti v 1930-e gody* (Moscow, 1995).

Khlevniuk, O. V., and Davies, R. W., 'The End of Rationing in the Soviet Union, 1934–1935', *Europe-Asia Studies*, 4 (1999), 557–609.

Kirmel', N. S., *Belogvardeiskie spetssluzhby v Grazhdanskoi voine, 1918–1922 gg.* (Moscow, 2008).

Kiseleva, E. L., 'Chistka gosudarstvennogo apparata, 1929–1932' gg., *Rossiiskaia istoriia*, 1 (2009), 96–109.

Kivinen, Marrku, 'Obzory OGPU i sovetskie istoriki', in G. N. Sevast'ianov, A. N. Sakharov, Ia. F. Pogonii, Iu. L. D'iakov, V. K. Vinogradov, L. P. Kolodnikova, T. Vikhavainen, M. Kivinen, and T. Martin (eds), *'Sovershenno Sekretno': Lubianka-Stalinu o polozhenii v Strane (1922–1934)* (8 vols. Moscow, 2001), i/1.

Knei-Paz, Baruch, *The Social and Political Thought of Leon Trotsky* (Oxford, 1978).

Kovalev, V. A., *Dva Stalinskikh Narkoma* (Moscow, 1995).

Kuromiya, Hiroaki, 'The Shakhty Affair', *South East European Monitor*, 2 (1997), 41–64.

Kuromiya, Hiroaki, *Stalin: Profiles in Power* (London, 2005).

Lewin, Moshe, *Lenin's Last Struggle* (London, 1969).

Lincoln, W. Bruce, *Red Victory: A History of the Russian Civil War* (London, 1991).

Long, John W., 'Plot and Counterplot in Revolutionary Russia: Chronicling the Bruce Lockhart Conspiracy, 1918', *Intelligence and National Security*, 1 (1995), 122–43.

McCagg, W. O., *Stalin Embattled, 1943–1948* (Detroit, 1978).

Maiolo, Joe, *Cry Havoc: The Arms Race and the Second World War, 1931–1941* (London, 2010).

Martin, Terry, 'The Origins of Soviet Ethnic Cleansing', *Journal of Modern History*, 4 (1998), 813–61.

Mawdsley, Evan, and White, Stephen, *The Soviet Elite from Lenin to Gorbachev: The Central Committee and its Members, 1917–1991* (Oxford, 2000).

Medvedev, Roy A., *Let History Judge* (London, 1972).

Merridale, Catherine, *Moscow Politics and the Rise of Stalin: The Communist Party in the Capital, 1925–1932* (Basingstoke, 1990).

Morozov, S.V., *Pol'sko-Chekhoslovatskie otnosheniia, 1933–1939* (Moscow, 2004).

Mozokhin, O. B., 'Iz istorii bor'by organov VChK-OGPU s terrorizmom', *Voenno-istoricheskii zhurnal*, 5 (2002).

Nove, Alec, *An Economic History of the USSR* (London, 1969).

Osokina, Elena, *Our Daily Bread: Socialist Distribution and the Art of Survival in Stalin's Russia, 1927–1941* (London, 2000).

Pipes, Richard, *Russia under the Old Regime* (London, 1974).

Pipes, Richard, *A Concise History of the Russian Revolution* (New York, 1996).

Plekhanov, A. M., *VChK-OGPU, 1921–1928gg.* (Moscow, 2003).

Priestland, David, *Stalinism and the Politics of Mobilization: Ideas, Power and Terror in Inter-War Russia* (Oxford, 2007).

Rayfield, Donald, *Stalin and his Hangmen* (London, 2005).

Rees, E. A., *Decision-Making in the Stalinist Command Economy* (Basingstoke, 1997).

Rees, E. A., 'Leaders and their Institutions', in Paul R. Gregory (ed.), *Behind the Façade of Stalin's Command Economy* (Stanford, Calif., 2001), 35–60.

Reese, Roger R., *Red Commanders: A Social History of the Soviet Army Officer Corps, 1918–1991* (Lawrence, Kan., 2005).

Reiman, Michal, *The Birth of Stalinism* (Bloomington, Ind., 1987).

Rigby, T. H., *Communist Party Membership in the U.S.S.R., 1917–1967* (Princeton, 1968).

Rigby, T. H., 'Early Provincial Cliques and the Rise of Stalin', *Soviet Studies*, 1 (1981), 3–28.

Rittersporn, Gabor, *Stalinist Simplifications and Soviet Complications: Social Tensions and Political Conflicts in the USSR, 1933–1953* (Chur, Switzerland, 1991).

Rossman, Jeffrey J., 'A Workers' Strike in Stalin's Russia: The Vichuga Uprising, 1930', in Lynne Viola (ed.), *Contending with Stalinism: Soviet Power and Popular Resistance in the 1930s* (Ithaca, NY, 2002), 44–83.

Rudgers, David F., 'The Origins of Covert Action', *Journal of Contemporary History*, 2 (2000), 249–62.

Sakwa, Richard, *Putin: Russia's Choice* (Abingdon, 2008).

Service, Robert, *The Bolshevik Party in Revolution: A Study in Organisational Change, 1917–1923* (New York, 1979).

Shearer, David, 'Elements near and Alien: Passportisation, Policing, and Identity in the Stalinist State, 1932–1952', *Journal of Modern History*, 4 (2004), 835–81.

Shearer, David, *Policing Stalin's Socialism: Repression and Social Order in the Soviet Union, 1924–1953* (New Haven, 2009).

Siegelbaum, Lewis, *Stakhanovism and the Politics of Productivity in the USSR, 1935–1941* (Cambridge, 1988).

Simonov, N. S., 'The "War Scare" of 1927 and the Birth of the Defense Industry Complex', in John Barber and Mark Harrison (eds), *The Soviet Defense Industry Complex from Stalin to Khrushchev* (Basingstoke, 2000), 33–46.

Skorkin, K.V., *NKVD RSFSR, 1917–1923* (Moscow, 2008).

Smith, Jeremy, 'Stalin as Commissar of Nationalities, 1918–1922', in Sarah Davies and James Harris (eds), *Stalin: A New History* (Cambridge, 2005), 45–62.

Spence, Richard B., 'Russia's *Operatsiia Trest*: A Reappraisal', *Global Intelligence Monthly*, 1 (1999), 19–24.

Steiner, Zara, *The Lights that Failed: European International History, 1919–1933* (Oxford, 2005).

Thurston, Robert, 'The Stakhanovite Movement: Background to the Great Terror in the Factories, 1935–1938', in J. Arch Getty and Roberta T. Manning (eds), *Stalinist Terror: New Perspectives* (Cambridge, 1993), 142–60.

Thurston, Robert, *Life and Terror in Stalin's Russia, 1934–1941* (New Haven, 1996).

Tsvetkov, V. Zh., 'Osobennosti antisovetskoi razvedyvatel'noi raboty podpol'nykh voenno-politicheskikh struktur belogo dvizheniia 1917–1918'gg., in A. A. Zdanovich, G. E. Kuchkov, N. V. Petrov, and V. N. Khaustov (eds), *Istoricheskie chteniia na Lubianke: 1997–2008* (Moscow, 2008), 36–50.

Tucker, Robert C., *Stalin as Revolutionary, 1879–1929* (London, 1974).

Ulam, Adam B., *Stalin: The Man and his Era* (New York, 1973).

Vert, Nikolia (Nicolas Werth), *Terror i besporiadok: Stalinizm kak sistema* (Moscow, 2010).

Viola, Lynne, 'The Campaign to Eliminate the Kulak as a Class, Winter 1929–1930: A Reevaluation of the Legislation', *Slavic Review*, 3 (1986), 503–24.

Viola, Lynne, *Peasant Rebels under Stalin: Collectivisation and the Culture of Peasant Resistance* (Oxford, 1996).

Whitewood, Peter, *The Red Army and the Great Terror: Stalin's Purge of the Soviet Military* (Lawrence, Kan., 2015).

Zubok, Vladislav, and Pleshakov, Constantine, *Inside the Kremlin's Cold War: From Stalin to Khrushchev* (Cambridge, Mass, 1996).

Index